Lecture Notes in Artificial Inte

Edited by J. G. Carbonell and J. Siekmann.

Subseries of Lecture Notes in Computer Science

Springer
Berlin
Heidelberg
New York
Hong Kong
London
Milan
Paris
Tokyo

Steve Renals   Gregory Grefenstette (Eds.)

Text- and Speech-Triggered Information Access

8th ELSNET Summer School
Chios Island, Greece, July 15-30 2000
Revised Lectures

 Springer

Series Editors

Jaime G. Carbonell, Carnegie Mellon University, Pittsburgh, PA, USA
Jörg Siekmann, University of Saarland, Saarbrücken, Germany

Volume Editors

Steve Renals
University of Sheffield, Department of Computer Science
Sheffield S1 4DP, UK
E-mail: s.renals@dcs.shef.ac.uk

Gregory Grefenstette
Clairvoyance Corp.
Pittsburg PA 15213-1854, USA
E-mail: g.grefenstette@clairvoyancecorp.com

Cataloging-in-Publication Data applied for

A catalog record for this book is available from the Library of Congress.

Bibliographic information published by Die Deutsche Bibliothek
Die Deutsche Bibliothek lists this publication in the Deutsche Nationalbibliografie;
detailed bibliographic data is available in the Internet at <http://dnb.ddb.de>.

CR Subject Classification (1998): I.2.7, I.2, F.4.2-3, H.5.5, H.3, H.2, H.4

ISSN 0302-9743
ISBN 3-540-40635-2 Springer-Verlag Berlin Heidelberg New York

Springer-Verlag Berlin Heidelberg New York
a member of BertelsmannSpringer Science+Business Media GmbH

http://www.springer.de

© Springer-Verlag Berlin Heidelberg 2003
Printed in Germany

Typesetting: Camera-ready by author, data conversion by Boller Mediendesign
Printed on acid-free paper   SPIN: 10928707   06/3142   5 4 3 2 1 0

Preface

This book originated from the 8th ELSNET Summer School on Language and Speech Communication that was held in the summer of 2000 on the island of Chios in Greece. ELSNET is the European Network in Human Language Technologies, a network of some 140 academic institutions and private companies from all over Europe, all active in language and speech technology, covering the whole range from basic research to industrial development and integration. It was created in 1991 with the objective to bring together the language and speech technology communities on the one hand, and the academic and industrial communities on the other.

The ELSNET Summer Schools have now become a tradition. They are different from other summer schools in that they are always dedicated to one specific topic area, always on the borderline of language and speech technology. They bring together a mixed audience of academic and industrial researchers, with backgrounds in language processing, speech processing, software engineering, and many other fields.

The topic selected for the 2000 Summer School was "Text- and Speech-Triggered Information Access." The underlying problem is well-known to all of us: we are continuously producing and storing enormous amounts of data in many different forms (such as text, speech, images, mixed modalities) – how can we ensure that these vast data collections remain accessible in an efficient and natural way?

The problem has of course many facets other than just accessibility, such as physical storage, data integrity, data acquisition, intellectual property rights and data management, but this Summer School focused on how language and speech technology can be deployed to get access to information.

We have found our Summer Schools to be an effective and efficient instrument for the transfer of knowledge. At the same time it should be noted that they can only accommodate a limited number of people, in a specific location, at a specific moment in time. In order to make the same knowledge accessible to a wider audience than just the happy few who were able to attend the School, we have adopted the policy of trying to transform the material taught at the School into a book. This book is the fifth ELSNET Summer School book, and the first one to be published in Springer-Verlag's LNCS Tutorials series.

The book attempts to give newcomers in the field a clear overview of the main technologies and problems and to give existing practitioners a concise review of the technologies used in state-of-the-art deployment of language and speech technology in information access.

We would like to thank the editors, Steve Renals and Gregory Grefenstette, for their efforts to make this book happen, all the authors for their contributions to the 2000 Summer School and to this book, and the European Commission for their financial support.

Steven Krauwer
ELSNET Coordinator
http://www.elsnet.org

Table of Contents

Text- and Speech-Triggered Information Access: Introduction

Gregory Grefenstette[1] and Steve Renals[2]

[1] Clairvoyance Corp., Pittsburgh PA, USA
g.grefenstette@clairvoyancecorp.com
[2] University of Sheffield, Sheffield, UK
s.renals@dcs.shef.ac.uk

Abstract. Years of speech and billions of characters are stored in various media including the Internet. How can we ever find useful information in such vast archives? Automatic procedures that can recognise speech accurately and linguistic tools that automatically take out essential information components may do the job.

1 Introduction: Accessing Information from Language

Research using computers to deal with human language grew from two different models of what the problem was. On one hand, some researchers in the 1960's saw the problem as controlling a robot with human speech. People wanted to be able to talk with a robot, have it understand the our commands, and to execute these commands accurately. Such a problem required language processing to be very accurate (so that the robot did not hand us a screwdriver when we asked for a hammer), to be able to do inferences and to be connected to a knowledge base (so we would not have to explain everything all the time), and to deal with mainly short utterances (i.e. the commands we gave). Terry Winograd's robot-controlling interface SHRDLU [6] was a paradigmatic example of this line of research. Much work in computational linguistics throughout the 1990s was still based on producing the faultless parsers that would be needed to control robots.

The other model that drove much research in natural language processing through the 1990s was the problem of finding information in a library. The requirements for natural language processing for treating this problem are different from those needed to control a robot. We expect the computer to digest the information in the library. As the library's content large, the language problem here is more difficult than that involved in using a limited set of commands to move a robot around a known, modelled space. On the other hand, the problem is easier because we do not need 100% accuracy; a ranked list of responses can usually suffice because we expect to make the final judgement of response relevance ourselves. Methods of text analysis used for such tasks were rudimentary; Frakes and Baeza-Yates [4] discuss many of the textual shortcuts used in these problems

In the 1990's, with the appearance of the Web, the quantity of information suddenly available outstripped all existing approaches to handling information. Database engineering soon solved the problems involving indexing strings from billions of Web

S. Renals, G. Grefenstette (Eds.): Text- and Speech-Triggered Info. Access, LNAI 2705, pp. 1-5, 2003.

documents[3],[2], leading to some successful search engines such as Google, Altavista, and AllTheWeb.

Speech is more difficult to process than text, not only due to the obvious problems relating to recognizing the acoustic signal. Spoken language is less grammatical, especially if the speech is uttered spontaneously (the usual situation), and is characterized by phenomena such as incomplete sentences, agrammatical phrasing, disfluency, hesitation and repetition, all of which serve to complicate spoken language processing.

Speech plays a role in information access both as an interface modality (eg a spoken query to a textual database), and as spoken archives. Speech interfaces are now realised in commercial systems for automated phone banking, directory lookup and many other applications. Such systems are based on the use of speaker-independent speech recognition systems, typically with large vocabularies, but operating in a limited domain.

Effective access of large collections of spoken data is more challenging—but it is a compelling task. It has been estimated that a large proportion of human-generated information is in spoken form: television and radio broadcasts, personal conversations, lectures, etc. [5]. While navigation and browsing of textual data is at the base of much consumer software, systems for tasks such as automatic extraction of information from radio and TV programmes are confined to the research laboratory: they work well for broadcast news, less well for films.

All these possibilities, and the growth of digital information, provides challenges and new opportunities for sophisticated speech and natural language processing approaches. The authors of the chapters presented here face these challenges head on.

2   Digital Libraries

The appearance of the Web and the widespread penetration of the Internet into people's homes during the 1990's begins to fulfil the hope of of having information accessible everywhere and at all times. The continuing success of storage and processing power, still following Gordon Moore's law of doubling in power every 18 months [1], means that more types of media are being stored in digital form. Though storing audio, images and video has become easier, accessing information embedded in these media still possesses many problems.

Current libraries still depend on human effort to catalog these media, converting their perceptions into text, which can then be handled digitally by known means of indexing. As we move to digital libraries, in which all the information in the library collection is accessible, we need automated techniques to convert images and discourse into searchable information.

Alex Hauptmann, in chapter 1, describes approaches to creating and exploiting Multimedia digital libraries. He covers issues related to capturing, processing, compressing, storing, indexing, searching, and retrieving various kinds of audio, video and image media. The intent is to provide a conceptual and technical framework for multimedia digital libraries.

3   Large Vocabulary Speech Interfaces

Understanding spoken language requires acoustic and language models to convert the speech signal into sequences of words. As we move beyond limited domains (such as telephone-based automated reservation systems) to less restricted domains (such as broadcast news), so the corresponding speech recognition problem becomes harder. While the reservation system may require a large vocabulary of place names, the underlying language that is modelled is relatively controlled. Additionally users are often aware that they are speaking to a computer and this can affect their behaviour.

In the case of "found speech", speech that is spoken for human ears, the problems are greater. The underlying language model is less restricted and the words are spoken with a greater degree of variability. In chapter 2, Eric Fosler-Lussier explores ways of addressing such variability in terms of pronunciation modelling. Pronunciation modelling refers to the way words, or sequences of words, are constructed from the basic units of speech (typically phones). Although modern speech recognition relies more on engineering notions of signal processing than theories of phonetics, pronunciation modelling is an area in which automatic speech recognition can be strongly informed by linguistics. Fosler-Lussier discusses approaches to pronunciation modelling based on linguistic theory, in contrast to more purely data-driven approaches. This chapter discusses online pronunciation models, in which the pronunciation of a word is dependent on the context of that word.

Speech recognition in unrestricted domains requires large statistical language models. Yoshi Gotoh and Steve Renals, in chapter 3, lay the foundations for understanding how such large language models are created and used. They show how language models can be created from large collection of texts, and how these models can be used to predict word combinations that have not been seen, i.e. how to compensate for incomplete or sparse data. After a presentation of the mathematical background of language modelling for speech, they also show some experimental results concerning recognizing named entities in text, an important part of the problem of finding information in large collections of audio files.

4   Dealing with Large Amounts of Text

The Web provides information access to anyone connected to the internet. Some this information in is images and some is in sound (as seen in the chapters mentioned above), in which case it must converted into text that a human can query. But much of the information on the Web is in text already.

Although we have some methods for dealing with text as we see when we use a web browser, the sheer size of the Web presents a challenge for capturing this information and digesting it into an efficient list of indexes that can link words to Web pages. David Hawking, in Chapter 4 presents how text-base information is performed on the Web. After a background on the field of information retrieval and its methodology, Hawking describes how the Web is spidered and indexed by web browsers. He describes what data structures must be used to store indexes for billions of URLs (addresses of Web pages), and how search engines can give an answer so quickly, even with such large indexes. Also discussed are issues of parallelizing and distributing indexing and retrieval processes.

Current browsers that access the large amount of text on the Web, already troubled by the mass of data they must manipulate, provide little normalization of the text that they index, other than conflating upper and lower case, and sometimes accented to unaccented letters. But the same ideas can be expressed with a wide variety of words and expressions. Agata Savary and Christian Jacquemin, in chapter 5, discuss the aspects of this language variation, and show how some aspects of it can be reduced. They describe terminology extraction, comparing systems such as ACABIT, LEXTER, TERMINO and Xterm, and compare indexing system that exploit terminology. They then show in detail how terminology can be extracted and normalized using the FASTR system, and give experimental results of the advantage of normalization of terms extracted from large information retrieval text collections.

In the final chapter, Jussi Karlgren reflects on information access and the current approaches being exploited. He discusses the limitations of current syntactic based approaches as compared to a semantic indexing of text. He touches about other, unused aspects of text, and wonders about how a model of the user might be integrated into a a new interactive interface to information. He also provides a list of research that he thinks needs to be done in the future to improve information access.

5   Conclusion

These chapters were originally presented as tutorials for students in linguistics and computer science during the 8th ELSNET Summer School, held in Chios Greece. ELSNET is the acronym for the European Network of Excellence in Human Language Technology (www.elsnet.org), a Europe-based forum dedicated to human language technologies. ELSNET sponsor activities that advance technologies involving both language and speech. The 8th ELSNET Summer School was organized by Stelios Bakamidis, George Carayannis, Vassilios Digalakis, Ioannis Dologlou, Sokrates Katsikas, George Kokkinakis, Panagiotis Konstantopoulos, Iraklio Yannis Kontos, George Kouroupetroglou, Ioanna Malagardi, Anastasios Patrikakos, Stelios Piperidis, Athanassios Protopapas, Timoleon Sellis, Gregory Stainhauer, Athanasios Tsakalidis. The members of the Program Committee were Gerrit Bloothooft, Koenraad de Smedt, Steve Renals, Gregory Grefenstette and George Carayannis. Other lecturers, not present in this volume, were Phil Woodland, Paul Taylor, Chris Brew, and Ido Dagan. Renata Da Silva Camargo helped with LaTeXing the final volume.

References

1. T.C. Bell, A. Moffat, I. H. Witten, and J. Zobel. Taking Moore's law into the next century. *IEEE Computer Magazine*, 32(1):43–48, 1999.
2. H.E. Blok, D. Hiemstra, S. Choenni, F. de Jong, H.M. Blanken, and P.M.G. Apers. Predicting the cost-quality trade-off for information retrieval queries: Facilitating database design and query optimization. In *Proceedings of the 2001 ACM CIKM International Conference on Information and Knowledge Management*, pages 207–214. ACM,, 2001.

3. Douglass R. Cutting and Jan O. Pedersen. Space optimizations for total ranking. In *Proceedings of RIAO'97*, pages 401–412, Montreal, 1997. CID.
4. William B. Frakes and Ricardo Baeza-Yates, editors. *Information Retrieval: Data Structures and Algorithms*. Prentice Hall, New Jersey, 1992.
5. P. Morrison and P. Morrison. The sum of human knowledge? *Scientific American*, July 1998.
6. Terry Winograd. *Understanding Natural Language*. Edinburgh University Press, Edinburgh, 1972.

Data Analysis for a Multimedia Library

Alexander Hauptmann, Rong Jin, and Howard Wactlar

Carnegie Mellon University, School of Computer Science, Pittsburgh, PA, USA

1 Introduction

This section describes the indexing, search, and retrieval of various combinations of audio, video, text, and image media and the automated content processing that enables it. The intent is to provide a framework for data analysis in multimedia digital libraries. The organization of this article is as follows: The introduction briefly distinguishes digital from traditional libraries and touches on the specific issues important to searching the content of multimedia libraries. The second section introduces the Informedia Digital Video Library as an example of a multimedia library, including a quick tour of the functionality. The next section discusses the processing of audio and image information, as it relates to a multimedia library. Section four illustrates the interplay between audio and video information using a video information retrieval experiment as an example. Section five discusses the exporting and sharing of metadata in a digital library using MPEG–7. Finally, section 6 presents one vision of a future digital library, where all personal memory can be recorded and accessed.

1.1 Traditional versus Digital Libraries

Traditional libraries have been in existence for thousands of years. Digital libraries must at least continue to serve the same functions as current paper libraries [12], as far as

- Collecting information
- Organizing and categorizing the information [cataloguing] and
- Allowing access and easy retrieval of desired information [distribution]

An essential function of traditional libraries is that they compile catalogs, which help users to access the individual documents. The catalog has so called 'metadata' , i.e. data about the documents, which in addition to author, publication details, copyright information, etc., may include keywords or phrases, summaries, abstracts, and cross-references [32]. Digital libraries allow for the introduction of more varied and comprehensive metadata description and complex cross-referencing of the metadata dimensions.

In addition, digital libraries can have higher capacity for collecting documents, broader means for delivering information to users and should provide new services that are possible through automatic analysis and synthesis or summarization of the complete content in their collections. For example, digital libraries are able to index every word in every one of their documents, something that was not available in a traditional library. Thus the grand vision of a universal digital library is to contain as much authored material as possible, created or converted to digital format, instantly available, to anyone, anywhere in the world, in any language [51].

S. Renals, G. Grefenstette (Eds.): Text- and Speech-Triggered Info. Access, LNAI 2705, pp. 6-37, 2003.

1.2 Multimedia Digital Libraries

According to the Concise Encyclopedia Britannica [11], multimedia is defined as a "computer-delivered electronic system that allows the user to control, combine, and manipulate different types of media, such as text, sound, video, computer graphics, and animation." A multimedia digital library therefore should contain authored video, image and audio work, in addition to text.

Why are multimedia libraries important in today's world? More and more our society

- *captures* its experience,
- *records* its accomplishments,
- *portrays* its past
- *informs* its masses

in pictures, audio and video. For many Americans, CNN has become the 'publication of record', replacing the New York Times as the standard reference for news. Multimedia digital libraries are also an essential component of formal, informal, and professional learning. They are crucial for growing fields such as distance education, and telemedicine.

Multimedia data is qualitatively different from text in that its data can have a time dimension and, most importantly, that the content cannot be directly indexed through words. Representing images and sounds in digital form also consumes much more disk space than does text. Thus both storage and bandwidth requirements in multimedia libraries are important, but techniques for multimedia data analysis are critical to help extract metadata and create textual descriptions of the image and audio content.

Nothing ever works perfectly in automatic multimedia data analysis; there is always a significant error rate. Sometimes the errors can be recovered, for some purposes they don't matter as much. At times domain-specific training data will reduce the error rate, but sometimes the processed data will just have unacceptably poor quality. This is especially true when the processing is transferred to new domains or new types of data, that are significantly unlike the original training data, even though the data appears to be similar, when e.g. it is speech and it sounds clear enough, but the microphones, domain of discourse and environmental conditions are subtly different. To compensate for these errors, alternative ways to search the content and good interfaces are critical.

Video is the ultimate multimedia data, subsuming audio, graphics, animations and still image data. Video is a veritable fire hose in producing large amounts of bits. To play one second of uncompressed 8–bit color, 640 × 480 resolution, digital video requires approximately 9 MB of storage. One minute would require about 0.5 GB. Data storage and transfer problems increase proportionally with 16–bit and 24–bit color playback. Without compression digital video would not be possible even with current advances in storage technology. Compression can reduce the video data to 18MB/second for high quality MPEG–2 compression that is comparable to digital cable or DVD quality. At the lowest end of video compression , the data is reduced to around 0.02 MB/second, typical in WWW video, drastically reducing image size, frame rate and with extreme image compression, resulting is blotchy video with jerky motion.

What makes multimedia digital libraries feasible, despite their large space requirements and their textually inaccessible audio and image content, are recent advances in compression and storage technology, as well as faster computer hardware and programs for content analysis that create searchable information from the audio and video. The Internet, especially the World Wide Web (WWW), makes it possible to deliver anywhere, virtually instantaneously or with low delay. We can expect this infrastructure to improve further over the next years and decades, reducing the creation, storage and transmission barriers to multimedia libraries.

2   The Informedia Digital Video Library (IDVL) as a Prototypical Multimedia Library

We will discuss various types of multimedia data that can be extracted from video, audio and images using the Informedia Digital Video Library as an example. The Informedia Digital Video Library [62] project focuses specifically on information extraction from video and audio content. Over a terabyte of online data has been collected in MPEG–1 format, with metadata automatically generated and indexed for retrieving videos from this library. The architecture for the project is based on the premise that real-time constraints on library and associated metadata creation could be relaxed in order to realize increased automation and deeper parsing and indexing for identifying the library contents and breaking it into segments. Library creation is an offline activity, with library exploration by users occurring online and making use of the generated metadata and segmentation.

The Informedia research challenge was how much can the information contained in video and audio be analyzed automatically and then made to be useful to a user. Broadly speaking, the Informedia project wants to enable search and discovery in the video medium, similar to what is widely available for text. One prerequisite for achieving this goal is the automated information extraction and metadata creation from digitized video. Once the metadata has been extracted, the system enables full-content search and retrieval from spoken language and visual documents. The approach that was ultimately successful was the integration of speech, image and natural language understanding for library creation and exploration.

2.1   Related Systems

Extraction of data from video has been getting attention by many researchers and entrepreneurs. There are now quite a few other systems similar to Informedia that analyze broadcast news and extract metadata into a database. BBN's *Oasis* system (formerly known as *Rough'n'Ready*) is a system for analyzing audio transcripts only [27],[28]. Oasis allows for speech recognition and indexing of the recognized transcripts, speaker identification, topic labeling, and extraction of "named entities" (i.e. names, places, and organizations). MITRE's Broadcast News Navigator (BNN) [34] works only from closed-captioned news and extracts named entities, but does not use speech recognition. Other similar projects include SRI's MAESTRO system [42], which features speech recognition and archiving, speaker tracking, optical character recognition (OCR), image

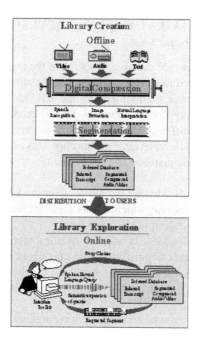

Fig. 1. The two phases of multimedia library processing: Library creation (offline) and library exploration (online) by users.

analysis (camera flash detection), natural language processing for sentence boundary identification, disfluency detection, and topic tracking. Físchlár is a system for recording, indexing, browsing and playback of broadcast TV programs developed at Dublin City University [54]. It emphasizes ease of recording, as well as browsing or querying as well as an integrated recommender system. The Físchlár news archive can, in addition, pre-process videos using IR techniques so that a small number of useful news segments (stories) for individual users can also be presented on a mobile interface, thus simplifying user interaction [31]. Commercial versions of similar video analysis software are marketed by companies such as Virage [57] and Sonic Foundry [56].

2.2　A Quick Tour of the Informedia Digital Video Library Interface

Figure 2 shows the Informedia Digital Video Library System (IDVLS) interface following a text query by a user. In this figure, a set of results is displayed at the bottom. The display includes a (yellow) pop-up window containing a title for a user-selected video segment, and a pictorial menu, labeled "Search Results (Page 1 of 67)", of the top fifteen matching video segments each represented with a thumbnail image at approximately 1/4–resolution of the video in the horizontal and vertical dimensions. The title window automatically pops up whenever the mouse is positioned over a result item; in this case the title window for the first result is shown. In addition to the headline for the segment, it describes the result as 4 minutes and 19 seconds long, and originating on 5/22/1998.

The Informedia Digital Video Library system (IDVLS) interface provides multiple levels of summaries and abstractions:

- Visual icons with relevance measure. Looking at the results in Figure 2, each keyframe has been selected to be representative for the story as it relates to the query. The keyframe has a little thermometer on the left side, which indicates the relevance of this video story to the user query. The different colors in the thermometer bar correspond to the different query words, so that the user can tell the contribution of each query word to the relevance of this clip. This allows a user to immediately see which query words matched in a story and query words are dominant in this story [6].
- Short titles or headlines. Moving the mouse over the keyframe brings up an automatically generated headline, which acts as a title for the story to summarize in text what this story is about. [20],[23].
- Topic identification of stories. In addition to titles, stories can also be assigned to topics, allowing a better categorization of the results [17].
- Filmstrip (storyboard) views. A story keyframe can be expanded into a complete storyboard of images, one per shot, which summarize the complete video story at a glance, as shown at the top of Figure 3 [7].
- Transcript following, even when the speech recognition is errorful. The bottom of Figure 3 shows the video playing and while it is playing, a transcription of the audio is visually synchronized by highlighting the words as they are spoken in the audio track [19].
- Dynamic maps. Sometimes the information in the video can best be summarized in a dynamic and interactive map, which dynamically shows the locations referenced in the video and allows the user to search geographically for video related to a given area [9].
- Active video skims allow the user to quickly skim through a video play playing interesting excerpts [7].

The interface was designed with the mantra of Shneiderman [52] in mind: Overview first, then zoom and filter, giving details on demand. IDVLS therefore supports multiple ways of navigating and browsing the digital video library. These "forgiving" and compensating navigation aids and interface features were essential to deal with the errors and uncertainties of the derived data generated by speech recognition, image processing, and natural language processing as encountered in the search and retrieval. Consider the filmstrip and video playback IDVLS window shown in Figure 3. For this video the segmentation process, which usually splits a news broadcast into individual, coherent stories of 3–4 minutes each, failed, resulting in a thirty-minute segment. This long segment was one of the returned results for the query "Mir collision." The filmstrip in Figure 3 shows that the segment is more than just a story on the Russian space station, but rather begins with a commercial, then the weather, and then coverage of Hong Kong before addressing Mir. By overlaying the filmstrip and video playback windows with information where the matching words occurred, the user can quickly see that the word matches don't occur until later in the segment, after these other clips that were irrelevant to the query. The match bars are optionally color-coded to specific query words; in Figure 3 "Mir" matches are in red and "collision" matches in purple. When the user

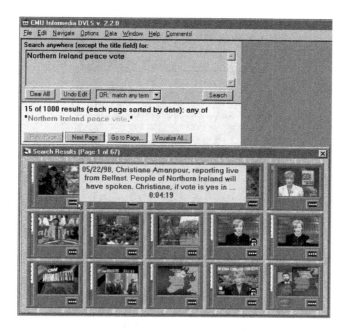

Fig. 2. The initial result of a query to the Informedia System

moved the mouse over the match bars in the filmstrip, a text window displayed the actual matching word from the transcript or video optical character recognition (OCR) metadata for that particular match; "Mir" is shown in one such text window in Figure 3.

By investigating the distribution of match locations on the filmstrip, the user can determine the location of a region of interest within the segment. The user can click on a match bar to jump directly to that point in the video segment. Hence, clicking the mouse as shown in Figure 3 would start playing the video at this mention of "Mir" with the overhead shot of people at desks. Similarly, IDVLS provides "seek to next match" and "seek to previous match" buttons in the video player allowing the user to quickly jump from one match to the next. In the example of Figure 3, these interface features allowed the user to bypass problems in segmentation and jump directly to the "Mir" story without having to first watch the opening video on other topics.

Since the Informedia system extracts place names from the spoken transcript using an approach described in [29], a gazetteer can place known locations on a map, shown in Figure 4. This map is active in that it highlights cities and countries as they are referred to in the video. The map is also interactive in that the user can manipulate the map, panning and zooming to any place in the world, and issue a 'spatial query' by selecting a region on the map and asking the system to retrieve relevant video the references the selected area [38].

Once a relevant video clip has been found, a user might want to make annotations for herself or others to later reuse what was learned. The library provides a simple mechanism that allows a user to type or speak any comment that applies to a user-selected

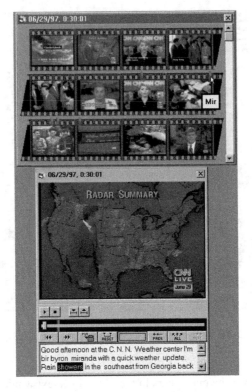

Fig. 3. Marking the filmstrip of a query with word location in the transcript and OCR for the query "Mir collision".

portion of the video. To this end, the indexing mechanism was modified to allow dynamic, incremental additions and deletions to the index. Finally, a fielded search capability enables the user to search only on selected fields, for example searching only the user annotation field, either through a statistical search or with a classic Boolean search expression. Since these combined requirements exceeded the functionality of available commercial text search engines, the project implemented its own, based on established and state-of-the-art techniques.

Further re-use of relevant video clips is enabled through a cut-and-paste mechanism that allows a selected clip to be extracted from the library and imported into PowerPoint slide presentations or MS Word text documents.

3   Content Analysis for Multimedia Data

In this section, we will elaborate on the application of audio and image processing technologies for extracting metadata from video and incorporating in into a content-searchable multimedia library. All processing is performed on MPEG–1 encoded video, which inherently sets limits on the accuracy and resolution of some of the processing

Fig. 4. A map display highlights locations as they are referenced in the video. Users can pan and zoom the map and select any region as a 'spatial query'.

steps. In each case, while the applied technologies may produce highly errorful intermediate results, one should remember that it is the integration of a number of different aspects that frequently overcomes the limitations of each technique. One of the best examples is speech recognition, where, despite getting every third or fourth word wrong, information retrieval is just minimally worse than retrieval from perfectly transcribed text.

3.1   Audio Analysis Functions

Audio processing supplies necessary information for library segmentation and multimedia abstractions. Specifically, from the audio track, we can automatically generate a transcript to enable text-based retrieval from spoken language documents. If a script is available, speech recognition can be used for alignment, and we can also identify changes in speakers and identify individual speakers. Through real-time speech recognition we can also provide a speech interface to speak queries to the digital video library, but this aspect will not be discussed here.

Speech Recognition for Alignment. One function for speech recognition in the Informedia Digital Video Library is to create a time aligned word index into the video through the accompanying audio track. We also use it for alignment of existing imperfect transcripts of the spoken words and for creating complete transcripts when none exist. This improves text synchronization to audio/video in the presence of scripts or closed-captions. The premise is that the speech generated transcripts for indexing/retrieval transcripts can then be searched effectively, despite errors.

Each word is spoken at a particular time in a video. If we know that point, we can facilitate browsing and navigation for users. For example, just because the user remembers that *"Frankly my dear, I don't give a damn"* was spoken in the movie *"Gone with the Wind,"* it would still be quite tedious to locate the exact scene and context of this phrase inside the movie. The missing information is the alignment of the transcript words to the location where the word is spoken. The process for this alignment is a simple dynamic time warping algorithm. Given a good-quality transcript and a speech recognition transcript, each of the words in both transcripts are aligned using a dynamic time warping (DTW) procedure. [37] Even for very low recognition accuracy, this alignment with an existing transcript provides sufficiently accurate timing information. The Informedia system uses this information to allow the user to jump directly to the location in the movie where a particular query term was spoken. Thus the user avoids viewing a complete video in order to find the words of a query.

Speech Recognition for Indexing and Retrieval. Information retrieval from speech recognition transcripts has received much attention in recent years in the spoken document retrieval evaluations at the Text REtrieval Conferences (TREC) between 1998 and 2000 [59]. The evaluations use a standardized evaluation format, a common corpus and test data to ensure different participants and their approaches can be compared fairly. The Spoken Document Retrieval (SDR) task eventually comprised 20,000 broadcast news stories (which translates to roughly 500 hours of audio), and 50 queries sought for information from these 20,000 stories. The consensus from a number of published experiments in this area is that as long as speech recognition has a word error rate less than 35%, then information retrieval from the transcripts of spoken documents is only 3–10% worse than information retrieval on perfect text transcriptions of the same documents. The most accurate recognizers to date produced a word error rate of just under 20% for broadcast news [13].

General insights from publications about speech retrieval :

Vocabulary size Speech recognizers like to have vocabularies less than 64,000 words, since that is easily stored and indexed in 16 bits of data. As the TREC experiments showed, typically only very few query words are outside the 64k vocabulary. Looking back at multiple sets of TREC queries (across different tracks), only about 1 word in 50 queries is really out-of-vocabulary. More frequently, there are issues with text conditioning, e.g. "CIA" might be transcribed by the recognizer as "C. I. A.", and "B–2" might be transcribed as "B. two" and thus not match the query [16].

Relation of Word Error Rate (WER) and Information Retrieval (IR) In general, WER predicts information retrieval accuracy very well. It also predicts how well named entities [29], that is names, organization, places, dates and numbers can be identified and extracted from the speech transcript. Beyond WER, other ways of measuring the relation of speech recognition accuracy and information retrieval show that metrics such as the Named Entity Error Rate, and the Term Error Rate (i.e. the word error rate after stop words are removed and words stemmed to their root) are no better predictor of performance than the straight WER [13].

Improving Information Retrieval from Speech Recognition Transcripts A big improvement in information retrieval for audio documents has come through document expansion. This idea was based on the fact that by looking at an errorful transcript, you still get a sense of what the document was about. Adding words or phrases from sections of other perfectly transcribed documents from a parallel collection about the same topic has helped improve retrieval performance. Blind relevance feedback is the practice of taking the top documents in a first retrieval run, and, assuming these documents are 'relevant' to the query, adding selected words from those documents to the query (e.g. add the top 5 terms from the top-ranked 15 documents retrieved to the original query and resubmit) in order to make the query longer and richer in the words it uses to describe the query topic. A number of variations of this technique have been shown to improve IR. In speech documents, parallel blind relevance feedback was found to be effective by using documents from a parallel, perfectly transcribed collection of documents to add new query terms in the relevance feedback step. These document and query expansion techniques can improve average precision by 17% or more. Eventually, the degradation in average precision due to a Word Error Rate (WER) of 25% is reduced to around 2% relative, when all methods are combined. Eliminating hard-to-recognize sections of the audio track has also been found to help accuracy. Thus when a system removes commercial advertisements, music and poor quality audio regions, word transcription accuracy improves as there are fewer miss-recognized words that spuriously match query words during retrieval.

While it is interesting to see how much information retrieval degrades with respect to a particular recognition word error rate, we also conducted experiments to estimate the retrieval effectiveness over a range of transcripts with different error rates. Given a set of perfect manually created transcripts and a set of speech-recognized transcripts with an average word error rate of 50.7%, we constructed a set of interpolated transcripts. To improve the transcripts to a better accuracy, we aligned the perfect transcripts with the speech transcripts and randomly replaced a substitution, deletion or insertion error with the corresponding aligned word entry in the perfect transcript. Thus we were able to create interpolated transcripts at any word error rate between 0% and 50.7%. This process of creating interpolated transcripts is only a very approximate model of the errors. Clearly, much more accurate error modeling could be performed using the actual recognition error statistics for insertions, deletions and substitutions, as well as the a-priori language model probabilities used in the recognizer. However, even with more accurate error modeling techniques, we would expect the shapes of the curves to be quite similar, and the same conclusions would apply.

To obtain error rates higher than the actual ones found in the speech recognized transcripts, we randomly deleted correctly recognized words from the speech transcripts, after aligning them to the perfect transcripts to determine which recognized words were correct and which were errors. WER measures the number of words inserted, deleted or substituted divided by the number of words in the correct transcript. Thus WER can exceed 100% at times. In the experiments described here, the stories being indexed were manually segmented, that is, the full news broadcasts were broken into individual stories by hand. Automatic segmentation methods can be expected to generate errors that are likely to decrease retrieval effectiveness.

Figure 5 shows the relationship between information retrieval precision and speech recognition accuracy plotted as relative degradation to retrieval from manually transcribed text documents. The performance of a "perfect" system is defined by the relevance judgments for documents and queries of a human judge of document relevance. In this figure, the quality of the information retrieval decreases as the speech recognition word error rate increases. For word error rates less than about 25 percent, there is only a very small decrease, but the information retrieval effectiveness starts to decline noticeably at increasing speech error rates.

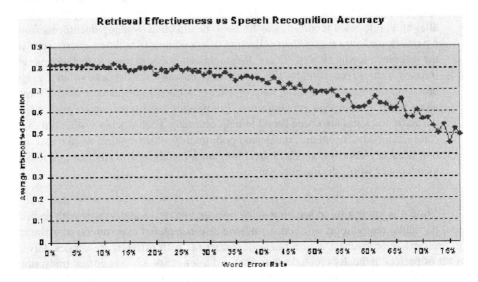

Fig. 5. Relative Information Retrieval Precision vs. Speech Recognition Accuracy. As word error rate in the speech documents increases, relative recall to a text retrieval system decreases.

Speaker and Audio Type Identification. Gaussian Mixture Models (GMM) have proven effective in speaker identification tasks in large databases of over 2000 speakers [26],[48]. Informedia uses similar techniques for processing the audio portion of a video stream to automatically extract additional metadata providing a description of the content of the audio channel. The GMM processing can be used to detect music and other non-speech sounds, e.g., laughter and applause. If we accurately label non-speech regions of the audio channel, then the output of the speech recognizer can be improved by removing these non-speech regions from the data passed to the recognizer. Current speech recognition systems are unable to deal with non-speech sounds and will output quasi-random transcription text. The GMM processing can also be used to distinguish male versus female speakers, so that the respective audio regions can be passed to more accurately trained gender-specific speech recognizers. We can also apply this technique to the identification of well-known speakers for which a significant amount of training data is available. For example, the techniques could easily identify President Bush as well as most of the news anchors. We segment the audio channel based on speaker change and classify regions that belong to the same speaker, even if the identity of that speaker is not previously known. The output is the identification of the region in which the first speaker spoke, followed by the region in which the second speaker spoke, and so forth [53]. The speaker change classification can be used to help break the video into coherent segments, and in general to characterize the audio channel of the data. Thus, video where one talker speaks for a long time can be labeled as a "speech," whereas an "interview" consists of two people switching back and forth, while a "forum" discussion includes many speakers. For news broadcast data, it is possible to detect which speaker remains present throughout the entire audio data, thus identifying the anchor or narrator. Furthermore, researchers have shown that audio classification as "clean", "noisy", or "telephone" can dramatically improve speech recognition accuracy [66].

Prior to classification, Mel-Frequency Cepstral Coefficients (or MFCC) features are extracted from the audio channel. For training, regions of audio are labeled with a speaker code, and then modeled in their respective class (speaker). For example, for the class labeled Music there may be 100 training examples, each from different sources. Once training models have been generated, the system must classify novel audio sections. The process begins by segmenting the audio channel into 1–second, overlapping regions. A GMM is then computed for each audio region. The resulting model is compared to existing trained models using a maximum likelihood distance function. Based on the comparisons to each class, a decision is made as to the classification of the data into speech, applause, laughter, known speaker X, etc. To detect speaker change, each region will be compared to the previous regions. The distance will be thresholded and combined with other features such as pitch. The combination of these features will allow accurate detection of speaker change. The final step involves clustering each user's audio data into the appropriate set. Each region bounded by a speaker change will be used to generate a new GMM. A clustering algorithm is then used to cluster the regions into one cluster for all the regions from the same speaker. Generally, about 4 seconds of speech are required to get reliable speaker identification, under benign environmental conditions.

3.2 Image Analysis

The goal of an automated visual analysis of the image or video is to characterize the type of image, extract image objects and perform similarity matching.

In the Informedia Digital Video Library, image understanding technology is applied to support:

- Similarity matching
- OCR on video text and titles
- Face detection and recognition
- Scene characterization
- Shot segmentation
- Camera motion determination and object tracking

The Image Similarity Challenge. The term "similarity" can have different meaning for different people. Even the same person uses different similarity measures in different situations. Images can be similar with respect to colors, shapes or content.

The above two pictures are very similar based on color, but different in content or object shapes. This is the easiest kind of similarity to determine.

For example, the above two pictures contain similar shapes and content (i.e. a horse jumping), but are very different in color, since one is indoors and one is outdoors. While some systems can extract shapes and match based on shapes, this is clearly a more difficult similarity match.

These last 2 pictures are similar only in content, but no color or shape similarity can be determined. Yet it is obvious that both are pictures of a soccer match. However, without keyword annotations, no system exists today that can determine that these last images are similar because they both contain soccer scenes.

If you have a picture and are supposed to find others like it, your success depends on how you define similarity. It could be a similar picture of an outdoor scene, something with a lot of sky and clouds, a similar picture with a plane, or a similar picture of the X–29 experimental plane in exactly the same position. Each one is similar according to some criteria. When people do image matching, they usually have a specific, semantic concept in mind that defines the similarity. However an image search engine is only given an image as a set of pixels without any interpretation to what is intended to be similar. This is complicated by the fact that an example picture is an unusual way to start a search, if you already have a picture of a girl flying a kite, then your marginal utility of finding a second picture is probably small. If you don't have any picture of a girl with a kite, and only the thought of one, current image similarity systems can't help, even if they allow you to draw a sample image. In most cases, the image search will be more successful with an environment or corpus that indexes images based on the keywords explicitly used to label the images.

QBIC – Query by Image Content: A Prototype Image Search Engine. The Informedia system combines a number of contributed and custom-implemented image indexing and retrieval methodologies; and is structured to enable researchers to compare and contrast to allow for highly informed relevance feedback. Instead of examining that structure in depth, we will discuss the IBM Query by Image Content (QBIC) system and it's features as a prototypical image retrieval system. While a complete discussion of image retrieval is clearly beyond the scope of this article, readers more interested in further details are referred to [55],[10]. First and best known among commercial image retrieval systems, QBIC was developed at the IBM Almaden Research Center [64],[22]. As is typical for many other image search engines, QBIC allows an image search by shape, color, texture, and keyword. QBIC queries can be based on:

- example images based on colors, textures, shapes or weighted combinations thereof,
- user-constructed sketches and drawings,
- or selected color and texture patterns
- as well as a combination of textures, colors and shapes.

A user can select colors and color distributions from a color wheel, select textures from a predetermined selection of textures, use shape features and adjust the relative weights among the features.

QBIC color analysis QBIC uses the standard 3–dimensional RGB (red, green, blue) color space. The color dimensions are quantized and clustered into a total of 256 color cells. The similarity between two images is determined by the similarity of their color histograms. In general, a variety of measures can be used to compare histograms, while some systems compute the distances between corresponding histogram bins, QBIC further weights the histogram computation by the perceptual color similarity between the different bins. A query image histogram is matched to the database image histograms by looking at the difference of the histograms. For each image pair, the difference histogram Z is computed, and a similarity measure is given by $||Z|| = Z^T A Z$, where A is a symmetrical matrix with $A(i, j)$ measuring the perceptual similarity of color bins i and j according to the Munsell color space. While a large collection of papers exists that experiment with image retrieval in different color spaces using different comparison metrics, it is generally not clear which one would be superior for a given collection. For QBIC, the image is also be partitioned into 256 regions, and a color histogram is computed for each region. This allows QBIC to compare color similarities in all regions individually (as well as only for user selected regions). The advantage is that a face with typical skin colors would only match to something with that histogram in the same location of the image, thus ensuring a match on the composition of the image as well as the overall colors.

QBIC texture analysis has 3 components: *coarseness*, *contrast*, and *directionality*. *Coarseness* measures texture scale, which is the average size of regions that have the same intensity. *Contrast* measure vividness of the texture, how dramatic the light and dark frequencies vary. Contrast thus depends on the variance of the gray-level histogram. *Directionality* reflects the eventual main direction (angle) of the image texture. Directionality depends on the number and the shape of the peaks of the distribution of gradient directions. The texture similarity between images is computed as a weighted Euclidian distance between the 3 component dimensions of texture.

QBIC shape analysis looks at 5 components related to the shape of the continuous colors. The *area* is determined by the number of pixels in shape body. The *circularity* is measured as the perimeter^2/Area. The *eccentricity* is the ratio of the smallest and the largest eigenvalues of the second order covariance matrix. The *major axis orientation* is the direction of the largest eigenvector of the second order covariance matrix. Finally a set of *algebraic moment invariants* are computed as the eigenvalues of predefined matrices, which consist of weighted factors of the central moments.

In general, research in image retrieval lacks standard test suites with human judgments to measure precision and recall. Frequently systems are only compared against specific internal and copyrighted subsets of a specific type, showing the benefit of various system specific features, without the possibility of external validation by others.

Extracting Text from Images.

Document Image Analysis through Optical Character Recognition Optical character recognition (OCR) can be viewed in a narrow way as just trying to recognize a linear stream of characters on a printed page. This implies that the marks on a page are converted into ASCII or Unicode characters. Obviously, the task is easier, if the text is machine typed as opposed to hand-written. Just recognizing the characters A–Z, a–z, and 0–9, may be not be enough, usually one would also like to have a transcription of the visible punctuation. A frequent source of error is the grouping of letters, trying to determine where the word separation is.

A broader view of OCR looks beyond the issue of characters, trying to understand page layout style, words and word flow. One task may be identifying the character set used, which also has implications for the language the text may be written in. Furthermore we may want to recognize the font style, the font size, and the actual font used. Looking at hand written text is clearly harder due to variations in individual writing style. Especially scribbles can pose a formidable challenge to OCR. More subtle issues involve the way the characters are placed in "sequence", identifying subscripts, superscripts. Some writing may not be left to right (Arabic and Hebrew is written right-to-left) and Chinese characters are often written top to bottom, as are some advertising texts. Under the heading of "grouping", we would like to recognize the text flow on a line, and across lines. Page formatting can be important, as newspapers may have multiple articles on one page, interspersed with graphics, or pictures. Trying to analyze the page layout geometry is a 2 dimensional problem, introducing a dimension not present in linear speech audio or text. If we can capture the logical structure we could output the marked-up text in XML or a page description language such as PDF. It is easy to describe how well characters and words are recognized, but the correctness of a description of the page layout is much harder to measure.

At some level it can be argued that OCR is inherently intractable because the text on a page is employed for intentional communications among people where the context is arbitrary and unpredictable, thus leaving the interpretation unclear without a specific content. Standard OCR on typical, printed text pages is usually excellent with a word error rate under 10%, but occasionally the results are totally unusable. Similar to what happens in speech recognition, catastrophic failures are commonplace: Noise bursts in the image quality (e.g. in fax transmissions), loss of reading order, and drop-outs result. What's worse is that these failures are hard to predict and identify automatically. Thus OCR systems can't ensure uniformly high performance. Evaluation of OCR errors can also be performed 'downstream'. It has been found that Information Retrieval which usually represents the text as a 'bag of words' vector is quite robust to OCR errors. However OCR errors are severely disruptive to machine translation systems, and combining OCT, machine translation and information retrieval has only resulted in dismal failures, since the errors compound. During the TREC evaluations, experiments have shown that information retrieval on documents recognized through OCR with a character error rate of 5% and 20% degrades IR effectiveness anywhere between 10% and 50% depending on the metric, when compared to perfect text retrieval [25].

Video OCR. A somewhat different textual representation is derived by interpreting the text that is present in video images using optical character recognition (OCR). The Informedia video optical character recognition system identifies and recognizes captioned text that appears in the image on the video [45],[46], as opposed to closed-captioning, which is separately embedded in machine readable form in the vertical blanking interval between frames. OCR technology has been commercially available for many years. However, reading the text present in the video stream requires a number of processing steps in addition to the actual character recognition (see Figure 3.2). First the text must be detected as present in a wide variety of scenes and backgrounds. Then it must be extracted from the image and finally converted into a binary black and white representation, since the commercially available OCR engines do not recognize colored text on a variably colored background. The video OCR is further complicated by the fact that the text has very low resolution, frequently only about 10 pixels of height per character. This resolution is due to the NTSC television standard of 325x248 pixels per image. The European PAL and SECAM standards have similar restrictions. Unlike text printed on white paper, the background of the image tends to be complex, with the character hue and brightness very near the background values. Among the solutions to these problems are interpolation filters, the integration of images across multiple frames and combinations of filters.

Text segmentation amounts to text area detection. Given the number of frames contained in typical broadcast news, it is not computationally feasible to process each and every video frame for text. For this reason a rough or quick text region detection is performed first. It searches for horizontal rectangular structure of clustered sharp edges using variable orientation differential filtering techniques. Different filters looking for horizontal, vertical, left diagonal, and right diagonal lines are combined, and blurred to a gray scale. The regions where edges were detected are grouped into clusters and bounding boxes are applied. Heuristics then identify text boxes based on their aspect ratio, absolute size and the fill factor of the bounding boxes.

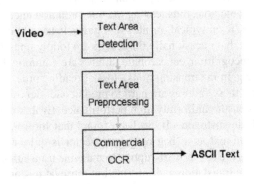

Fig. 6. Video OCR Block Diagram consisting of text area detection, text area preprocessing, and commercial OCR

Once a text area is detected, enhancement takes place. Multi-frame integration looks at the potential bounding boxes over several frames and finds the minimal (white) pixel values across that range. Potential text regions are sequentially filtered across all detected frames, effectively increasing the resolution of the each caption. This uses an assumption that the text is stable in the image, i.e. overlaid, while the background may be moving inside the image. Only text that is on the screen for at least 1 second is readable by humans. The box is magnified and sub-pixel interpolation performed to increase resolution without incurring jagged edges as artifacts of the magnification.

Character segmentation occurs at the troughs on the histogram. The detected text characters are normalized for size. Segmentation of characters is performed at the troughs in the color histogram. Individual text areas are combined into a region. Adaptive thresholding on the gray-scale histogram is then used to create binarized black on white text.

Fig. 7. Text regions as detected in a single image, web service provided by C. Wolf at http://telesun.insa-lyon.fr/~wolf/demos/textdetect.html

The potential text region is extracted as a tiff image and submitted to a commercial optical character recognition package for the final stage of recognizing the text. Since the extraction and binarization steps are quite noisy and do not produce perfect results, our system runs the OCR engine on every 3rd frame where text was detected. Thus we obtain over 100 OCR results for a single occurrence of text on the screen that might last for just over 10 seconds. Frequently many of the results would be only slightly different from each other.

In internal evaluations, the OCR word accuracy once text was detected in the video stream video was estimated to be 27% [15]. Despite the high error rate, OCR is very useful for video retrieval, as evidenced by the video retrieval experiments discussed in the next section. The text can be incorporated into the video metadata and indexed as if it were a transcript. Since only about half the words visible on the screen in a typical news broadcast are also spoken in the audio, the VOCR has the potential to allow retrieval of material that could never be derived from the speech recognition transcript.

Once text is recognized by an OCR system, a post-processing step can attempt to correct some of the inevitable errors. Our method for OCR correction involves the dictionary spelling correction method provided in MS Word. Through an application program interface to the features of MS Word 2000, an OCR recognized string is expanded into its possible "corrected" spellings. The system proceeded in a very conservative fashion, only expanding words that MS Word had flagged as incorrectly spelled. This dramatically reduced the number of spurious word candidates and avoided false matches.

Object Detection (Faces). Face detection is one class from a set of object detection tasks that are useful for image and video analysis. At the core is a simple recognition

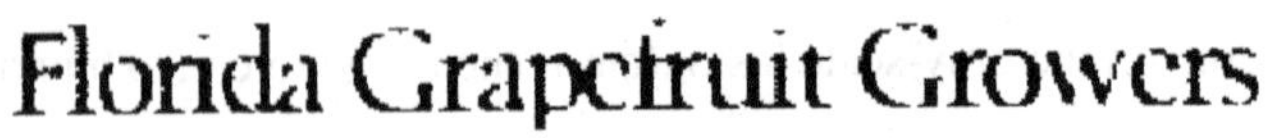

Florida Grapefruit Growers

Fig. 8. Typical binarized output of detected text for the OCR system. The difficulty in separating foreground from background in the video becomes apparent.

problem: does this image or region contain a face or not. There are some more subtle aspects to faces, such as the facial activities, expressions and emotions, which we ignore. What we really want to know is whose face is in the picture, and knowing that a face is there is a partial step towards the true goal. Even though one could think of many other object recognition tasks, as humans we are predisposed to view the task of finding faces more interesting as a class in general than maybe trees or clouds, or buildings. Other objects for which attempts at recognition have been made include cars, people's shapes, buildings, quadrupeds, military vehicles.

Extensive work in face detection has been done at CMU by Rowley [43]. This approach modeled the statistics of appearance implicitly using an artificial neural network. The neural network was trained on multiple 'face' windows templates, each 20x20 pixels. Images that might contain larger faces were subsampled to reduce their size. Training was done on a large set of rotated, scaled, translated and mirrored faces. The training also incorporated negative examples from false alarms in training. To increase confidence, overlapping detected faces were merged.

Currently Informedia uses an implementation of [49], which applies statistical modeling to capture the variation in facial appearance. This approach tries to learn the statistics of both object appearance and "non-object" appearance using a product of histograms. Each histogram represents the joint statistics of a subset of wavelet coefficients and their position on the object. Our approach is to use many such histograms representing a wide variety of visual attributes. The detector then applies a set of models that each describe the statistical behavior of a group of wavelet coefficients.

Face matching was used in Name-It [47] with the 'Eigenface' approach. Meanwhile there have been several commercial systems offering face detection and identification, such as Visionics [58]. In the Informedia Digital Video Library implementation we use the Schneiderman face detector and 'Eigenfaces' [41] for matching similar faces. Eigenfaces treat a face image as a two-dimensional N by N array of intensity values. From a set of training images, a set of eigenvectors can be derived that constitute the Eigenfaces. Every unknown new face is mapped into this eigenvector subspace and we calculate the distance between faces through corresponding points within the subspace. Only the first 30 eigenvectors are used to get a distance estimate.

The combination of face detection, matching and Video OCR enables an interesting application which puts a name to an unknown face or finds the face that goes with a particular name [47]. While the original Name-It system correlated similar faces with names referenced in audio track, OCR extracted (and corrected) text has proven to be a much more productive face labeling approach [21].

Detection of Video Shot Breaks. One step in video processing that is common to all video analysis systems is camera shot detection. A shot is defined as a continuous

Fig. 9. Example of face and text detection in one video image.

camera operation, terminated by an editing action such as a cut, fade, dissolve or wipe. Comparative difference measures are used in processing the video to mark potential shot boundaries or film editing cuts. Adjacent image frames with small color histogram disparity are considered to be relatively equivalent. By detecting significant changes in the weighted histogram of each successive video frame, a sequence of images can be grouped into a single shot. This simple and robust method for segmentation is fast and can detect 90% of the editing cuts in video. [18]. Techniques for shot break detection have been widely studied and can be considered very robust [33].

Camera Motion Analysis. Camera motion detection is an important element for automated video analysis that can be achieved with reasonable levels of success, unlike object motion detection or tracking. A standard video camera can pan left or right while recording, tilt up and down and zoom in or out. In principle, camera motion can also rotate around a focal point in the image, however this is a relatively infrequent event. Most methods approach the problem of camera motion by deriving parameters proportional to the zoom, pan, rotate and tilt given a set of motion blocks. The methods usually determine an empirical threshold that classifies the derived parameters as representative for a particular camera motion.

Numerous approaches have been developed to analyze camera motion of video sequences based on analyzing the optical flow computed between consecutive images [24],[3]. Optical flow relies on tracking a large number of characteristic points across adjacent frames. A few methods directly manipulate MPEG compressed video to extract camera motion [63],[40],[1]. These approaches use the MPEG motion vectors as an alternative to optical flow. MPEG–1 and MPEG–2 streams [35] encode one quantized motion vector per block. Though these motion vectors are not directly equivalent to the true motion vectors of a particular pixel in the frame, there are typically hundreds of motion vectors in one frame, sufficient to estimate camera model parameters.

3.3   Text Processing

Three types of text analyses are routinely performed in the video system using the text extracted from video OCR and speech recognition or captioning: headline creation, topic classification and named entity extraction.

Headlines and Summaries. To provide an overview over multiple video stories, it is helpful to have a short text representation of the story, which can be quickly scanned by a user. Ideally, providing a good, automatically generated title satisfies this need. While the traditional approaches have used a 'parsing' system to understand the document [30] and extract the title [14],[44], more recently statistical approaches have been used [65]. These approaches learn from training data by looking at many thousands of title and document pairs, and build probabilistic models of the type of title that may be suitable for a particular document, given the words in the document. The Informedia system has experimented with rule-based titles, which function in almost any domain, and statistical title approaches using Naive Bayes learning, and K-nearest neighbors to 'learn' good titles for a video story [23]. As with topic classification, the statistical methods depend on good training data, which closely resembles the actual data for their success. Fortunately, current news documents and titles can easily be harvested from the web, so the statistical classification remains up to date.

Topic Classification. In order to summarize and browse through stories quickly, it is convenient to assign stories to particular topic classes. We have implemented two separate topic classification schemes, one that uses HMMs in the spirit of [50] to assign one of about 3200 topic labels to a video story [17]. However, since the approach is dependent on training data, we found that the topic classes and the conditional word evidence for each class were strongly influenced by the events that occurred during the period from which the training data was derived. Thus, O.J. Simpson and Princess Diana dominated news during particular years in the mid 1990s. Later on, the topic assignment was overly biased to topics related to these events, when words about British royalty or DNA testing appeared in the news. To remedy this bias, it would be necessary to either retrain the system on a regular basis with new stories and topics, or to use a smaller set of topics. Currently we are only assigning video stories to general categories such as entertainment, politics, international affairs, sports, weather, business, medicine and human interest.

Named Entity Extraction and Geocoding. Named entity extraction refers to the process of identifying those phrases in the text which refer to people, places, organizations, dates, times, percentages, numbers and monetary amounts. The named entity extractor used in Informedia is in part based on one of the first versions of BBN's NYMBLE system, as described in [2],[29]. Our current version extracts names, locations and organizations. One of the major advantages of NYMBLE is that training produces a different language model for each type of entity, i.e., co-occurrence probabilities between word pairs differ across entity types, and the probability of a word being the first word of an entity (as in "*New* findings were discovered today" and "*New* York is one of the largest cities") also differs. Entities are extracted from text by parsing each sentence, one at a time, and using a Viterbi search to tag each word as belonging to one of four entities (people, places, organizations and other) so that, given the probabilities derived during training, the transitional probabilities from one state (word/entity) to another are maximized.

The hidden Markov model for our entity extractor was trained using training data consisting of approximately 100 hours of news broadcasts. It is important to note that we use only uncapitalized and unpunctuated text, i.e., transcripts that do not contain commas, periods and semicolons. Punctuation provides significant clues for entity extraction, as does word capitalization. Including prior probabilities and the training data our entity extraction model consists of about 39,000 unique words and 240,000 word pairs.

The extracted location entities are then retrieved from a gazetteer, which maps text names to latitude and longitude, and identifies the administrative type of the location (e.g. city, province/state, country, continent). The gazetteer used for geocoding in Informedia is a subset of ESRI's world gazetteer. This subset currently consists of all countries and administrative areas worldwide, as well as approximately 81,000 cities, towns and villages. Each record in the address coverage includes other information on a place. Columns used for geoprocessing in Informedia are the country name, the type of place, the administrative area and the province, country, and continent.

A heuristic disambiguation scheme is used to resolve ambiguous locations (e.g. *Paris*, Texas vs. *Paris*, France or *Georgia* the U.S. state vs. *Georgia*, the former Soviet republic), based on the amount of other location evidence in the textual vicinity of the location entity, which supports a particular location interpretation [38].

4 Experiments in Video Information Retrieval

In this section we discuss an experiment in video information retrieval from a video library, which involves a number of the processing steps described earlier.

The Text REtrieval Conference (TREC) has sponsored contrastive evaluations of information retrieval systems for the last 10 years. In 2001 the first video information retrieval evaluation was performed. The 2001 TREC Video Retrieval evaluation made a corpus of 11 hours of MPEG–1 encoded broadcast video available to all participants [61]. The data consisted of NIST project and promotional videos, documentary material from NASA and the Bureau of Reclamation and Land Management, a series of videotaped lectures, as well as BBC stock footage.

Two types of queries were used, known item and interactive queries. There were 36 general search queries and 34 known item queries. The 34 known item queries are distinguished from the remaining 'general search' queries in that the information need tended to be more focused and all instances of query-relevant items in the corpus are known. For general search queries, the top 20 results were evaluated for precision by human judges, but no evaluation for recall was performed due to the lack of a sufficiently large pool of results. For known-item queries, the top 100 results were scored.

In the following analysis of video retrieval we will elaborate only on the known item query set, because comprehensive relevance judgments were available for this set

allowing automatic estimation of precision and recall for variations of our video retrieval system. This allows an experimental comparison of system variations without
the need for further human evaluations.

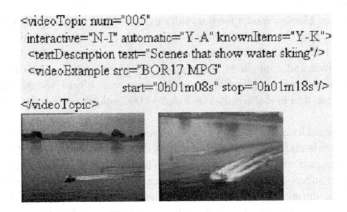

Fig. 10. A Video Trec query specified through a text description and a video sequence, for which
only two frames are shown.

The general unit of retrieval (or relevant 'document' to be found), was a 'shot', in
other words a time range between two shot changes. Systems had to determine shot
changes automatically. An item was considered relevant if at least 33% of the length
of the returned item overlapped with the target item in the list of shots relevant to this
query and less than 33% of the time range for the returned item was outside the target
range. This requirement ensured a reasonable overlap of the returned shot with the
target shot. An example of a typical query is shown in Figure 7. This query is to be used
for automatic systems, but not for interactive evaluations. It is a known item query,
indicating that all results are known inside the video collection. According to the text
description, the query is looking for video scenes of water skiing, and gives an example
of the type of video that is desired. Two images from the example video are extracted
and also shown in Figure 7.

From the 11 hours of video, Informedia extracted about 8000 shots using color
histogram differences. We aggregated the MPEG I-frames for each shot to be alternative
images for each shot. Whenever something matched to an image within a shot, the
complete shot was returned as relevant. In total, there were about 80,000 images to be
searched.

Because the collection contains only small numbers of relevant items, we adopted
the average reciprocal rank (ARR) as our evaluation metric, similar the TREC Question
Answering Track [60]. ARR is defined as follows: For a given query, there are a total
of N_r items in the collection that are relevant to this query. Assume that the system
only retrieves k relevant items and they are ranked as $r_1, r_2, \ldots, r_k$. Then, the average
reciprocal rank is computed as

$$ARR = \{\sum_{i=1}^{k} i/r_i\}/N_r \ .$$

(1)

As shown in Equation 1, there are two interesting aspects of the metric: first, it rewards the systems that put the relevant items near the top of the retrieval list and punish those that add relevant items near the bottom of the list. Secondly, the score is divided by the total number of relevant items for a given query. Since queries with more answer items are much easier than those with only a few answer items, this factor will balance the difficulty of queries and avoid the predominance of easy queries.

Table 1. Results of video retrieval for each type of extracted data and combinations. [from [15]]

Retrieval using:	Avg. Reciprocal Rank	Recall
Speech Recognition Transcripts only	1.84%	13.2%
Raw Video OCR only	5.21%	6.10%
Raw Video OCR + Speech Transcripts	6.36%	19.30%
Enhanced VOCR with dictionary post-processing	5.93%	7.52%
Speech Transcripts + Enhanced Video OCR	7.07%	20.74%
Image Retrieval only	14.99%	24.45%
Image Retrieval + Speech Transcripts	14.99%	24.45%
Image Retrieval + Face Detection	15.04%	25.08%
Image Retrieval + Raw VOCR	17.34%	26.95%
Image Retrieval + Enhanced VOCR	18.90%	28.52%
Image Retrieval + Face Detection + Enhanced VOCR	18.90%	28.52%
Image Retrieval + Speech Transcripts + Enhanced VOCR	18.90%	28.52%
Image Retrieval + Face Detection + Speech Transcripts + Enhanced VOCR	18.90%	28.52%

4.1 Results for Individual Types of Metadata

The results are shown in Table 1. The average reciprocal rank (ARR) and recall for retrieval using only the speech recognition transcripts was 1.84% with a recall of 13.2%. Since the queries were designed for video documents, it is perhaps not too surprising that information retrieval using only the OCR transcripts show much higher retrieval effectiveness to an ARR of 5.21% (6.10% recall). The effects of post-processing on the OCR data were beneficial, the dictionary-based OCR post-processing gave a more than 10% boost to 5.93% ARR and 7.52% recall. Again, perhaps not too surprisingly, the image retrieval component obtained the best individual result with an ARR of 14.99% and recall of 24.45%. Since the face detection could only provide a binary score in the results, we only evaluated its effect in combination with other metadata.

4.2   Results when Combining Features

When the various sources of data were combined for information retrieval, we used a linear interpolation with very high weights on the binary features such as face detection or speaker identification. This allowed these features to function as almost binary filters instead of being considered more or less equal to OCR, speech transcripts or image retrieval. Combining the OCR and the speech transcripts gave an increase in ARR and recall at 6.36% and 19.30% respectively. Again post-processing of the OCR improved performance to 7.07% ARR and 20.74% recall. Combining speech transcripts and image retrieval showed no gain over video retrieval with just images (14.88% ARR, 24.45% recall). However, when face detection was combined with image retrieval, a slight improvement was observed (15.04% ARR, 25.08% recall).

Combining OCR and image retrieval yielded the biggest jump in accuracy to an ARR of 17.34% and recall of 26.95% for raw VOCR and to an ARR of 18.90% and recall of 28.52% for enhanced VOCR. Further combinations of image retrieval and enhanced OCR with faces, and speech transcripts yielded no additional improvement. The probable cause for this lack of improvement is the redundancy to the other extracted metadata.

4.3   Insights from the Video Information Retrieval Experiment

What have learned from this first evaluation of video information retrieval? Perhaps it is not too surprising that the results indicate that image retrieval was the single biggest factor in video retrieval for this evaluation. Good image retrieval was the key to good performance in this evaluation, which is consistent with the intuition that video retrieval depends on finding good video images when given queries that include images or video. One somewhat surprising finding was that the speech recognition transcripts played a relatively minimal role in video retrieval for the known-item queries in our task.

Overall, the queries presented a very challenging task for an automatic system. While the overall ARR and recall numbers seem small it should be noted that about one third of the queries were unanswerable by any of the automatic systems participating in the Video Information Retrieval task. Thus for these queries nothing relevant was returned by any method or system.

The overall results of this experiment indicate the difficulty of searching a multimedia collection, despite all the processing techniques available. While no one technique provides a complete solution, it is the integration of multiple approaches and methods that give at least some hope for finding relevant content in a multimedia library.

5   Metadata Exchange for Interoperability

A number of video analysis and retrieval systems have been developed in recent years. In general, these video systems do some form of video analysis but their results remain locked in an internal database. Inaccessible to the world, the video metadata lies hidden behind proprietary data formats and cannot be re-used by any other party. Many very impressive video analysis modules are unable to share their insights into the video data due to the lack of common exchange formats. Yet, there have been efforts to standardize the exchange of video data, most notably in the ISO MPEG–7 standard for multimedia content description.

The Informedia processing components automatically extract information from the video. As described earlier, we segment the video into individual shots, each with a representative **key frame** as a summary image. Shots are grouped into semantic **video paragraphs** or **segments**. The audio is transcribed using speech recognition, resulting in a **time-aligned word transcript**. From the transcript **locations** are extracted and geo-coded for map displays. **Topics** are identified for each video paragraph. **Faces** are detected within individual frames and a characteristic vector is extracted for each face. **Image text** is also located on the image, then extracted and recognized through OCR. A variety of **standard descriptors, annotations and labels** can also be manually added. All this data is stored in the schemas of the Informedia database in a form suitable for efficient access by the Informedia client programs.

MPEG–7 [39] is an ISO/IEC standard formally named "Multimedia Content Description Interface" developed by the Moving Picture Experts Group (MPEG). It describes the multimedia content using a comprehensive set of audiovisual description tools to enable effective access (search, filtering and browsing) to multimedia content. Metadata elements and their structure and relationships are defined in four types of normative elements: Descriptors (D), Description Schemes (DSs), a Description Definition Language (DDL), and coding schemes.

The MPEG–7 Descriptors primarily describe low-level audio or visual features such as color, texture, motion, audio energy, and so forth, as well as attributes of AV content such as location, time, quality, and so forth. The MPEG–7 DSs are designed primarily to describe higher-level AV features such as regions, segments, objects, events; and other fixed metadata related to creation, production, and usage. In MPEG–7, the DSs are categorized as pertaining to the multimedia, audio, or visual domain. The multimedia DSs describe content consisting of a combination of audio, visual data, and possibly textual data, whereas the audio or visual DSs refer to features unique to the audio or visual domain, respectively.

The MPEG–7 standard in its textual form uses XML, the eXtensible Markup Language defined by the world wide web consortium [XML, 1998] to allow interoperable searching, indexing, filtering and access of audio-visual (AV) content. The top-level **annotations** that cover the entire video document were easy to instantiate. Both Informedia and the MPEG–7 standard cover creation information such as producer, copyright owner, production data, and usage information with textual abstracts, summary and collection information at the top level. We recently engaged in an effort that mapped the Informedia metadata into an MPEG–7 content representation.

Informedia **video paragraphs or segments** were found to map most appropriately into the AudioVisualSegment DS, which includes both video-only and audio-only segments. Titles and Topics for video paragraphs are represented by the TextAnnotation Datatype. Extracted **Image Text and OCR results** had a direct corresponding mapping to the VideoText DS which describes a region of video corresponding to text or captions. Since the VideoText DS derives from the MovingRegion DS, text location can also be represented.

```
<VideoText id="VideoText1" textType="Superimposed">
  <MediaTime>
    <MediaTimePoint> T0:0:0:0 </MediaTimePoint>
    <MediaDuration> PT6S </MediaDuration>
  </MediaTime>
  <Text xml:lang="en-us">CNN World News</Text>
</VideoText>
```

Fig. 11. Example Informedia OCR output mapped into the MPEG–7 VideoText DS.

Time-aligned transcripts, where each word recognized by the speech system has a time stamp were found to map into the TextProperty Descriptor.

```
<TextProperty>
  <FreeText xml:lang="en"> World Today </FreeText>
  <SyncTime>
    <MediaRelTimePoint>PT01N30F </MediaRelTimePoint>
    <MediaDuration> PT2S </MediaDuration>
  </SyncTime>
  </SyncTime>
</TextProperty>
```

Fig. 12. Speech-recognized words and time mapped into the MPEG–7 TextProperty DS.

Geocoded locations can be described in MPEG–7 XML through the Place DS as shown in Figure 10.

```
<Place>
  <Name xml:lang="en">Kabul</Name>
  <GPSCoordinates type="latlon">69.137E 34.531N
  </GPSCoordinates>
  <Country>Afghanistan</Country>
  <Region>Velayat</Region>
  <AdministrativeUnit type="city"> Kabul </AdministrativeUnit>
</Place>
```

Fig. 13. Geocoded locations mapped into the MPEG–7 Place DS.

Informedia camera shots (cuts/fades/dissolves) found their analogy in the MPEG–7 VideoSegment DS, while the representative summary keyframe for a shot could be mapped into the FrameProperty D.

Unfortunately, the FaceRecognition DS in MPEG–7 functions differently from our faces, in that it assumes a particular type of vector data to characterize the face. Instead we mapped our face locations into the parent StillRegion DS, which allows us to describe a spatial mask and coordinates for the face location. The 30–dimensional Eigenface vector which Informedia uses to describe the face is stored as an MPEG–7 Vector data type.

It was initially quite difficult to find the correct correspondence for structured Informedia metadata objects among the many MPEG–7 XML description variants. Once the correct mapping was found, it was trivial to produce an XML version of our metadata objects in the MPEG–7 specification format [39]. Some of the XML notation is not the most efficient way to represent the data (see the text annotation in Figure 9, which requires many lines of XML for each transcript word), but they are easy to generate.

MPEG–7 represents a viable standard for the exchange of video metadata, for the Informedia project as well as similar video analysis systems [5]. It is important to utilize a global standard for sharing metadata; thus making it accessible to other groups for research, processing and display [8]. MPEG–7 is clearly the most appropriate format for this purpose at this time.

6   A Vision of Multimedia Libraries: Digital Human Memory

Suppose digital storage was infinite and *everything* that you did, saw and heard was saved for posterity. In an era of ever-increasing data collection and archiving, the existence of yet more information stored somewhere is of no use to you *unless* you could access it easily and efficiently. Within ten years it will be feasible to create a continuously recorded, digital, high fidelity record of your whole life.A future research challenge is the development of life memory aids; the creation of a digital human memory machine that transforms this personal history into a meaningful, accessible information resource. Personal experience might be captured as audio and video through wearable portable microphones and cameras, personal annotations, location (GPS) and other relevant electronic information sources (e.g., email, PDAs), which can also be annotated by human participants. This data could then be incorporated into a structured multimedia resource as in [36] containing multiple synchronized streams of information. A memory integration environment could synthesize data from many personal records into a "collective experience"—a global perspective of ongoing and archived personal events. This fulfills the vision of Vannevar Bush's personal Memex [4], capturing and remembering whatever is seen and heard, and quickly returning any item on request, but recognizing that automated search, presentation, and summarization are technologies key to its realization. Combining data analysis technology such as speech recognition and image analysis, together with event tracking, could enable abstract models to be built and used for organizing the source material. The result could impact daily life in a number of different ways:

Perfect memory and digital immortality for an individual. The capture and abstraction of personal experiences recorded through audio, video, GPS and electronic communication can serve as a form of personal memory. Digital human memory becomes the substrate for an intelligent assistant that can provide memory refreshers as needed. Query and recall should be automatically configured and summarized to augment either short or long-term memory lapses, drawing from recent or lifelong events. For instance, an earphone can remind an Alzheimer's patient of the identity and relationship of familiar visitors. Video "memory" of the visitor, which is annotated with date, location, and names, will provide more context. Your life history will then outlive your physical existence. Intelligent processing will allow an extraction of "interesting" events in the personal history, which can be composed into a form of biographical documentary, which allows us to survey a person's life in 5 minutes or 2 hours.

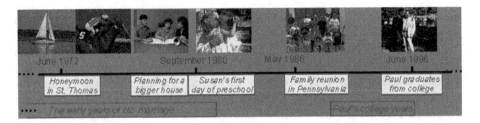

Fig. 14. A hypothetical biography generated from collected digital human memory

Expertise synthesized across individuals and maintained over generations.
Integrating experience data across a number of individual sources enables the creation of example-based learning environments and expert systems. Situations encountered and reacted to by one person can become training examples for others who need to learn how to deal with similar instances. For example, law enforcement officers and field medical personnel can relive and learn from critical response cases recorded in others' personal histories without direct exposure to the same dangerous circumstances. Relevant episode segments will need to be retrieved accurately despite imperfect processing of voluminous source data. Redundancy will have to be minimized to avoid flooding the user with irrelevant material.

The establishment of a historical sense of truth. A past event could be re-established from multiple captured personal histories to enable true time travel and teleportation: a place or time could be re-visited without being restricted to the filtered view left behind by limited newspaper accounts or video productions. It will be possible to establish a historical sense of "truth" as an objective record of what really was seen and heard will now be accessible, not subject to reinterpretation through imperfect individual memory.

In the not-too-distant future, capabilities such as digital human memory will clearly come to pass. These esoteric capabilities raise a number of social and ethical questions. As a society, we will have to find ways of managing these issues. It is inevitable that technological progress is increasingly substituting multimedia information for the space, time and matter it represents, and it will alter the way we live and work.

References

1. E. Ardizzone, M. La Cascia, A. Avanzato, and A. Bruna. Video indexing using MPEG motion compensation vectors. *IEEE International Conference on Multimedia Computing and Systems*, 2:725–729, 1999.
2. D.M. Bikel, S. Miller, R. Schwartz, and R. Weischedel. Nymble: A high performance learning name-finder. In *Proc. 5th Conference on Applied Natural Language Processing*, pages 194–201, 1996.
3. P. Bouthemy, M. Gelgon, and F. Ganansia. A unified approach to shot change detection and camera motion characterization. *IEEE Trans. Circuits and Systems for Video Technology*, 9:1030–1044, 1999.

4. V. Bush. As we may think. *The Atlantic Monthly*, 176(7):101–108, 1945.
5. S.-F. Chang, T. Sikora, and A. Puri. Overview of the MPEG-7 standard. *IEEE Transactions on Circuits and Systems for Video Technology*, 2001.
6. M. Christel and D. Martin. Information visualization within a digital video library. *Journal of Intelligent Information Systems*, 11(3):235–257, 1998.
7. M.G. Christel, A.G. Hauptmann, A.S. Warmack, and S.A. Crosby. Adjustable filmstrips and skims as abstractions for a digital video library. In *Proc. IEEE Advances in Digital Libraries Conference*, pages 98–104, 1999.
8. M.G. Christel, B. Maher, and A. Begun. XSLT for tailored access to a digital video library. In *Proc. Joint Conference on Digital Libraries*, pages 290–299, 2001.
9. M.G. Christel, A.M. Olligschlaeger, and C. Huang. Interactive maps for a digital video library. *IEEE MultiMedia*, 7(1):60–67, 2000.
10. A. Del Bimbo. *Visual Information Retrieval*. Morgan Kaufmann Publishers, 1999.
11. Encyclopedia Britannica. http://www.britannica.com, 2002.
12. E. A. Fox and G. Marchionini. Toward a worldwide digital library. *Communications of the ACM*, 41(4):22–28, 1998.
13. J.S. Garofolo, C.P. Auzanne, and E.M. Voorhees. The TREC spoken document retrieval track: A success story. In *Proc RIAO–2000: Content-Based Multimedia Information Access Conference*, pages 12–14, 2000.
14. J. Goldstein, M. Kantrowitz, V. Mittal, and J. Carbonell. Summarizing text documents: Sentence selection and evaluation metrics. In *Proc. ACM SIGIR*, 1999.
15. A.G. Hauptmann, R. Jin, and T.D. Ng. Multi-modal information retrieval from broadcast video using OCR and speech recognition. In *Proc. Joint Conference on Digital Libraries*, 2002.
16. A.G. Hauptmann, R.E. Jones, K. Seymore, M.A. Siegler, S.T. Slattery, and M.J. Witbrock. Experiments in information retrieval from spoken documents. In *Proc. DARPA Workshop on Broadcast News Understanding Systems*, 1998.
17. A.G. Hauptmann and D. Lee. Topic labeling of broadcast news stories in the Informedia digital video library. In *Proc. ACM Conference on Digital Libraries*, 1998.
18. A.G. Hauptmann and M. Smith. Text, speech and vision for video segmentation: The Informedia project. In *Proc. AAAI Fall Symposium, Computational Models for Integrating Language and Vision*, pages 10–12, 1995.
19. A.G. Hauptmann and M. Witbrock. Informedia: News-on-demand - multimedia information acquisition and retrieval. In M. Maybury, editor, *Intelligent Multimedia Information Retrieval*. AAAI Press/MIT Press, 1998.
20. A.G. Hauptmann, M.J. Witbrock, and M.G. Christel. Artificial intelligence techniques in the interface to a digital video library. In *Proc. Conference on Human Factors in Computing Systems*, pages 2–3, 1997.
21. R. Houghton. Named faces: putting names to faces. *IEEE Intelligent Systems*, 14(5):45–50, September-October 1999.
22. Q. Huang, B. Dom, M. Gorkani, J. Hafner, D. Lee, D. Petkovic, D. Steele, and P. Yanker. Query by image and video content: the QBIC system. *IEEE Computer*, 28(9):23–32, September 1995.
23. R. Jin and A.G. Hauptmann. Headline generation using a training corpus. In *Proc. International Conference on Intelligent Text Processing and Computational Linguistics (CI-CLING'01)*, pages 208–215, 2001.
24. K. Jinzenji, S. Ishibashi, and H. Kotera. Algorithm for automatically producing layered sprites by detecting camera movement. In *Proc. International Conference on Image Processing*, volume 1, pages 767–770, 1997.
25. P. Kantor and E.M Voorhees. Report on the confusion track. In *Proc. Fifth Text Retrieval Conference, (TREC-5)*, 1997.

26. O. Kimball, M. Schmidt, H. Gish, and J. Waterman. Speaker verification with limited enrollment data. In *Proc. ICSLP*, volume 2, pages 967–970, 1996.
27. F. Kubala, S. Colbath, D. Liu, and J. Makhoul. Rough'n'Ready: A meeting recorder and browser. *ACM Computing Surveys*, 31(2es):7, 1999.
28. F. Kubala, S. Colbath, D. Liu, A. Srivastava, and J. Makhoul. Integrated technologies for indexing spoken language. *Communication of the ACM*, 43(2):48–56, 2000.
29. F. Kubala, R. Schwartz, R. Stone, and R. Weischedel. Named entity extraction from speech. In *Proc. DARPA Broadcast News Workshop*, 1998.
30. J. Kupiec, J. Pedersen, and F. Chen. A trainable document summarizer. In *Proc. ACM SIGIR*, pages 68–73, 1995.
31. H. Lee and A. Smeaton. Searching the Físchlár-NEWS archive on a mobile device. In *Proc. ACM SIGIR*, pages 11–15, 2002.
32. B. M. Leiner. The scope of the digital library. *Draft Prepared for the DLib Working Group on Digital Library Metrics*, 1998.
33. R. Lienhart. Comparison of automatic shot boundary detection algorithms. In *Storage and Retrieval for Still Image and Video Databases VII*, 1999. Proc. SPIE 3656-29.
34. I. Mani, D. House, M. Maybury, and M. Green. Towards content-based browsing of broadcast news video. *Intelligent Multimedia Information Retrieval*, 1998.
35. MPEG Moving Pictures Expert Group. Standards ISO/IEC 13818-2:2000, and ISO/IEC 11172-2. http://mpeg.telecomitalialab.com/standards.htm, 1993.
36. ISO/IEC JTC1/SC29/WG11 N4509. Overview of the MPEG-7 standard (version 6.0), 2000.
37. H. Ney. The use of a one stage dynamic programming algorithm for connected word recognition. *IEEE Transactions on Acoustics, Speech and Signal Processing*, AASP-32(2):262–271, April 1984.
38. A.M. Olligschlaeger and A.G. Hauptmann. Multimodal information systems and GIS: The Informedia digital video library. *ESRI User Conference*, 1999.
39. MPEG-7 Schema Page. http://pmedia.i2.ibm.com:8000/mpeg7/schema/, 2001.
40. J.I. Park, S. Inoue, and Y. Iwadate. Estimating camera parameters from motion vectors of digital video. *IEEE Workshop Multimedia Signal Processing*, pages 105–110, 1998.
41. A. Pentland, T. Starner, N. Etcoff, N. Masoiu, O. Oliyide, and M. Turk. Experiments with Eigenfaces. In *Proc. IJCAI Looking at People Workshop*, 1993.
42. Z. Rivlin, R. Bolles, D. Appelt, A. Cheyer, D.Z. Hakkani-Tur, D. Israel, L. Julia, D. Martin, G. Myers, K. Nitz, B. Sabata, A. Sankar, E. Shriberg, K. Sonmez, A. Stolcke, and G. Tur. MAESTRO: Conductor of multimedia analysis technologies. *Communications of the ACM*, 43(2):57–74, 2000.
43. H. Rowley, S. Baluja, and T. Kanade. Human face detection in visual scenes. Technical Report CMU-CS-95-158, Carnegie Mellon University, Pittsburgh, PA, 1995.
44. G. Salton, A. Singhal, M. Mitra, and C. Buckley. Automatic text structuring and summary. *Info. Proc. And Management*, 33:193–207, 1997.
45. T. Sato, T. Kanade, E. Hughes, and M. Smith. Video OCR for digital news archives. In *IEEE International Workshop on Content-Based Access of Image and Video Databases*, pages 52–60, January 1998.
46. T. Sato, T. Kanade, E.A. Hughes, M.A. Smith, and S. Satoh. Video OCR: Indexing digital news libraries by recognition of superimposed caption. *ACM Multimedia Systems*, 7(5):385–395, 1999.
47. S. Satoh and T. Kanade. NAME-IT: Association of face and name in video. IEEE CVPR97, Puerto Rico, 1997.
48. M. Schmidt, J. Golden, and H. Gish. GMM sample statistic log-likelihoods for text-independent speaker recognition. In *Proc. Eurospeech-97*, volume 2, pages 855–858, 1997.
49. H. Schneiderman and T. Kanade. Probabilistic modeling of local appearance and spatial relationships of object recognition. *Proc IEEE CVPR*, 1998.

50. R. Schwartz, T. Imai, F. Kubala, L. Nguyen, and J. Makhoul. A maximum likelihood model for topic classification in broadcast news. In *Proc. Eurospeech-97*, 1997.

51. M. Shamos. Vision for the universal library. http://www.ul.cs.cmu.edu/, 2002.

52. B. Shneiderman. *Designing the User Interface*. Addison-Wesley, 1998.

53. L. Slaughter, D.W. Oard, V.L Warnick, J.L. Harding, and G.J. Wilkerson. A graphical interface for speech-based retrieval. In *Proc. Digital Libraries-98*, pages 305–306, 1998.

54. A. Smeaton, N. Murphy, N. O'Connor, S. Marlow, H. Lee, K. Mc Donald, P. Browne, and J. Ye. The Físchlár digital video system: A digital library of broadcast TV programmes. In *Proc. Joint Conference on Digital Libraries*, 2001.

55. A.W.M. Smeulders, M. Worring, S. Santini, A. Gupta, and R. Jain. Content-based image retrieval at the end of the early years. *IEEE Trans. Pattern Analysis and Machine Intelligence*, 22(12):1349–1380, 2000.

56. SonicFoundry. http://sonicfoundry.com/, 2002.

57. Virage. http://www.virage.com/, 2002.

58. Visionics. http://www.visionics.com, 2002.

59. E.M. Voorhees and D.K. Harman. *The Ninth Text Retrieval Conference (TREC-9)*. 2001.

60. E.M Voorhees and D.M. Tice. The TREC-8 question answering track report. In *The Eighth Text Retrieval Conference (TREC-8).*, 2000.

61. VTREC. The Video TREC track home page. http://www-nlpir.nist.gov/projects/trecvid/, 2001.

62. H. Wactlar, M. Christel, Y. Gong, and A. Hauptmann. Lessons learned from the creation and deployment of a terabyte digital video library. *IEEE Computer*, 32(2):66–73, 1999.

63. R. Wang and T. Huang. Fast camera motion analysis in the MPEG domain. *International Conference on Image Processing*, 3:691–694, 1999.

64. QBIC web site. http://wwwqbic.almaden.ibm.com, 2002.

65. M. Witbrock and V. Mittal. Ultra-summarization: A statistical approach to generating highly condensed non-extractive summaries. In *Proc. ACM SIGIR*, 1999.

66. P.C. Woodland, M.J.F. Gales, D. Pye, and S.J. Young. Development of the 1996 broadcast news transcription system. In *Proceedings of the 1997 ARPA Workshop on Speech Recognition*, February 1997.

A Tutorial on Pronunciation Modeling for Large Vocabulary Speech Recognition

Eric Fosler-Lussier*

Columbia University, New York, NY 10027, USA,
fosler@ee.columbia.edu

Abstract. Automatic speech recognition (ASR) research has progressed from the recognition of read speech to the recognition of spontaneous conversational speech in the past decade, prompting some in the field to re-evaluate ASR pronunciation models and their role of capturing the increased phonetic variability within unscripted speech. Two basic approaches for modeling pronunciation variation have emerged: encoding linguistic knowledge to pre-specify possible alternative pronunciations of words and deriving alternatives directly from a pronunciation corpus. This tutorial is intended to ground the reader in the basic linguistic concepts in phonetics and phonology that guide both of these techniques and to outline several pronunciation modeling strategies that have been employed through the years. The chapter will conclude with a summary of some promising recent research directions.

1 Introduction: What Are Pronunciations and Pronunciation Modeling?

In automatic speech recognition (ASR), statistical modeling is used to convert spoken input into a text transcript.[1] In small-vocabulary situations where the vocabulary of the recognizer consists of tens or hundreds of words, independent statistical models can be developed for each word. For example, one might implement a system where every word has a number of sub-parts (*e.g.*, beginning, middle, and end) and then train a model to recognize each of the sub-parts; when the recognizer sees a beginning followed by a middle followed by an end part, then it would postulate that the input speech was that particular word.

There is a limit to this approach, however: statistical modeling requires a sufficient number of examples to get a good estimate of the relationship between speech input and the parts of words. If the task is recognizing digit strings, then one presumably has hundreds or thousands (or millions!) of examples of each digit. However, in large-vocabulary tasks, one may see only one, or even zero, examples of a word in the training

---

* The material in this chapter was developed while the author was at the International Computer Science Institute, Berkeley, CA, and was written while the author was at Bell Labs, Lucent Technologies, Murray Hill, NJ.

[1] Unfortunately, this article cannot go into depth on the construction of acoustic models. For more information, see either [85] or [45].

S. Renals, G. Grefenstette (Eds.): Text- and Speech-Triggered Info. Access, LNAI 2705, pp. 38–77, 2003.
© Springer-Verlag Berlin Heidelberg 2003

set. Thus, it is not feasible to train a model for each word. We need to share information across words: for example, *cat*, *cab*, *cap*, and *can* share the same initial sounds, while *cat*, *bat*, *mat*, and *vat* have the same sounds word-finally.

Thus, large vocabulary speech recognition is usually accomplished by classifying the speech signal into small sound units (or sub-word units), and then combining them into words, and eventually phrases and utterances. Figure 1 depicts this process at a very coarse level. The glue that binds words to their corresponding sound units is the *pronunciation model*, the subject of this chapter. The following sections of this chapter review the history of and techniques for building pronunciation models for ASR systems.

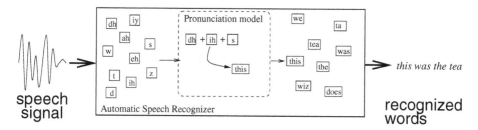

Fig. 1. Pronunciation modeling in the ASR system

As speakers and listeners, humans have an intuitive feel for pronunciation — people chuckle when words are mispronounced and notice when a foreign accent colors a speaker's pronunciations. Yet it is often difficult to pin down exactly how a word is composed of sub-word units. In isolation, words are usually pronounced clearly in what is said to be a *canonical* fashion. However, when found in a sentence context, the pronunciation of a word can change due to (among other things) the influence of neighboring words, a process called *coarticulation*. A particularly picturesque example of this phenomenon is the American English phrase *jeetyet?*, which corresponds to the longer phrase *did you eat yet?*

Pronunciation modeling is rooted deeply in the science of linguistics. Two fields of inquiry detail the production of pronunciation: *phonetics*, which studies the range of vocal sounds made during spoken language generation, and *phonology*, which models the variation in phonetics by finding a smaller set of underlying categories and determining how these categories relate to phonetic phenomena.[2] System builders often look to phonology for tools to represent this variation. A bit of caution is necessary, though: it is not clear that machines perceive patterns of phones as humans do. Some phonological models may not carry over to the ASR domain completely.

The pronunciation model determines how subword units can be combined to make words. The typical ASR system uses the linguistic concept of *phones*[3] to represent

---

[2] In fact, the boundaries between phonetics and phonology are often blurred; some authors [77] suggest that there is no separation between these two fields.

[3] See Section 3.1 for more detail.

subword units; thus, it is the job of the pronunciation model to determine what phone sequences constitute valid words. For example, one model might allow the phonetic sequence [d ow n n ow] to represent *don't know*. Much of the modeling done within speech recognition systems is intended to capture the variation in pronunciations; for instance, triphone[4] acoustic models within Hidden Markov Model (HMM) systems [121] are often used to model acoustic contexts because phones have different acoustic realizations depending on the context of surrounding phones. Some system builders also introduce reduced word forms, such as *alotta* for *a lot of*, in order to capture some phonetic variations [104]. Pronunciation modeling is usually intended to give an account of significant phonetic changes that are not easily described by simple triphone (or quinphone) models – in other words, wholesale changes in the phonetic structure of utterances.

In this chapter, we will examine some of the connections between linguistics and ASR pronunciation modeling, and outline the techniques commonly used today. The following section gives a review of the statistical underpinnings of speech recognition and the relationship of the pronunciation model to the rest of the ASR process. Section 3 covers the basic tenets of linguistics that underly the choices of sub-word units in ASR systems, as well as formal representations of linguistic variation. The subsequent section shows how these formal representations are employed in describing pronunciation variation within ASR systems. In particular, Section 4 covers both knowledge-based pronunciation learning, where linguistic theories are injected into the ASR system, and data-driven pronunciation learning, where linguistic rules are inferred from annotated corpora. Section 5 describes algorithms for online pronunciation modeling, where the pronunciation model changes during the recognition process in response to external conditioning variables. Finally, Section 6 describes a set of problems yet to be solved for current ASR pronunciation models.

Unfortunately, space does not permit a full review of the literature in either phonology or pronunciation modeling; the reader is invited to consult [106, 105] for a history of pronunciation modeling, and [60] or other introductory linguistics texts for more details on phonetics and phonology.

2   Statistical Underpinnings for Pronunciation Modeling

Speech transcription, as generally defined in the literature, is the problem of writing down what someone has said. This definition makes no distinction regarding the agent that processes the utterance — whether human or machine. For speech transcription to be accomplished automatically, models of the utterances in a language are required, so that the best model can be selected as the transcription. This section discusses the various components of the typical automatic speech recognition system and how pronunciation models fit into the system.

Utterances that are the input to an ASR system are recorded as acoustic signals and digitally quantized into some representational vector $X = x_1, x_2, \ldots, x_T$, where x_i is a

---

[4] A triphone is a context-dependent representation of a phone which depends on the previous and next phones. The word *cat* would be represented as [k ae t] with *monophones* (no context dependency), whereas [#k^{ae} $^k ae^t$ $^{ae}t^#$] would be the triphonic representation.

multidimensional vector of coefficients that encapsulates information in a small portion of speech (often around 25 msec); later time segments are represented by an increase in i, up to the length of the utterance T. See [49] for an overview of Viterbi alignment; more details about the algorithm can be found in [85] or [45].

If the range of possible utterances (word sequences for speech transcription) in the universe is $\mathcal{M}$, the speech recognition problem can be stated formally as:

$$M^* = \underset{M \in \mathcal{M}}{\operatorname{argmax}} P(M|X) \ . \tag{1}$$

In other words, what is the string of words M^* that has the highest probability given the acoustic waveform that was input into the computer? This probability is, in general, intractable to compute; Bayes' rule, however, is applied to break up this probability into components:

$$\underset{M \in \mathcal{M}}{\operatorname{argmax}} P(M|X) = \underset{M}{\operatorname{argmax}} \frac{P(X|M)P(M)}{P(X)} \tag{2}$$

$$= \underset{M}{\operatorname{argmax}} P(X|M)P(M) \ . \tag{3}$$

During recognition, the prior probability of the acoustics $P(X)$ in the denominator of Equation 2 may be removed from consideration because the argmax operator does not depend on X at all, that is, $P(X)$ is constant over all hypothesized utterances (M). Thus, the ASR system must model two probability distributions: (1) the probability of the acoustics matching the particular hypothesis $P(X|M)$, and (2) the prior probability of the hypothesis $P(M)$.

Of course, it is difficult to model the likelihood $P(X|M)$ directly — this would involve modeling the relationship between all acoustic sequences and all possible utterances. In order to make the models more tractable, in large vocabulary speech recognition we invoke conditional independence assumptions to subdivide the models. Words in utterances are represented by discrete subword units, which are further subdivided into *HMM states*.[5] Models of utterances are reconstructed into an HMM state sequence Q, representing the total joint probability of the acoustics X and model M with three separate models, each with its own linguistic correlate.[6] X is an acoustic representation that might correspond to a model of human acoustic perception (*e.g.*, models of cochlear transfer functions), whereas the M vector is usually representative of a sequence of words. Three different terms that comprise the complete probability distribution map onto different subfields of linguistics:

$P_A(X|Q)$: The probability of acoustics given phone states (known as the *acoustic model*) is similar to psychological models of categorical perception, in the sense that it is a mapping between a continuous domain (the acoustic vector) and a categorical domain (state identities).

---

[5] HMM states can be thought of as nodes in a large search graph; arcs between the nodes represent transitions from one phonetic state to another.

[6] The linguistic correlates given here are to allow readers with a linguistics background to draw parallels to the appropriate ASR models, but should not be taken as a claim that the ASR system actually implements a psychological or linguistic model.

$P_Q(Q|M)$: This is the probability of phone states given the words, encompassing the *pronunciation model*, *context-dependence model* and *duration model*, which maps onto the fields of phonetics, phonology, and to some extent, morphology.[7] We will shortly see how these models are further decomposed into separate models.

$P_L(M)$: The prior probability of word sequences (the *language model*) has a correlate in the linguistic areas of syntax and semantics.

These three models, P_A, P_Q, and P_L, are related to $P(X|M)P(M)$ as follows:

$$\operatorname*{argmax}_{M} P(X|M)P(M) = \operatorname*{argmax}_{M} \sum_{Q} P(X|Q,M)P(Q,M) \tag{4}$$

$$\approx \operatorname*{argmax}_{M} \sum_{Q} P_A(X|Q)P_Q(Q|M)P_L(M) \tag{5}$$

$$\approx \operatorname*{argmax}_{M} \max_{Q} P_A(X|Q)P_Q(Q|M)P_L(M) . \tag{6}$$

Equation 4 follows directly from probability theory; the subsequent equation makes the assumption that the acoustic likelihood is independent of the word models given the state sequence. This approximation provides a representational savings since the number of words in the lexicon is often in the tens of thousands, but the number of different states in a system is only on the order of 40 to 8000, depending on the complexity complex the acoustic model. A *Viterbi approximation* is often employed in the recognition process (Equation 6), where the summation is replaced with a maximum over the state sequences; this allows the system to find the best state sequence over all of the models.

i	can't				stay			words (M)
ay	k	ae	n	t	s	t	ay	baseforms
$^{\#}$ay^k	^{ay}k^{ae}	^{k}ae^n	^{ae}n^t	^{n}t^s	^{t}s^t	^{s}t^{ay}	^{t}ay$^{\#}$	triphones
8-8-8-	8-8-8-	8-8-8-	8-8-8-	8-8-8-	8-8-8-	8-8-8-	8-8-8-	HMM states (Q)

Fig. 2. The decomposition of $P_Q(Q|M)$ showing the mapping from words to HMM states in a standard cross-word triphone recognizer.

As noted above, the choice of state sequence in the HMM is influenced by several models, including the pronunciation model, the context dependence model, and the duration model. Figure 2 shows a typical decomposition of the word sequence *I can't stay* in a recognition model with single pronunciations. Each word is represented with a baseform pronunciation composed of phones; these phones are transformed into context-dependent triphones, and the duration of each triphone is represented by the

---

[7] The morphology of a word is the structure of its composition (or how it is constructed). For example, the English word *bedrooms* is composed of three morphemes (*bed+room+s*), since it is both a compound word and carries a plural inflection.

transition probabilities in the HMM states.[8] Typically, the pronunciation model is concerned with producing the baseform phone sequence given the set of words.

Fig. 3. Entries from a typical pronunciation dictionary

The pronunciation model of a recognizer is usually specified as a pronunciation dictionary (also known as a pronouncing dictionary, or pronunciation lexicon),[9] which is a list of words followed by acceptable pronunciations specified in terms of the *phoneset* of the recognizer. Figure 3 illustrates the contents of a typical dictionary file.

The one-pronunciation-per-word model, however, is often too rigid to capture the variation in pronunciations seen in speech data. Often, phones are changed from the canonical ideal in continuous speech; this means that the acoustic realization of phones will not match the acoustic models corresponding to the individual HMM states well. For example, the word *I* is often pronounced [ah] rather than [ay]. Furthermore, the phone [t] is often deleted between [n] and [s], especially when speaking quickly.[10] Thus, a speaker saying *I can't stay* might pronounce this sentence [ah k ae n s t ay].

---

[8] Most systems actually use three states to represent the parts of a triphone (initial, middle, final), but some systems will increase or decrease the number of states to give the HMM different durational properties.

[9] Technically, a lexicon is just a list of words used by the recognizer, but the two terms dictionary and lexicon are often used interchangeably in this field.

[10] The reason for [t] deletion between [n] and [s] is a consequence of the physiology of the vocal tract. Think about the position of your tongue when your are saying [n], then [t], and then [s] – notice that the tongue stays in the same place. What happens during [t] deletion is that voicing of the [n] continues through the (usually) silent part of the [t]; the burst part of the [t], where one usually exhales, is merged into the gesture for the [s]. This process can also happen in reverse, which produces an *epenthetic stop*. For example, *dance* can often be pronounced as *dants*, especially when speaking slowly; this is caused by the voicing of the [n] stopping

Several options are available to the pronunciation modeler. For example, one can introduce new alternate pronunciations of *I*=[ah] and *can't*=[k ae n] to represent this variation; these pronunciations would replace (or augment) the baseforms in Figure 2. Of course, this means that the words *can't* and *can* are now homophonous under all circumstances, increasing the load for the language model in disambiguating the two words. A second option is to learn mapping rules to transform the baseform phones into a "surface" representation (Figure 4). This allows for context dependence in the pronunciation model, but is often difficult to include in a first pass of a decoder. Several methods can be employed to implement this transformation; an overview of this method can be found in Section 5.

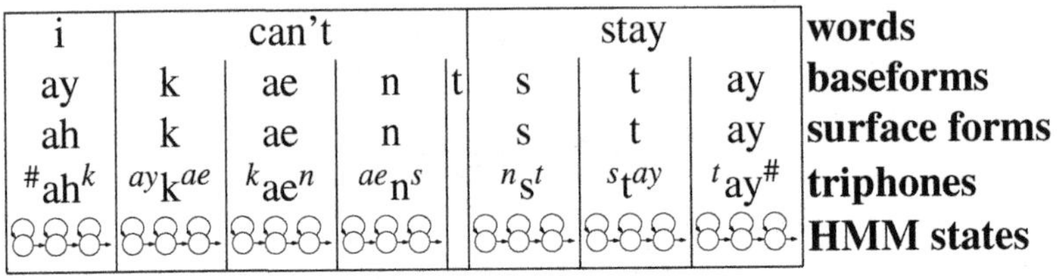

i		can't				stay			
ay	k	ae	n		t	s	t	ay	**baseforms**
ah	k	ae	n		s	t	ay	**surface forms**
${}^{\#}ah^{k}$	${}^{ay}k^{ae}$	${}^{k}ae^{n}$	${}^{ae}n^{s}$		${}^{n}s^{t}$	${}^{s}t^{ay}$	${}^{t}ay^{\#}$	**triphones**
⊗-⊗-⊗-	⊗-⊗-⊗-	⊗-⊗-⊗-	⊗-⊗-⊗-		⊗-⊗-⊗-	⊗-⊗-⊗-	⊗-⊗-⊗-	**HMM states**

The first column on the right is labeled **words**.

Fig. 4. Transforming from baseform pronunciations to surface pronunciations in ASR decoding.

Other variations on this theme exist, such as modeling phone deletions as zero-length phones [122], modeling optional phonetic elements in French (*e.g.*, optional schwas and liaison) [2, 13], or describing pronunciation variation on the state level rather than the phone level [95].

The pronunciation model serves an important role: it acts as the interface between acoustic models and words, creating mappings between these two models. What is often overlooked is the fact that the pronunciation model is actually compensating for *two* separate effects. The discussion up to this point has focused on *linguistic pronunciation variation*: changes in sound unit sequences that are notatable by trained linguists (or even lay people). One can think of these as variations that are inherent in the speech signal. However, it is important to remember that ASR signal processing algorithms are *not* exact substitutes for the human auditory system. They are susceptible to variations in the signal channel (*e.g.*, background noise, or signal bandwidth limitations as in a telephone channel). These factors may decrease the likelihood of a correct acoustic model corresponding to a particular subword unit to the point where another subword unit has a higher probability; if this pattern of change in subword units is regular, the pronunciation model may be used to capture this *statistical pronunciation variation*[34].[11]

---

before the [s] sound begins: the silence is similar to that produced by the beginning portion of [t].

[11] This viewpoint is somewhat unorthodox, as some researchers would object to variations due to channel conditions being called pronunciation variation, but from the ASR recognizer point-of-view, the pronunciation model is just a set of subword units, and the pronunciation model doesn't care about the source of variation in these subword units.

In Section 4, we will discuss the difference between *knowledge-based* and *data-driven* modeling techniques, which primarily deal with this point: knowledge-based methods will restrict possible variations to known linguistic phenomena, whereas data-driven techniques will infer regular patterns of variation derived from the acoustic model.

3   Linguistic Formalisms and Pronunciation Variation

Research in ASR pronunciation modeling is derived almost completely from linguistic theory. In this section, we discuss some of the basic elements in phonetics and phonology.

3.1   Phones and Phonemes

In linguistic theory, sound units are divided into two basic types: phones and phonemes. *Phones* are the fundamental sound categories that describe the range of acoustic features found in languages of the world. While the actual set of phones used to describe sound patterns in a language may vary slightly from linguist to linguist, phoneticians in general do have a system for codifying these sounds: the International Phonetic Alphabet (IPA).

Phonemes, on the other hand, are more abstract, language-specific units that correspond to one or more phones. The field of phonology is dedicated to describing which phone one would expect to see in particular instances. For example, there are (at least) two types of p sounds in English: an aspirated p ([pʰ]), as in the word *pit*, and an unaspirated p ([p]), as in the word *spit*. The difference between these two phones is the amount of air expelled at the release of the mouth closure.[12] However, if one were to substitute an aspirated p into *spit*, the meaning of the word would not change. This means that these two p phones are *allophones* of the phoneme /p/; in other words, the phoneme /p/ can have two realizations, [pʰ] and [p], depending on the context.[13] Compare this with [p] and [l] — substituting [l] for [p] changes the word to *slit*, so /p/ and /l/ are different phonemes. As the reader may have observed, to distinguish phones from phonemes in text, one uses different delimiters. Phones are set off using brackets (*e.g.*, [p]), whereas for phonemes we use slashes (*e.g.*, /p/).

What sometimes makes the difference between phones and phonemes confusing for speech recognition researchers is the fact that most systems use neither phones nor phonemes, but something in between. The most common representation of sound segments in ASR systems is very much like a set of phonemes (around 40 units for English), although some systems use separate representations for stop closures, bursts and flaps, as such representations facilitate discrimination between these acoustically disparate situations.

---

[12] In fact, native speakers of American or British English (and other dialects) can feel the difference between aspirated p and unaspirated p by holding your hand in front of your mouth and saying *pit* and *spit*.

[13] The situation is more complicated than as it first appears. In fact, if the /s/ were removed from *spit*, the resulting word would sound more like *bit* than *pit*. Thus, context plays a large role in how phones are realized.

ASR researchers also vary from linguists in their choice of phonetic transcription alphabet. There are three basic features that are desirable in alphabets: each sound should be represented by a one-character symbol, symbols should be easy to remember, and, for ease of use with computers, symbols should be ASCII characters. Unfortunately, it's not really possible to achieve all three of these goals, since the number of sounds in any language (*e.g.*, roughly 40 in English) outstrips the number of letters in the alphabet. Linguists typically choose to use IPA as it uses one symbol per sound, and many the symbols added beyond the Roman character set are reminiscent of standard characters, adding to the ease of learning. The IPA covers the sounds in many (but not all) of the world's languages. In the ASR domain, though, the need for computer-processable characters led researchers to develop ASCII representations, which were usually language-dependent; these alphabets are commonly referred to as *phonesets*. The most common standard in the U.S. is the ARPABET (and its extended cousin, TIMITBET); the British English Example Pronunciation Dictionary (BEEP) [91] extends these with phones specifically found in British English. A number of phonesets are also available for multiple languages, *e.g.*, WorldBet [40] or SAMPA [112]. Further information about phonesets can be found in [38]. This chapter utilizes ARPABET symbols for phonetic transcription.

3.2 Articulatory Features

Neither the phone nor the phoneme are linguistically atomic units, although they are generally treated as such for the purposes of automatic speech recognition. Linguists generally agree that there is a set of *articulatory features* that describes commonalities among phone units. Jakobson first proposed a set of *distinctive features* [44] that form a matrix describing each phone; the exact constituents of the set of features has been debated extensively.[14] One often-cited (but also controversial) set of features is that of Chomsky and Halle [17]; the description of features in this chapter is similar to their paradigm.

Phones are often divided into two broad classes: consonants and vowels. Unfortunately, the line between them is often not very distinct; some consonants behave much the way vowels do. Consonants are formed by constricting the oral cavity in some fashion with the tongue or lips; they are usually described with three main feature categories: the *place* of articulation, the *manner* of articulation, and the *voicing*. The place of articulation is defined as the place in the mouth with the constriction forming the consonant. Types of articulation place from the front of the mouth to the back include *labial* (at the lips [p]), *labiodental* (between the lips and teeth [f]) *dental* (at the teeth [th]), *alveolar* (on the ridge behind the teeth [t]), *palatal* (at the hard palate [ch]), *velar* (at the soft palate, or velum [k]), *uvular* (at the uvula – the soft fleshy part hanging at the back of the mouth; no English sound corresponds), and *glottal* (near the vocal cords – as in the small silence in "uh-oh").

The manner of articulation describes the type of mechanism used to produce the sound, relating to the movement of air in the vocal tract. Types of consonant manner

---

[14] For a detailed discussion on the history of this debate, see [5].

include *stops* (where the air is completely blocked [d]), *fricatives* (where the air is allowed to pass, but the constriction creates turbulence [s]), *affricates* (a combined stop and affricate release [ch]), *nasals* (where the air is stopped in the oral cavity, but allowed to pass through the nose instead [n]), and *liquids* and *glides* (which are vowel-like consonants that are shaped by the positioning of the tongue and lips [r],[w]).

Finally, consonants can be *voiced* or *unvoiced*, indicating whether the vocal folds are vibrating when the consonant is produced. Different consonants can have the same manner and place and still differ in voicing (*e.g.*, unvoiced [s] versus voiced [z]).

Vowels are usually described in three terms: *height*, *frontness*, and *roundedness*. Height refers to how close the tongue is to the top of the mouth, and can be high (as in beet or boot), low (as in bought), or somewhere in the middle (as in but). Frontness describes how close the constriction is to the front of the mouth; again there is a continuum from the front of the mouth (beet) to the back of the mouth (boot). The lips can also be rounded (boot) or unrounded (beet). In English, roundedness tends to correlate with the frontness, with back vowels usually being rounded and front vowels not rounded, but in other languages these are independent features (*e.g.*, in German, the umlauted vowels ü and ö are rounded front vowels).

Vowels can carry other subsidiary features such as nasality (*e.g.*, *can't* in New York and *bon* in French), and rhoticization (*e.g.*, *bird* and *bard* in most North American and Scottish dialects). For a further description of articulatory features, the reader is invited to peruse Ladefoged's *A course in phonetics* [60].

3.3 Phonological Rules

Linguists' efforts in the field of phonology are devoted to capturing the variation of surface forms of pronunciation. There are two basic parts to a phonological system: a hypothesis of the underlying (phonemic) pronunciations of words, and a system for deriving the surface (phonetic) representation from this underlying form. One historically popular system is the derivation of surface pronunciations by transformational phonological rules [17]. In this system, rewrite rules are used to express transformations from an underlying form to a surface form. In general, the form of a phonological rule is:

$$A \to B \quad / \quad C \underline{\quad} D \; . \tag{7}$$

This transformational rule can be read as "change A to B when it follows C and precedes D." The context (C and D) can be specified as a class of phones instead of phone identities, for generality. As an example, the commonly known "flapping" rule that differentiates the /t/ in British *butter* ([b ah t ax]) from American *butter* ([b ah dx axr]) can be written as:

$$/t/ \to [dx] \quad / \quad [+\text{vowel}] \underline{\quad} \begin{bmatrix} +\text{vowel} \\ -\text{stress} \end{bmatrix} \; . \tag{8}$$

This rule reads: change the phoneme /t/ to a flap ([dx]) when preceded by a vowel and followed by an unstressed vowel. A good phonological representation describes phonological alternatives with as concise, general rules as possible.

3.4   Finite State Transducers

Phonological rules have a connection with finite state automata (FSA). Johnson [47] showed that phonological rules of the form A→B/C _ D, while appearing to be general rewrite rules, were equivalent to the much smaller set of finite state languages under the assumption that the output of a rule was never fed back into the rule (*i.e.*, *recursive* phonological rules were disallowed). The equivalent type of automaton is a *finite state transducer* — an FSA that associates pairs of input and output symbols. In the case of phonological rules, the inputs are phonemes and the outputs are phones.

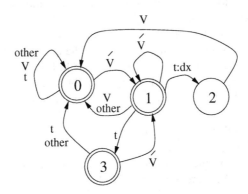

Fig. 5. Finite-state transducer for the English flapping rule, after Jurafsky and Martin [49]. Input-output pairs are indicated on each arc, separated by colons. V́ indicates a stressed vowel, V is an unstressed vowel, other represents any feasible pair of input-output relations. Arcs without a colon indicate only a constraint on the input, not the output. The initial state is state 0, and final states are indicated by double circles.

A simple transducer for the flapping rule is shown in Figure 5. The state path 0-1-2-0 shows the main part of the phonological rule: if there is a stressed vowel on the input and the following input phoneme is a /t/, then transform the /t/ to a [dx] if the following input phoneme is an unstressed vowel. State 3 is necessary for explaining what happens if an unstressed vowel does not follow: the realization of /t/ is left unspecified. State 2 is the only non-final state in this transducer because if /t/ occurs at the end of a word, a flap is not allowed.

Figure 6 shows the result of composing[15] a finite state automata containing the canonical pronunciation of *attenuated* ([ah t eh n y uw ey t ax d]) with the flapping transducer in Figure 5. The initial [t] is not changed to a flap ([dx]) because the stressed vowel precondition is not met, whereas the final [t] is flapped, as it occurs between a stressed and unstressed vowel.

---

[15] Composition of two finite state transducers is a mathematical operation where the output symbols of one transducer (say, A) are matched up against the input symbols of another transducer (B). The resulting transducer (A ∘ B) contains all of the paths consistent with this output-input matching; the paths are labeled with the input symbols of A and the output symbols of B. See [49] for more details.

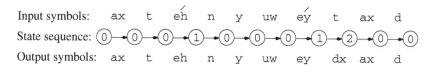

Fig. 6. Output from flapping transducer on the word "attenuated". A finite state acceptor containing the phones from the canonical pronunciation of attenuated was composed with the flapping transducer in Figure 5. The resulting transducer shows the input-output mappings; states are annotated with the state path followed in the flapping transducer.

Kaplan and Kay [52] observed that finite state transducers are closed under serial composition (see also [53]). This means that if one has an ordered set of phonological rules $\{R_1, R_2, \ldots, R_n\}$, corresponding to transducers $\{T_1, T_2, \ldots, T_n\}$, then when a string is given to T_1, and the output of T_1 is fed into T_2, the output from T_2 into T_3, and so on down to T_n, this series of operations will produce an output equivalent to the output from the input applied to the single transducer $T_1 \circ T_2 \circ \ldots \circ T_n$, where $\circ$ is the composition operator. Using this technique, all of the phonological rules of a language can be compiled into one large transducer. Koskenniemi [58] developed a similar approach to transduction in his thesis, called *two-level morphology*.[16] In his paradigm, the transducers are used as parallel constraints, instead of applied serially as in [52]; rules are specified slightly differently to accommodate this parallelism. The advantage of this specification is that there is no rule ordering within the system. Finite state transducers are *invertible*, which means that they can be used not only for generation of pronunciations, but also for phonological parsing by interchanging the input and output of the system. Transducers may be induced directly from data [78], but Gildea and Jurafsky [39] showed that for phonological-rule learning, seeding the transducers with linguistic knowledge will allow induction of more compact models. For a further introduction to finite state transducers and their use in phonology and morphology, see [54, 49].

The relevance of finite state transducers to ASR is that finite state grammars form the backbone of most pronunciation models; the state sequence of a Hidden Markov Model is a finite state automaton. When derivational models such as phonological rules or decision trees are used to construct new pronunciation models, underlying this transformation are the implicit grammar operations described above. Some researchers (*e.g.*, [103, 72, 89, 74, 13]) have chosen to make this representation more explicit in ASR by searching the space of utterance hypotheses directly using transducers; this often makes murky transformational operations in phonological models clearer.

4   ASR Models: Predicting Variation in Pronunciations

As suggested by the introduction, speech recognition systems require a pronunciation model to match words with sub-word acoustic units. Many recognizers use only one pronunciation per word (also known as a single pronunciation lexicon). When the task

---

[16] Although Koskenniemi's thesis dealt primarily with morphology, this system applies to phonology as well.

of the recognizer is to transcribe spontaneous speech with a large vocabulary, however, the variability of pronunciations cannot be captured by such a simple model; multiple pronunciation lexicons are required. For example, in an English transcription task, the word *read* will differ in pronunciation depending on the tense of the verb (*he will read the book* versus *he has read the book*). Homographic words will require multiple pronunciations. Furthermore, faster speaking rates and coarticulation will change the pronunciations of words (*e.g.*, *could have been* becomes *coulda been*).

The knowledge provided by linguistic theories can assist in deriving new pronunciation lexicons. This knowledge can be integrated into a system in several ways. Knowledge-based approaches attempt to include linguistic observations directly in the model, while data-driven approaches (often) use linguistic knowledge to help discover patterns in phonetic corpora. In this section, we will explore several standard techniques for building pronunciation dictionaries.

4.1   Knowledge-Based Approaches

Hand-Crafted Dictionaries. One primary source of pronunciations is a hand-built lexicon, in which experts carefully craft pronunciation models for each word. When care is taken to minimize dictionary confusions and ensure consistency of pronunciation across similar words, the resulting lexicon is often excellent. Still, the work, being manual in nature, is very time-consuming; incorporating a new vocabulary into a recognizer can often be prohibitively expensive. Moreover, it is difficult to transfer the knowledge from expert to expert to ensure the consistency of a lexicon. One can, however, construct tools [61] to improve the consistency across phoneticians.

Linguistic data repositories, such as the Linguistic Data Consortium (LDC) or the European Language Resource Association (ELRA), keep dictionaries for a number of languages; there are also a number of publicly and privately available resources as well. For American English, experiments often start with the Pronlex database[63][17] or the CMU dictionary[18][18]; several investigators have also reported work starting from the LIMSI dictionary [61] as a baseline.

Usually, hand-crafted dictionaries only have one or two canonical pronunciations per word. This makes them a good starting point for inducing additional pronunciations by automatic means. Dictionaries have also been constructed by linguists specifically for the purpose of modeling pronunciation variation: the SRI Switchboard system [104] includes pronunciations provided by a linguist for 1389 multi-word phrases; including these variants in the system reduced the error rate of the recognizer by almost 10% (from an absolute 49.0% word error rate to 44.5%).

Letter to Sound Rules. Pronunciation dictionaries can also be obtained from text-to-speech (TTS) systems. Many of these systems have a component which can derive phonetic transcriptions for a lexicon of words. One of the most thorough reviews of these types of systems was produced by Klatt [57]. A text-to-speech system usually contains a hand-compiled pronunciation dictionary for the most common words, as well as a set

---

[17] available from the LDC (http://www.ldc.upenn.edu)
[18] available from http://www.speech.cs.cmu.edu/cgi-bin/cmudict

of rules for generating pronunciations not in the dictionary based on the morphology, syntactic location, and orthography of the word. For some languages (*e.g.*, Italian), the mapping between orthography and canonical pronunciation is straightforward. English, due to its many foreign borrowings and the changes in the spoken language since the inception of the writing system, has a more complicated relationship between pronunciation and spelling.

Klatt suggests that, for English, hand-written rules have performed the best [11], presumably because rare exceptions can be encoded using human knowledge, rather than being lost as statistical noise in a learning technique. However, automatically induced letter-to-sound (LTS) rules can produce nearly as good results. In general, these systems attempt to predict the probability of each phone in the pronunciation given the corresponding letter and some surrounding context. In some of the first automatic induction work, Lucassen and Mercer [66] proposed a decision tree model for prediction of a phone given a window of nine letters. This model predicted the correct phone 94% of the time;[19] when coupled with a speech recognizer to choose the correct phone from a spoken corpus, the accuracy increased to 97%. NETtalk [100], a similar system that utilized neural networks instead of decision trees, predicted the correct phone 95% of the time (without any speech recognizer assistance). This research has given rise to the NETtalk database, which has been used to compare different LTS algorithms (*e.g.*, [46, 59, 4]).[20]

In English LTS systems, some of the difficulties in predicting correct pronunciation include word compounding (Klatt explains that *houseboat* is difficult, because the *e* is silent), determining the syntactic function of words (*e.g.*, *project* is pronounced differently as a verb than as a noun), and discovering the language of origin of the word. Proper nouns are particularly difficult because of this last problem – for example, in my extended family, there exist two pronunciations of *Fosler* and three pronunciations of *Lussier*, depending on which generation and which part of the family they are in. While some work has focused particularly on the proper noun generation problem [21, 25], this remains a largely unsolved problem.

Phonological Rules. Phonological rules have been used extensively in ASR systems to model phonetic variations due to coarticulation and fast speech by expanding the range of pronunciations represented within the lexicon. The first studies describing the need for capturing phonological regularities appeared in a special issue on speech recognition in the IEEE Transactions on Acoustics, Speech, and Signal processing; two papers cited

---

[19] Letter-to-sound systems are usually judged by taking a large hand-constructed pronunciation dictionary, sub-selecting a number of word/pronunciation pairs for training, and then testing on the remainder of the dictionary. In these experiments, a correspondence between the letters in the word and the sounds they produced was determined in the dictionary beforehand. For example, *cat* would have the correspondence *c:k a:ae t:t* and *rough* would likely be *r:r o:ah u:- g:f h:-*, with - corresponding to a null phone. Thus, 94% accuracy means that for 94% of the letters in the words in the test dictionary, the correct phone was output by the system. Some systems also report per-word accuracies, which will (necessarily) be lower than the per-letter accuracies.

[20] Researchers in this area also report results training and testing on the CMU Dictionary [18].

the inclusion of phonological rules in their systems [79, 35], although neither paper reported recognition results.[21] However, phonological rules were a part of early speech recognition systems, including a system at IBM [8], the BBN HWIM system [117], and CMU HARPY system [65].

With the development of relatively large corpora that were manually annotated with phonetic transcriptions (corpora such as TIMIT [37]), investigations into phonological phenomena became feasible. Cohen [19] provided one of the first comprehensive phonological analyses of TIMIT data and used the results to build pronunciation networks for the SRI Decipher recognizer. These insights were used to build probabilistic pronunciation networks for the Resource Management task [84]; performance on an early version of the Decipher system went from 63.1% word accuracy to 65.5% accuracy with the new pronunciation models. In a later version of the system with better acoustic models, the networks were pruned[22] to realize an increase in performance (from 92.6% accuracy with unpruned models to 93.7% with pruned models).[23] In a similar vein, probabilistic rules have been used to describe pronunciation variation in English in the Wall Street Journal and Switchboard domains [107, 108, 27, 29], as well as in German in the Verbmobil domain [97], and within a Dutch rail service system [115]. Schiel [96] used probabilistic phonological rules to describe speaker differences in a German system that adapted to individual speakers; the use of phonological rules as an speaker-adaptive technique has also been implemented by Imai *et al.*[43] and DeMori *et al.*[23].

One of the problems that can occur with phonological rule generation of pronunciations, however, is that rules can over-generalize, leading to an explosion of possible surface forms. Various methods can be used to reduce the number of generated forms; in one study [108], my colleagues and I developed a method for calculating the probability of rules so that the pronunciations produced by the model could be ranked according to their probabilities, thus allowing for pruning. A number of phonological rules found in the literature were used to expand a baseline dictionary; each new pronunciation was tagged with the rules that caused its creation. A forced-Viterbi alignment of a training corpus using this large dictionary produced the best-matching pronunciations. From the counts of tagged pronunciation instances, the probability of a rule firing could be calculated. The rules we used in this experiment, derived from [123, 124, 125, 51], are shown in Table 1, along with the probability estimates that we derived for some of the rules.

The fast-speech pronunciation rules were used to expand the number of pronunciations in a baseline dictionary; the new dictionary was subsequently integrated into a recognition system for the Wall Street Journal database [70]. These rules provided an average of 2.41 pronunciations per word for the 5K WSJ test set lexicon. The results of running a recognition with this lexicon were insignificantly worse than the base system. When performing an error analysis on the results, we noted that the difference in error rate on a sentence-by-sentence basis between the two systems varied widely; for

---

[21] Cohen and Mercer [20] described a contemporaneous phonological rule system within the IBM recognizer; a description of their work can be found in [42].

[22] Pruning is the process of eliminating unlikely pronunciations from a model; see Section 4.4 for more details.

[23] See also Weintraub *et al.*[111] for a discussion of these results.

Table 1. Phonological rules with probabilities from Tajchman *et al.*[108]. Probabilities marked with *n/a* were considered for later use, but not calculated in this study.

Name	Rule	Example	Prob
Syllabic Rules*			
Syllabic n	[ax ix] n → en	button	.35
Syllabic m	[ax ix] m → em	bottom	.32
Syllabic l	[ax ix] l → el	bottle	.72
Syllabic r	[ax ix] r → axr	butter	.77
Flapping	[tcl dcl] [t d]→ dx /V ___ [ax ix axr]	button	.87
Flapping-r	[tcl dcl] [t d]→ dx /V r ___ [ax ix axr]	barter	.92
H-voicing	hh → hv / [+voice] ___ [+voice]	ahead	.92
L-deletion	l → Ø/ ___ y [ax ix axr]	million	*n/a*
Gliding	iy → y / ___ [ax ix axr]	colonial	*n/a*
Nasal-deletion	[n m ng] → Ø/ ___ [-voice -consonant]	rant	*n/a*
Function words			
h-deletion	h → Ø/ # ___	he, him	*n/a*
w-deletion	w → Ø/ # ___	will, would	*n/a*
dh-deletion	dh → Ø/ # ___	this, those	*n/a*
Dental-deletion	[tcl dcl] [t d] → Ø/ [+vowel] ___ [th dh]	breadth	*n/a*
Final dental-deletion	([tcl dcl]) [t d] → Ø/ [+cons +continuant] ___ #	soft (as)	*n/a*
Slur	ax → Ø/ [+consonant] ___ [r l n] [+vowel]	camera	*n/a*
Stressed slur	[+vowel +stress] r → er	warts	*n/a*
Pre-stress contraction	ax → Ø/ [+cons] ___ [+cons] [+vowel +stress]	senility	*n/a*
Ruh-reduction	r ax → er / [-word bdry] ___ [-word bdry]	separable	*n/a*
Transitional stops			
t-introduction	Ø→ tcl / [+dental +nasal] ___ [+fricative]	prin[t]ce	*n/a*
t-deletion	[tcl] → Ø/ [+dental +nasal] ___ [+fricative]	prints	*n/a*

* Syllabic rules can also be implemented as hyperarticulation rules, depending on the baseform representation. For instance, if the baseform for *button* were [b ah t en], then a hyperarticulation rule could be written as [en]→[ax n].

some sentences the base lexicon did much better, and for others, the new dictionary had up to 75% fewer errors. It has been reported by other researchers [101] that modifying the word models by using pronunciation rules has not resulted in any improvements for fast speech in the Wall Street Journal read-speech database. One reason that these fast-speech rules were ineffectual may be that the phonetic reductions and deletions that they model are more often observed in conversational than read speech. Another possibility is that the rules must be applied judiciously to a subset of words (such as words that occur frequently), instead of the whole lexicon. Finally, rules may need to be applied at more limited times, depending, for instance, on more local rate estimates, and on previous words or phones.

With probabilistic phonological rules, it is difficult to dynamically change the probabilities of individual rules at run-time. One can compute rule probabilities for several *classes* of inputs that one might see (such as dialect variation), but these must be known beforehand, and data for each condition are not shared easily across conditions. For example, in the New England dialect of American English, the phone /r/ is often deleted in the same contexts where in a Midwest accent the /r/ would remain, so a speech researcher might want to build two models — one for /r/-less and one for /r/-ful dialects. The use of two models may present a new difficulty, though: if the flapping of /t/ occurs at about the same rate in both dialects, then the data for the estimation of probabilities are split across each class, possibly resulting in poorer probability estimation.

Moreover, when it comes to integrating continuous variables like speaking rate (measured in syllables per second, for instance), it is not clear how to build separate models for fast and slow speech — how does one decide where the cutoff for fast or slow lies? Ideally, one would like the data to indicate what the optimal cutoff point is. Here, there is also a data fragmentation problem: speaking rate tends have a roughly Gaussian distribution, so the number of very fast and very slow utterances for rule probability estimation may actually be quite low. Data sharing across models is imperative in this case.

The solution proposed by Ostendorf et al.[81] was to incorporate all of the factors that could affect pronunciation into a single hidden variable, called a *hidden speaking mode*;[24] pronunciation probabilities were learned for each word dependent on the mode. The features used to determine mode included speaking rate, fundamental frequency, energy, and word duration. Finke and Waibel [29] extended this work by incorporating mode dependence in phonological rules, yielding 6–7% relative gains on the Switchboard corpus (28.7% WER to 26.7%) and the CallHome English corpus (38.6% to 36.1% WER).

4.2 Data-Driven Approaches I: Automatic Baseform Learning

Researchers have been examining ways to build dictionaries in a more automatic fashion. Two components are needed for a pronunciation modeling system: a source of data, and a method of capturing variation seen in the data. Pronunciation data can be provided from either hand-annotated speech, or (more frequently) from automatic phonetic transcriptions provided by a speech recognizer. In most of the systems below, a hand-crafted dictionary is used as a type of "phonological" representation; deviations from this canonical form are induced from the data. The linguistic formalisms discussed in the previous section have provided pronunciation modelers many tools for modeling this variation.

The simplest method of learning pronunciation variants is to learn each word's various pronunciations on a word-by-word basis. Typically, a phone recognizer is utilized to determine possible alternatives for each word by finding a best-fit alignment between the phone recognition string and canonical baseform pronunciations provided by a baseline dictionary, although hand-transcribed data can also be used for this task [19].

In the phone-recognition-based learning methodology, the recognizer is instantiated with a small vocabulary; instead of a lexicon of words, the lexicon consists of all of the phones in the phone set (on the order of 40 to 60 phones). A phone bigram or phone trigram grammar is often trained either from a dictionary or transcribed data.

---

[24] The hidden aspect refers to the fact that this mode is statistically inferred, rather than directly observed by an annotator.

This grammar helps to filter out unlikely phonetic sequences. A training corpus is then fed through the recognizer to produce the most likely phonetic sequence. For example, the phone recognizer might choose to transcribe the phrase *a baseball game* as [ax b eh ey s b el g eh m] rather than the canonical [ax b ey s b ao l g ey m]. The canonical phone sequence can be found by replacing the word sequence with its most likely dictionary pronunciation, or by performing a forced Viterbi alignment[25] of the speech to the word sequence.

a	baseball	game	**word sequence**
ax|b| ey |s|b|ao|l	g|ey|m		**canonical phone sequence**
ax|b|eh ey|s|b| el	g|eh|m		**aligned surface phones**
ax| b eh ey s b el	g eh m		**proposed new pronunciations**

Fig. 7. Deriving new pronunciations via baseform learning

Once canonical and surface pronunciation sequences have been determined for an utterance, aligning the two phonetic sequences provides the word boundaries for the surface pronunciations. This alignment can either be accomplished by comparing the times of individual phones, or via a dynamic programming alignment between the sequences.[26] Figure 7 illustrates the result of an alignment for the two strings representing *a baseball game*. Every phone in the canonical phone string is mapped to zero or more phones in the surface pronunciation. A mapping of zero phones is said to be a phone deletion; when two or more surface phones correspond to a single canonical phone, we have a phone insertion.

After an entire training corpus has been annotated in this fashion, the learned pronunciations for each word can be collected into a dictionary. Without pruning, however, recognizing with this dictionary will give poor results, as phone recognition is often noisy: since phone recognition is a statistical process that includes no lexical information, critical phones are sometimes changed or deleted so that the word is no longer recognizable out of context. Thus, most system designers choose to augment the canonical dictionary with learned pronunciations, and only include instances that occur a certain number of times. It is often advisable to limit the number of pronunciations per word [19]. Many designers believe that only frequently occurring words should receive multiple pronunciations: one rule of thumb in common use is that the number of pronunciations of a word should be proportional to the log of the number of instances

---

[25] See [49] for an overview of Viterbi alignment; more details about the algorithm can be found in [85] or [45].

[26] Algorithms for string alignment via dynamic programming can be found in Sankoff and Kruskal's book [93] or Jurafsky & Martin [49]. For aligning phonetic sequences, however, it is best to use a cost matrix weighted by phonetic features, or by a confusion matrix, rather than just the standard Levenshtein distance [62]. See [34] for details on how to compute a phonetic distance matrix.

of that word in the training corpus. More complex methods of selecting pronunciations can be employed, and are described in Section 4.4.

Wooters [119] and Westendorf and Jelitto [113] used alignments between baseform pronunciations and frequent pronunciations derived from a phone recognizer to create a set of word-recognition baseforms. Others have used phone recognition output constrained by orthography-to-phone mappings [66, 10], or by generalizing phone recognizer output to broad phonetic categories (such as stops and fricatives) [98].

One can also generalize over the set of pronunciations learned by these techniques, using techniques such as HMM Generalization [118, 119], which allows induction of new baseforms not seen in the training data by finding common variations among pronunciations seen during training. Eide [26] used a similar technique in their Broadcast News speech recognizer, finding improvements in word error rate for spontaneous and fast speech.

One problem with word-based techniques is that they do not model coarticulation between words well. For example, the fact that the second /d/ in "Did you eat?" often gets realized as /jh/ (as in "Didja eat?") is conditionally dependent on the fact that the following word is "you"; a word-by-word technique would not have access to this dependence. Sloboda and Waibel [102] address this problem by adding common phrases (*tuples*) to their dictionary, allowing for coarticulation modeling across word boundaries in German.[27] They found that adding tuples reduced word error rate about 3% relative (increasing word accuracy from 65.4% to 67.5% on the Verbmobil[28] task), and learning multiple pronunciations brought relative improvement to 4% (68.4% word accuracy). Compounding words is a technique that has been used for language modeling for some time (*e.g.*, [69, 87]), but the use of this technique within pronunciation modeling has only recently become commonplace [1, 83, 29, 75, 67, 12, 104].

Another problem in word-by-word learning is that generalizations cannot be learned across words. For instance, the phoneme /t/ in *butter*, *flutter*, and *mutter* shares the same phonemic environment in each word; however, in a word-by-word setting, the probability for flapping the /t/ must be learned independently for each word; such probability estimations may run into problems due to the sparseness of data.[29] One solution to this problem may be to smooth pronunciations with the probabilistic phonological rules described above. Another possibility is to learn phonological rules automatically across words, in procedures described in the next section.

4.3   Data-Driven Approaches II: Automatic Induction of Pronunciation Rules

One can incorporate the generalization power of linguistic rules while retaining the advantages of a data-driven approach by automatically learning pronunciation rules from a training corpus. One way to conceptualize this is as a change in the focus of the modeling from "How is this word pronounced?" to "How is this phoneme pronounced?"

---

[27] This technique is generally called *multi-word* modeling in the literature.

[28] A speech recognition task that operates as a first stage for a human-to-human appointment-making translation system.

[29] Note that this the same problem discussed in the introduction that led to the use of sub-word units in large-vocabulary speech recognition.

Consider the alignment presented in Figure 7: the simplest model using a phone-based perspective would incorporate statistics of how each baseform phone is realized as a surface phone throughout the training corpus independent of any other considerations. Let us assume that each word has a canonical pronunciation $c_1 c_2 \ldots c_n$, and that variants of each canonical phone c_j can be represented as phone or cluster of surface phones s_j. s_j can also be empty, indicating a phone deletion. We can then define a set of possible surface pronunciations of this word, $\{S^i = s_1^i \ldots s_n^i\}$, with a probability distribution over this set of alternative pronunciations:

$$P(S^i) = \prod_{j=1}^{n}(P(s_j^i|c_j)) \ .$$

For example, if $P(\text{dh}|\text{dh}) = 1$, $P(\text{iy}|\text{iy}) = .8$, and $P(\text{ax}|\text{iy}) = .2$, then we would predict that the word *the* (canonical pronunciation [dh iy]) would have two pronunciations, with $P([\text{dh iy}])=.8$ and $P([\text{dh ax}])=.2$. In general, this type of system would derive a large number of pronunciations for long words; probabilities can be used to help decide which word pronunciations are the most likely.

This is, of course, a very simplistic model, since how phone variations are realized depends on the context in which they occur. Given the training pattern in Figure 7, we probably don't want to suggest that [ah] can be realized as [el] under all circumstances; rather, only when it is followed by [l]. Therefore, we would like to have a model that estimates the probability of a surface pronunciation S^i as:

$$P(S^i) = \prod_{j=1}^{n}(P(s_j^i|\text{context}_j)) \ .$$

The context, of course, will likely contain the canonical phone c_j, but it is the job of the pronunciation modeler to provide the definition of context_j. In early systems of this type, Chen [16] and Randolph [86] chose to model the context as a function of the surrounding canonical phones. In other words, they estimated the probability of a pronunciation as:

$$P(S^i) = \prod_{j=1}^{n}(P(s_j^i|c_{j-1},c_j,c_{j+1})) \ .$$

This formulation makes a statistical independence assumption – the realization of each surface phone is independent of all others given the canonical phone sequence. In the *baseball* example above, [ax] should only be transformed into [el] only if we delete the canonical phone [l] (otherwise, we get [b ey s b el l]). Riley [88] noted that the previous transformation could be taken into account, *i.e.*:

$$P(S^i) = \prod_{j=1}^{n}(P(s_j^i|c_{j-1},s_{j-1}^i,c_j,c_{j+1})) \ .$$

One consequence of this formulation is that it is infeasible to model the probability distribution of $P(s_j|\text{context}_j)$ directly from data. Assuming that there are roughly 40 canonical phonemes and, on average, there are five surface realizations of each phone,

$5(40^3) = 320,000$ parameters are needed to estimate the direct distribution without including the previous transformation as context. Machine learning techniques are therefore used to learn an estimate of this probability distribution.

Decision Tree Models. In the systems mentioned above [16, 86, 88], classification and regression trees (CART) [14], a particular form of decision trees, was the machine learning methodology of choice for this estimation. A full description of decision tree algorithms can be found in [49, 92], but the intuition behind decision tree algorithms for this problem is to find a set of descriptors (or *features*) that best represents the set of contexts that influence the probability of how each canonical phone is realized. Thus, the transformation of [ax] into [el] in *baseball* is dependent on whether [l] follows [ax] or not, but is independent of whether [b] proceeds [ax].

The selection of features is accomplished by recursively partitioning (or splitting) the training data into two groups.[30] In the beginning, all of the training examples are pooled into one distribution. The algorithm then asks binary questions about the context (*i.e.*, "Is the next canonical phone [l]?") and attempts to find the best question according to two criteria:

- Which question produces the most pure split?
- Which question produces the most balanced split?

A binary question acts as a partition of the distribution: for each example, if the answer to the question is true, then we throw it into the "true" distribution, or into the "false" distribution otherwise. Purity refers to the proportions of the different surface phone realizations within each distribution – if one allophone dominates the distribution, the distribution is purer than if all allophones have equal probabilities.[31] A balanced split has similar numbers of training samples in the true and false distributions. Both of these criteria are important: if we have 100 samples, half being of type A and half type B (maximally impure), in creating an unbalanced split of 99 trues and 1 false, even though the false node could be purely A, we haven't gained much because we still have 49 A's and 50 B's in the true distribution. Likewise, if we have a balanced split of 50 trues and 50 falses, but each node still has 25 A's and 25 B's, we still haven't improved the predictive capability of the system. The quantization of this measure is called the *information gain*.

As described above, the decision tree algorithm finds the best question to ask at every step of the derivation. How to formulate the questions is left to the design of the researcher. One option is to allow questions of the form "is the {next,previous} phone Z?" This formulation, however, has two problems; imagine the situation where phone X transforms to Y after a vowel. The trees encoding this rule will need to be large (Figure 8).

Furthermore, this encoding can miss some cases due to lack of training data (*i.e.*, if we never saw the combination [uw X] we would not know to transform it to [uw Y].) A more efficient encoding of this tree is to ask if the previous phone was a vowel – this

---

[30] One can also use *n*-ary partitions without loss of generality.

[31] The purity is actually the entropy of the probability distribution.

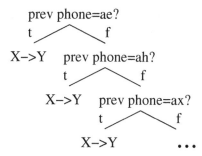

Fig. 8. Decision tree for X→Y after a vowel, with only phone identity questions.

produces a much shorter tree (with height one). Thus, questions are usually formulated using the phonological distinctive features described in Section 3.2 [86, 88, 90, 110]. This allows the injection of linguistic knowledge into the automatic decision process, and is key in building robust estimates of the probability distributions given sparse data. This model is very similar to the concepts of building *generalized triphones* and *HMM state tying* [76], where context-dependent acoustic models are clustered together using decision trees (*e.g.*, all of the [t] models with a high vowel to the left may share one acoustic model).[32]

Another approach is to construct the feature sets automatically, by finding groups of phones that behave similarly in different phonetic contexts. The "feature" in this paradigm corresponds to a subset of the set of phones: if a phone ϕ is an element of some subset of phones $S = \{\phi_1, \phi_2, \ldots\}$, then the feature $f_S(\phi)$ is true.

The number of possible features in this paradigm is quite large: since any possible subset of phones is a feature, there are $O(2^n)$ possible features, where n is the number of phones in the phoneset. In practical terms, one cannot search the space of all possible phone subsets in a reasonable amount of time. The pronunciation modeling work described in [16] uses a hierarchical clustering algorithm that measures the mutual information between training set allophones and potential feature clusters to find feasible candidates.

Other Machine Learning Techniques. Decision trees are not the only possible machine learning technique for pronunciation models. Neural networks, for example, can be used to estimate pronunciation probabilities [36]. Neural nets have both advantages and disadvantages as compared to decision trees. Decision trees perform feature subselection automatically as part of the training algorithm, whereas irrelevant features in a neural network, at best, just increase the number of parameters in the system, and at worst will decrease performance by adding noise to the statistical model. Consequently, it is also easier to analyze which features are relevant in decision trees. On the other hand, features can work in concert within a neural network, while features are assumed independent in a decision tree. The benefits and risks seem to balance each other; to date no compelling argument has been made for one paradigm over the other.

---

[32] See [85] for more details on triphone acoustic models in large vocabulary speech recognition.

Cremelie and Martens [22] proposed a framework to learn pronunciation rules directly from data (work which was extended in [120]). In their algorithm, two types of rules are learned, positive and negative rules. In the phonological rule format discussed in section 3.3, these rules are of the form:

$$A \rightarrow B \quad / \quad C \underline{\quad} D \quad \text{with } P(B|A,C,D) \quad \textbf{positive rule}$$
$$A \rightarrow \text{not } B \quad / \quad C \underline{\quad} D \text{ with } 1 - P(B|A,C,D) \text{ } \textbf{negative rule} \text{ .}$$

The prior context C and subsequent context D can be a series of phones, rather than just one. This allows negative rules, for example, to specify exceptions to the positive rules, refining transformations learned with smaller amounts of context. The algorithm has the flavor of the Brill part-of-speech tagger [15], in which transformations that remove the greatest amount of modeling error are learned first; subsequent transformations refine the model, possibly undoing a previous rule in a more specific context.

4.4   Pruning: Selecting Candidate Pronunciations

So far, we have discussed word-based and phone-based models of pronunciation variation. Using such a model in a standard speech recognizer requires creating a pronunciation dictionary (such as in Figure 3).[33] Baseform learning techniques will often overgenerate candidate pronunciations because of noise in the training set; pronunciation generation by rule will usually produce too many candidates as well, since pronunciation rules usually can fire independently of each other. Having too many pronunciations for each word leads to increased decoding time, since the number of HMM paths that must be searched increases during decoding. Furthermore, there is often an increase in the recognizer error rate with too many pronunciations, as the larger number of pronunciations increases the chance that words will be confusable with each other. Thus, it is important to prune the set of candidate pronunciations to produce a dictionary optimal for recognition.

One method is to choose a maximum number of pronunciations that would be allowed per word. The probability of each candidate pronunciation is calculated using either pronunciation rules or the output of forced alignment with a training corpus (possibly smoothed with a back-off model — the canonical dictionary — to improve probability estimates); the n candidate pronunciations which have the highest probability for a word w are included in the lexicon. Alternatively, the maximum number can be a function of the unigram frequency of the word $f(u(w))$ (or, similarly, a function of the training counts $f(\text{count}(w))$); this allows the pronunciation model to contain many variants for frequent words while only having a few (or one) pronunciation for rarely seen words. The exact form of this function is usually left to experimentation, but as mentioned earlier, some of our previous work [33] suggests that using $f(\text{count}(w)) \propto \log(\text{count}(w))$ works well.

---

[33] Researchers have also employed rule-based models directly in a transformation-based pronunciation model, which does not require the creation of a standard recognizer dictionary; see Section 5 for more details.

Another option for pruning is to remove variants that occur with a probability less than a predetermined threshold. In [88], for example, phonetic variants occurring less than 10% of the time in the training corpus were removed from the decision tree leaves. While effective in the word-based learning techniques for pruning pronunciations for frequent words, with infrequent words this technique suffers from the problem of poor probability estimation. Assume that a relatively rare word is only observed four times in the training corpus, with three different pronunciation variants. Two variants would occur 25% of the time, and the other would have an occurrence rate of 50%, according to naive probability estimation. A probability threshold would have to be high ($> 25\%$) to eliminate the other two candidates; but this threshold may eliminate too many candidates for frequent words. Therefore, thresholding should be frequency-dependent; furthermore, a cap on the absolute number of pronunciations for a word may still be needed (*e.g.*, in the case where a word has four equiprobable pronunciations, either all would be retained or all would be pruned in a pure thresholding scheme).

A third option for probability-based pruning is to use "relmax" (relative-to-maximum) pruning: pronunciations with probabilities less than some fraction of the most likely pronunciation are discarded. Stolcke *et al.* [104], for example, found that deleting pronunciations from their lexicon that occurred less than 0.3 times as the most likely pronunciation for that word did not have a significant effect on recognition accuracy, while speeding up the decoder search. This type of pruning alleviates some of the issues with absolute thresholding: the probability threshold is relative for each word, allowing words with many pronunciations to keep several close alternatives. While, in theory, the three-variant situation described above could arise, in practice it is a good compromise over having to limit the number of pronunciations per word *a priori*.

Pruning algorithms may use criteria other than the corpus probability of a pronunciation to determine the rank ordering of pronunciations. In word baseform learning, for instance, one determines the probability of the pronunciations of a word from a corpus, where each instance of a word is labeled with one and only one pronunciation (through a forced Viterbi alignment). Instead of having a hard decision that pronunciation p applies for an instance of word w in the corpus, one can measure the relative merits of a set of $P = \{p_1, p_2, \ldots\}$ pronunciations, giving some weight to the second-best (and other) pronunciations. In maximum-likelihood (ML) pronunciation modeling [41], one attempts to select the set of pronunciations that maximizes the likelihood of the training corpus. Given a predetermined limit on the number of baseform pronunciations to be learned, the algorithm selects the best set of baseforms by iterative clustering, using the ML criterion to guide the search strategy. This criterion can also be used to prune pronunciation rules [3]. Another pruning approach [33], similar in spirit, optimizes an acoustic confidence score criterion: for every instance of a word w_i, a confidence score $C(p_j, w_i)$ is computed which represents the probability that the word is actually pronounced as p_j according to the acoustic model.[34] The set of baseform pronunciations P (again with some predefined limit on membership size) is selected that maximizes the confidence scores over all instances of word w.

---

[34] This might seem to be the same criterion as maximum likelihood, but it is not: the probability computed is a posterior probability rather than a likelihood. See [116] for more details on posterior acoustic confidence scores.

5 Online Transformation-Based Pronunciation Modeling

To this point, we have only discussed pronunciation models which are static in nature: during the training phase, we select a set of candidate pronunciations for each word (perhaps pruning the dictionary to improve performance). At test time, however, this dictionary is fixed – one cannot change pronunciation probabilities based on context.

Diagnostic experiments [68, 95] suggest that allowing the dictionary to be dynamic – that is, changing the dictionary to include pronunciations seen in the test utterance – has the potential to greatly improve performance, cutting the error rate on some of the hardest ASR tasks in half. In the experiments described in [95], an ASR system was used to recognize the test set of the Switchboard corpus; the word error rate on this corpus was 47%. A second recognition system was also developed where the correct pronunciation for each word in an utterance (according to the recognizer) was inserted into the dictionary.[35] Each utterance had its own specific dictionary; the word error rate in this system dropped to 27% (43% relative improvement). The fine-grained control of the dictionary (*i.e.*, adapting on an utterance-by-utterance level) was crucial in this experiment; when all of the correct pronunciations for the entire test set were inserted into the dictionary, the recognition error rate was a respectable, but more modest 38% — thus, it is important to not only know what pronunciations to add to a dictionary, but also when to add them.

One example of a dynamic dictionary (already described in Section 4.1) is that of Finke and Waibel [29], where pronunciation rule probabilities were allowed to vary based on the speaking mode (a combined estimate of speaking rate, fundamental frequency, duration, and other factors).

Dynamic pronunciation probabilities can also be incorporated through online transformation-based modeling. The general technique of transformation-based modeling was pioneered by Riley and Ljolje [90]; the main thrust of the algorithm is to use encoded pronunciation rules directly during decoding, rather than expanding the rules out into separate pronunciations for each word. Figure 9 gives a schematic view of the ASR decoding process from the (perhaps unorthodox) view of the underlying phonetic graph – from the top, a word hypothesis will generate a phonetic sequence via dictionary lookup; this sequence is then matched against the acoustic models to produce an acoustic score. In a transformation-based model (Figure 10), this canonical phonetic sequence is expanded via pronunciation rules learned previously.

Some expansions of the phonetic graph can be handled statically, when only prior knowledge is required (*e.g.*, phonological rules that only depend on the previous, current, and next baseform phones). On the other hand, when the expansion depends on the acoustic input (*e.g.*, when a phonological rule depends on the rate of speech) or long-range context (such as a dependency on the previous or following word identities), as indicated by the dashed box in Figure 10, the network expansion must happen online; the proper expansion can only happen after seeing the acoustic input. One additional advantage of this "delayed expansion" of the dictionary is that even in the case where

---

[35] Note that this type of experiment, known colloquially as a "cheating experiment," is only useful as a diagnostic tool, and not as a deployable system, because you are inserting information about the test set into the recognizer's models.

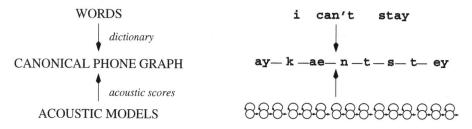

Fig. 9. A schematic view of traditional decoding

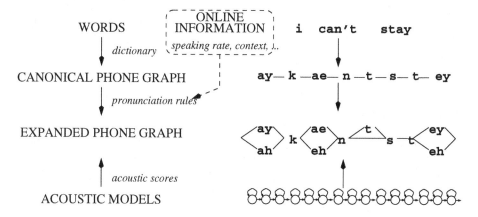

Fig. 10. A schematic view of transformation-based pronunciation modeling

phonological rules depend only on local phonemic context, cross-word effects to be modeled more accurately. For example, Riley and Ljolje's model predicts that the [d] sound and the [j] sound in "did you" combine to form [jh], as in "didja eat?" With static dictionaries, it is not possible to model this type of word-juncture effect.

These models are often implemented as finite state transducers (Section 3.4). Riley et al. [89], for example, convert decision-tree based phonological rules into finite state transducers (one algorithm to do such is [103]); Livescu and Glass [64] represent non-native phonological rules directly as confusion transducers. In Figure 10, the transformation from the canonical phonetic graph to the phonetic graph with alternative pronunciations (both of which are, in fact, finite state acceptors) can be effected by composition with the phonological rule transducer.[36] The resulting phonetic graph is usually rescored by decoding with traditional ASR acoustic models; in theory, one can build a complete decoder using only finite state technology [71, 74], although in practice specialized algorithms, such as on-the-fly transducer composition, are required for efficient operation.

---

[36] If C is the canonical graph, A is the alternative pronunciation graph, and R is the phonological rule transducer, then $A = \text{Proj}_{\text{out}}(C \circ R)$, where the Proj_{out} function projects a resulting transducer to an acceptor containing its output symbols (equivalently, removing its input symbols).

Baseform pronunciations derived directly from phone recognition can be quite noisy statistically (as described in Section 4.2). An advantage to the transducer formulation is that one can iteratively refine phone recognition outputs to eliminate some of the statistical noise, a process called "smoothed phone recognition" [110, 34]. A spoken training corpus, transcribed at the word level, is first aligned using canonical pronunciation models, as well as passed through a phone recognizer (providing the noisy phonetic transcription). Phonological rules are then induced with a machine learning technique (*e.g.*, decision trees). Unlikely rules are pruned (cf. Section 4.4) and the rules are compiled into a transducer. A second round of phonetic transcription occurs, this time expanding the forced alignment phonetic transcription with the rule transducer, producing an alternative phonetic graph. A forced Viterbi alignment of the graph produces a new "best" alternative pronunciation sequence; statistical noise is reduced because the pruning in the previous step constrains the possible answers that the Viterbi alignment process can produce. This procedure can be repeated several times, successively refining the pronunciation model.[37]

6   Five Problems Yet to Be Solved

The techniques described in the previous section are effective for learning new pronunciations: study after study has shown improvement of the prediction of test set pronunciations. Yet the ASR word error improvements have been somewhat more discouraging, with 10 to 15 percent error reductions maximally in large vocabulary tasks, rather than the 50% possible error reductions suggested by diagnostic studies [68].

This section outlines five problems with the above models, as well as some current research in the field attempting to address these issues.

6.1   Confusability and Discriminability

The issue of confusability has been brought up frequently as a problem for adding new baseforms to a pronunciation model (see [19] *inter alia*). The primary issue is that it is not clear what the effect of adding a new pronunciation to the dictionary is on the entire recognition process. A new pronunciation added to the dictionary may cause a previously correctly recognized word to be misrecognized as the new word, for example. Some types of confusability are easy to eliminate: some researchers choose to eliminate learned baseforms that exactly match pronunciations for other words that are already in the dictionary [102]. Despite this effort, a new pronunciation, particularly one containing phonetic deletions, can still match parts of other words well. Since the recognizer has no preconceived notion of where word boundaries occur, these novel pronunciations can introduce more recognition errors by combining with other words in the dictionary.

In [114], Mirjam Wester and I introduced a metric which attempts to characterize the confusability inherent in a lexicon using a (spoken) text corpus. In this system, each

---

[37] Smoothed phone recognition bears some resemblance to the embedded training technique of Wooters [119], which also refined baseform probabilities using successive model estimation and forced alignment decoding.

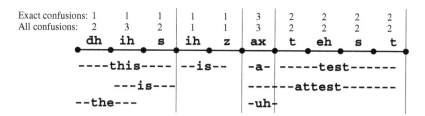

Fig. 11. Alignment for computing confusions in a dictionary (from [114])

sentence in the text corpus is converted into a reference phonetic sequence, as given by the dictionary.[38] The idea behind the confusion metric is to find words whose pronunciations correspond to substrings in the reference string. A search is conducted matching the dictionary against all substrings of the reference string, producing a confusion alignment (Figure 11).

For every phone, we can then compute the number of words in the confusion alignment that correspond to each phone, as shown in Figure 11 in the row marked "All confusions." By averaging this score over the number of confusable phones in each word, we can obtain an estimate of which words are likely to be confused with other ones. The confusability of an entire lexicon is obtained by averaging the phone-level confusion over all words in the lexicon.

This metric overestimates the number of possible confusions, since it doesn't take into account that some words would be pruned during decoding because of a dead-end path in the word lattice: for example, the word *the* in the figure doesn't have any appropriate following word in the lattice. An "exact confusion" metric ameliorates this somewhat by only counting confusions that occur at the word boundaries provided by the forced alignment – an underestimate of the amount of confusion in the lexicon. In our experiments [114], we found that this metric did not correlate well with the word error rate or the speed of ASR decoding; however, it was useful in selecting non-confusable pronunciation variants, providing an 8% reduction in word error rate (reducing 10.9% to 10.1% WER) on the Dutch Rail Corpus task.

There are some problems inherent in this metric. First, it takes only the Viterbi path into account in creating the confusion lattice. As discussed above, the overlap between acoustic models means that introducing a variant can create confusion with another model, even if the two phone strings do not completely match. A second problem is that unlikely paths in the confusion lattice are given as much weight as likely paths. Incorporating language model information into the lattice would provide a more accurate reflection of the decoding process, and hence a more accurate picture of the possible lexical confusions. We are currently extending this paradigm to address some of these problems.

---

[38] One can either choose a random pronunciation from the dictionary for each word, or, in the case of a spoken corpus, perform forced alignment to find the best phonetic sequence.

6.2   Hard Decisions

Another problem with many of the pronunciation learning paradigms is that decisions are made in a "hard" manner: at some point in the learning process, one model is chosen over another, and the information about the unselected model is discarded. One instance of this phenomenon is prevalent in models that use forced Viterbi alignment to choose the most likely pronunciation for each instance. In this case, the losing models in the alignment are given no weight towards their inclusion in the pronunciation dictionary, although they may be good representations nonetheless. Using the Viterbi criterion for pronunciation selection may partially account for the frequently-seen lack of recognition improvement, despite improved pronunciation prediction, as the model as a whole is not taken into account.[39] Mokbel and Jouvet [73] proposed deriving pronunciations from n-best phonetic decodings, which gave encouraging results on isolated-word tasks, but it is not clear how to use their framework in large-vocabulary situations.

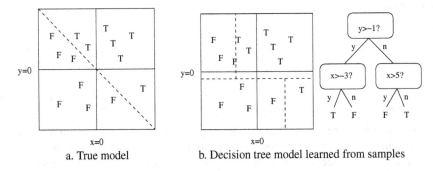

Fig. 12. True model and decision tree model learned from samples of $x + y > 0$.

Another instance of hard decisions occurs in the decision tree learning algorithm. The greedy nature of feature selection (*i.e.*, at every step, the best feature is taken) has two implications. First, features are considered independently and are not allowed to act jointly to determine probability distributions. In theory, this is not a problem, since with infinite training data, any joint distribution can be modeled using a tree. However, in practice, there may be some difficulty in determining a good probability estimate. If there are n features in the system, each decision tree question acts as a hyperplane in n-dimensional space that is parallel to the axes of the other features. Consider the expression $x + y > 0$, which can be modeled as a single hyperplane in 2-space (*i.e.*, a line) separating two classes (Figure 12a); since training data is usually finite, however,

---

[39] The advanced selection criteria discussed in Section 4.4 (maximum-likelihood pronunciation modeling [41] and maximum-confidence pronunciation modeling [33]) are some of the ways that researchers are relaxing the Viterbi assumption. Schramm and Aubert [99] have incorporated merging hypotheses arising from multiple pronunciations, suggesting that this might lead to new pronunciation selection criteria, but they still use the Viterbi criterion for pronunciation selection.

a decision tree model can only approximate the function (Figure 12b). This is a general problem that has received much attention in the machine learning literature; to date, however, there has not been much work in addressing this issue within pronunciation modeling.[40]

The second implication is a corollary of the first: successive partitioning can mean poor probability estimation. After the best question is found for each node, the data in that node are partitioned into two groups; the data in one group can no longer influence probability estimation in the other group. Thus, as we get further down the tree, the data for estimating probability distributions becomes sparser and sparser. One solution is to smooth the probability distributions at the leaves with that of its ancestors; other techniques for making soft decisions are also available in the literature [48].

6.3 Consistency

Many pronunciation modeling techniques suffer from the problem of inconsistency: decisions within a model are often made independently from each other, so the influence of one decision (*e.g.*, whether a pronunciation rule fires, or whether a particular baseform variant is used) does not affect later decisions. As noted above, some models [90] will condition the output of rules on the previous decision. However, this is only a local effect; pronunciation variation can be affected by longer-term factors such as speaking rate, or dialect of the speaker.

The hidden-state pronunciation modeling technique [81] discussed in Section 4.1 is one attempt to encapsulate long-term factors into a single variable. While the factors incorporated into that model definitely correlate with pronunciation variation, one important factor is left out of that and other models: the speaker's dialect. If one had a lot of data for a given speaker, speaker-dependent pronunciation models could be constructed.[41] Usually data is too scarce for such an application. One alternative is to construct accent-specific pronunciation models, which cover particular dialect regions. Fitt [30] proposed an approach to accent modeling which maintains consistency in a lexicon by tying together pronunciations of morphologically related words. Several systems have transformed pronunciation dictionaries from one regional/national variant to another [42], or modeling the variations made by non-native speakers [109, 64, 3], although less work across the field has gone into detecting the appropriate accent model for a speaker (see [50, 6]).

---

[40] Solutions might be found in related fields, however: for example, maximum entropy models have proven useful in language modeling, see [82] *inter alia*.

[41] Pronunciation variation can be a speaker-dependent phenomenon: while a speaker's dialect will give general indications of pronunciation tendencies, dialect regions tend not to be distinct areas, but rather overlap with each other. The geographical boundaries for two types of pronunciation variation may not, in fact, coincide. Furthermore, some speakers have moved from dialect region to dialect region, picking up some traits in the new area, but retaining some variations seen in the old dialect.

6.4 Information Structure

When modeling the sub-parts of words, it is often difficult to remember that spoken language is meant to carry semantic information from the speaker to the listener. Redundancy of information is built into the speech signal, allowing the speaker to change or leave out some cues at the phonetic level. For example, words that are easier to predict from context usually have higher phonetic variability in human to human conversations [32]; since the hearer can infer from context the phonetic content of the word, it is not necessary for the speaker to give the full, canonical pronunciation of the word. The effect of information content can be seen in syllable structure as well: onset consonants, which begin syllables, are much less likely to be modified than the vowel (nucleus) or coda (ending) consonants of the syllable [31]. Humans process language in a roughly linear fashion as they hear it. It is likely that once the hearer has enough information to disambiguate a word from another word (via the hearer's internal lexicon of words, syntactic and semantic information, or other means), the full phonetic specification of the rest of the word on the part of the speaker is not necessary.

Researchers in this area have only begun to investigate the rich information structure available in the speech signal and its effects on pronunciation variation. As noted above, speaking rate has proven to be an important correlate of pronunciation variation (and has been used in several models [122, 29, 34]), as well as the predictability of a word [34]. It is likely that the semantic information structure of a sentence, indicating which words and concepts are important to the spoken message, will also indicate where variability is permitted. The prosodic structure of the sentence, including the pitch contour and timing of words, is also critical: speakers often use prosodic cues to indicate the important parts of an utterance, and these cues may correlate with pronunciation variation. There are many other possible influences on pronunciation realization, such as discourse structure, or familiarity of the speaker with the listener; some of these factors are good targets for inclusion in a dynamic model of pronunciation.

6.5 Moving Beyond Phones as Basic Units

Many of the models discussed here have assumed that the phone is an appropriate sub-word unit for modeling pronunciation variation, but this assumption is being questioned more and more frequently.[42] The search for alternative representations dates back at least to IBM's concept of fenones [9], which were groups of automatically clustered acoustic vectors. A system designer would decide that a certain number of fenones were required for a system (typically on the order of 100), and the algorithm would induce the phonetic structure given some training data. Unfortunately, for a new word not seen in the training set, it was difficult to predict the appropriate set of fenones for that word. A solution to this was proposed by Bacchiani and Ostendorf [7]; in this work, the acoustic sub-word units and a dictionary capturing pronunciation variants were modeled jointly.

Pronunciation variation, however, may happen at too fine a scale to be captured accurately in a model where phonetic identity is treated atomically. Saraclar *et al.* [94]

---

[42] See [80] for an expanded discussion of the issues surrounding phonetic representations in ASR systems.

showed that if a phone [x] is said to change to phone [y] perceptually, the acoustic vectors corresponding to this phone are not the same as a canonical [y]. Rather, the changed phone vectors usually lie somewhere between [x] and [y] (and often closer to [x]!). This led them to model pronunciations at the HMM state level [95]. A new model [x+y] was created for each variant; the Gaussians from [x] and [y] were shared to create the acoustic distribution for the state.

Other researchers have taken a slightly different approach: modeling pronunciation variation as changes in distinctive features (cf. Section 3.2). Kirchhoff [56], for example, trained neural networks to predict probability distributions for five articulatory features (voicing, manner, place, frontness, and lip rounding). These feature probability streams were combined at the frame level to produce a probability of a phone for that frame. King and Taylor [55] performed similar experiments using a number of different phonological feature sets based on different linguistic theories. Finke *et al.* [28] also used a similar framework, but incorporated pronunciation modeling by introducing alternative acoustic vectors for phones. Thus, [ax] could be modeled by [+voicing,+nasality], [+voicing,+nasality,+back], or [+voicing,+back]; the choice of alternative vectors is dependent on the neighboring feature vectors and is learned from the training data. Also along these lines, Deng [24] proposed a model in which variation is modeled by inferring the position of the vocal tract (i.e, how the lips, tongue, velum, and glottis are positioned) and the consequences of the coarticulation between phones.

7 Summary

The pronunciation model of an ASR system is the bridge between the acoustic model and the language model, linking words to their sub-word units. In this chapter, we have discussed various methods of constructing pronunciation models and the tradeoffs inherent in each model. Using linguistic knowledge to create multiple pronunciation dictionaries by hand is usually the most effective, but most time consuming option. One can induce pronunciation models for individual words directly from a phonetically transcribed corpus (either manually or automatically transcribed), but words seen infrequently are poorly modeled, and the power of generalization of phonological phenomena across words is lost. Pronunciation-by-rule systems (either automatic decision-tree rules or hand-coded phonological rules) have the opposite problem: with the ability to generalize comes the possibility of overgeneralization; typically rules are not allowed to be word-dependent. Within this genre, there are also tradeoffs; phonological rules encode linguistic knowledge derived from years of research, but it is difficult to specify all of the possible variations that one might see. Decision-tree rules (or rules other machine learning methods) can represent data well, but might also encode noise from the statistical learning process.

With all of these tradeoffs, there has been no consensus in the field as to the best overall mechanism for deriving a pronunciation model. The choice of modeling process depends on the amount of time, available linguistic expertise, amount and quality of the training data, and the diversity of vocabulary for the particular task. Whatever path is followed, however, it is clear that ASR researchers have and will need to continue to rely on the insights provided by phoneticians and phonologists.

The current mediocre performance of conversational speech recognizers has highlighted some of the deficiencies in current pronunciation models, providing a road map for the pronunciation model of the future. If the pronunciation model were certain to contain the correct pronunciation at the right time, the errors made in current recognition systems would greatly decrease; but adding a large number of pronunciations indiscriminately increases the lexical confusion (and hence the error rate and decoding time) for recognizers. An ideal model would be dynamic and adaptive, integrating knowledge of previously seen pronunciation patterns for a speaker to provide consistency, and incorporating higher-level factors such as the semantics of the message and the speaking rate to predict exactly when changes from the canonical pronunciation are likely to appear. Such a model might also operate on a sub-phonetic level, as phonetic changes may be too subtle to capture when phones are treated as atomic units. The construction of this ideal model presents a formidable but surmountable challenge to ASR researchers.

References

1. G. Adda, L. Lamel, M. Adda-Decker, and J.L. Gauvain. Language and lexical modeling in the LIMSI Nov96 Hub4 system. In *Proceedings of the DARPA Speech Recognition Workshop*, February 1997.
2. M. Adda-Decker and L. Lamel. Pronunciation variants across systems, languages, and speaking style. In *ESCA Tutorial and Research Workshop on Modeling Pronunciation Variation for Automatic Speech Recognition*, pages 1–6, Kerkrade, Netherlands, 1998.
3. I. Amdal, F. Korkmazskiy, and A. C. Surendran. Joint pronunication modelling of non-native speakers using data-driven methods. In *Proceedings of the 5th Int'l Conference on Spoken Language Processing (ICSLP-2000)*, Bejing, China, 2000.
4. O. Andersen, R. Kuhn, A. Lazaridès, P. Dalsgaard, Jürgen Haas, and Elmar Nöth. Comparison of two tree-structured approaches for grapheme-to-phoneme conversion. In *Proceedings of the 4th Int'l Conference on Spoken Language Processing (ICSLP-96)*, Philadelphia, PA, October 1996.
5. S. Anderson. *Phonology in the Twentieth Century: Theories of Rules and Theories of Representations*. University of Chicago Press, Chicago, 1985.
6. L. Arslan and J. Hansen. Language accent classification in American English. *Speech Communication*, 18(4):353–367, August 1996.
7. M. Bacchiani and M. Ostendorf. Joint lexicon, model inventory, and model design. *Speech Communication*, 29:99–114, 1999.
8. L. R. Bahl, J. K. Baker, P. S. Cohen, F. Jelinek, B. L. Lewis, and R. L. Mercer. Recognition of a continuously read natural corpus. In *Proceedings IEEE Int'l Conference on Acoustics, Speech, & Signal Processing (ICASSP-78)*, pages 422–424, Tulsa, 1978.
9. L. R. Bahl, J. R. Bellegarda, P. V. de Souza, P. S. Gopalakrishnan, D. Nahamoo, and M. A. Picheny. A new class of fenonic Markov word models for large vocabulary continuous speech recognition. In *Proceedings IEEE Intl. Conf. on Acoustics, Speech, and Signal Processing*, Toronto, Canada, May 1991. IEEE.
10. L. R. Bahl, S. Das, P. V. deSouza, M. Epstein, R. L. Mercer, B. Merialdo, D. Nahamoo, M. A. Picheny, and J. Powell. Automatic phonetic baseform determination. In *Proceedings IEEE Int'l Conference on Acoustics, Speech, & Signal Processing (ICASSP-91)*, volume 1, pages 173–176, 1981.

11. J. Bernstein and D. B. Pisoni. Unlimited text-to-speech system: description and evaluation of a microprocessor-based device. In *Proceedings IEEE Int'l Conference on Acoustics, Speech, & Signal Processing (ICASSP-80)*, pages 576–579, 1980.

12. K. Beulen, S. Ortmanns, A. Eiden, S. Martin, L. Welling, J. Overmann, and H. Ney. Pronunciation modelling in the RWTH large vocabulary speech recognizer. In H. Strik, J.M. Kessens, and M. Wester, editors, *ESCA Tutorial and Research Workshop on Modeling Pronunciation Variation for Automatic Speech Recognition*, pages 13–16, Kerkrade, Netherlands, April 1998.

13. G. Boulianne, J. Brousseau, P. Ouellet, and P. Dumouchel. French large vocabulary recognition with cross-word phonology transducers. In *Proceedings IEEE Int'l Conference on Acoustics, Speech, & Signal Processing (ICASSP-2000)*, Istanbul, Turkey, 2000.

14. L. Breiman, J.H. Friedman, R.A. Olshen, and C.J. Stone. *Classification and Regression Trees*. Wadsworth, Belmont, 1984.

15. Eric Brill. Automatic grammar induction and parsing free text: A transformation-based approach. In *Proceedings of the 31st Meeting of the Association for Computational Linguistics*, 1993.

16. F. Chen. Identification of contextual factors for pronounciation networks. In *Proceedings IEEE Int'l Conference on Acoustics, Speech, & Signal Processing (ICASSP-90)*, pages 753–756, 1990.

17. N. Chomsky and M. Halle. *The Sound Pattern of English*. Harper and Row, New York, 1968.

18. CMU. The Carnegie Mellon Pronouncing Dictionary. Carnegie Mellon University, 1993–2002.

19. M. H. Cohen. *Phonological Structures for Speech Recognition*. PhD thesis, University of California, Berkeley, 1989.

20. P. S. Cohen and R. L. Mercer. The phonological component of an automatic speech-recognition system. In R. Reddy, editor, *Speech Recognition*. Academic Press, 1975.

21. The ONOMASTICA Consortium. The ONOMASTICA interlanguage pronunciation lexicon. In *4th European Conference on Speech Communication and Technology (Eurospeech-95)*, pages 829–832, Madrid, Spain, September 1995.

22. N. Cremelie and J.-P. Martens. In search for better pronunciaiton models for speech recognition. *Speech Communication*, 29:115–136, 1999.

23. R. De Mori, C. Snow, and M. Galler. On the use of stochastic inference networks for representing multiple word pronunciations. In *Proceedings IEEE Int'l Conference on Acoustics, Speech, & Signal Processing (ICASSP-95)*, pages 568–571, Detroit, Michigan, 1995.

24. L. Deng. Integrated-multilingual speech recognition using universal phonological features in a functional speech production model. In *Proceedings IEEE Int'l Conference on Acoustics, Speech, & Signal Processing (ICASSP-97)*, Munich, Germany, 1997.

25. N. Deshmukh, J. Ngan, J. Hamaker, and J. Picone. An advanced system to generate pronunciations of proper nouns. In *Proceedings IEEE Int'l Conference on Acoustics, Speech, & Signal Processing (ICASSP-97)*, Munich, Germany, 1997.

26. E. Eide. Automatic modeling of pronunciation variations. In *DARPA Broadcast News Workshop*, Herndon, Virginia, March 1999.

27. M. Finke. The JanusRTK Switchboard/CallHome system: Pronunciation modeling. In *Proceedings of the LVCSR Hub 5 Workshop*, 1996.

28. M. Finke, J. Fritsch, D. Koll, and A. Waibel. Modeling and efficient decoding of large vocabulary conversational speech. In *6th European Conference on Speech Communication and Technology (Eurospeech-99)*, Budapest, Hungary, September 1999.

29. M. Finke and A. Waibel. Speaking mode dependent pronunciation modeling in large vocabulary conversational speech recognition. In *5th European Conference on Speech Communication and Technology (Eurospeech-97)*, 1997.

30. S. Fitt. Morphological approaches for an English pronunciation lexicon. In *Proceedings of Eurospeech*, Aalborg, Denmark, 2001.

31. E. Fosler-Lussier, S. Greenberg, and N. Morgan. Incorporating contextual phonetics into automatic speech recognition. In *International Congress of Phonetic Sciences*, San Francisco, California, August 1999.

32. E. Fosler-Lussier and N. Morgan. Effects of speaking rate and word frequency on pronunciations in conversational speech. *Speech Communication*, 29:137–158, 1999.

33. E. Fosler-Lussier and G. Williams. Not just what, but also when: Guided automatic pronunciation modeling for broadcast news. In *DARPA Broadcast News Workshop*, Herndon, Virginia, March 1999.

34. John Eric Fosler-Lussier. *Dynamic Pronunciation Models for Automatic Speech Recognition*. PhD thesis, University of California, Berkeley, 1999.

35. J. Friedman. Computer exploration of fast-speech rules. *IEEE Transactions on Acoustics, Speech, and Signal Processing*, ASSP-23(1):100–103, February 1975.

36. Toshiaki Fukada, Takayoshi Yoshimura, and Yoshinori Sagisaka. Automatic generation of multiple pronunciations based on neural networks. *Speech Communication*, 27:63–73, 1999.

37. J. Garofolo, L. Lamel, W. Fisher, J. Fiscus, D. Pallett, and N. Dahlgren. DARPA TIMIT acoustic-phonetic continuous speech corpus. Technical Report NISTIR 4930, National Institute of Standards and Technology, Gaithersburg, MD, February 1993. Speech Data published on CD-ROM: NIST Speech Disc 1-1.1, October 1990.

38. D. Gibbon, R. Moore, and R. Winski, editors. *Handbook of Standards and Resources for Spoken Language Systems: Spoken Language Reference Materials*, volume 4. Mouton de Gruyter, Berlin, 1998.

39. D. Gildea and D. Jurafsky. Learning bias and phonological-rule induction. *Computational Linguistics*, 22(4):497–530, December 1996.

40. J. Hieronymous. ASCII phonetic symbols for the world's languages: Worldbet. *Journal of the International Phonetic Association*, 1993.

41. T. Holter and T. Svendsen. Maximum likelihood modelling of pronunciation variation. *Speech Communication*, 29:177–191, 1999.

42. J. J. Humphries. *Accent Modelling and Adaptation in Automatic Speech Recognition*. PhD thesis, Trinity Hall, University of Cambridge, Camridge, England, October 1997.

43. T. Imai, A. Ando, and E. Miyasaka. A new method for automatic generation of speaker-dependent phonological rules. In *Proceedings IEEE Int'l Conference on Acoustics, Speech, & Signal Processing (ICASSP-95)*, volume 6, pages 864–867, 1995.

44. R. Jakobson. Observations sur le classment phonologique des consonnes. In *Proceedings of the 3rd International Congress of Phonetic Sciences*, pages 34–41, 1939.

45. F. Jelinek. *Statistical Methods for Speech Processing*. Language, Speech and Communcation Series. MIT Press, Cambridge, MA, 1997.

46. J. Jiang, H.-W. Hon, and X. Huang. Improvements on a trainable letter-to-sound converter. In *5th European Conference on Speech Communication and Technology (Eurospeech-97)*, Rhodes, Greece, 1997.

47. C.D. Johnson. *Formal Aspects of Phonological Description*. Mouton, The Hague, 1972. Monographs on Linguistic Analysis No. 3.

48. M. I. Jordan. A statistical approach to decision tree modeling. In *International Conference on Machine Learning*, pages 363–370, 1994.

49. D. Jurafsky and J. Martin. *Speech and Language Processing: An Introduction to Natural Language Processing, Computational Linguistics, and Speech Recognition*. Prentice Hall, Upper Saddle River, New Jersey, 2000.

50. D. Jurafsky, C. Wooters, G. Tajchman, J. Segal, A. Stolcke, E. Fosler, and N. Morgan. The Berkeley restaurant project. In *Proceedings of the 3rd Int'l Conference on Spoken Language Processing (ICSLP-94)*, pages 2139–2142, Yokohama, Japan, 1994.

51. E. Kaisse. *Connected Speech: the Interaction of Syntax and Phonology*. Academic Press, 1985.

52. R.M. Kaplan and M. Kay. Phonological rules and finite-state transducers. Paper presented at the annual meeting of the Linguistics Society of America, New York, 1981.

53. R.M. Kaplan and M. Kay. Regular models of phonological rule systems. *Computational Linguistics*, 20(3):331–378, 1994.

54. L. Karttunen. Finite state constraints. In J. Goldsmith, editor, *The Last Phonological Rule*, chapter 6, pages 173–194. University of Chicago Press, Chicago, 1993.

55. S. King and P. Taylor. Detection of phonological features in continuous speech using neural networks. *Computer Speech and Language*, 14:333–353, 2000.

56. K. Kirchhoff. Combining articulatory and acoustic information for speech recognition in noisy and reverberant environments. In *Proceedings of the 5th Int'l Conference on Spoken Language Processing (ICSLP-98)*, Sydney, Austrailia, 1998.

57. D. Klatt. A review of text-to-speech conversion for English. *Journal of the Acoustical Society of America*, 3:737–793, 1987.

58. K. Koskenniemi. Two-level morphology: A general computational model of word-form recognition and production. Technical Report Publication No. 11, Department of General Linguistics, University of Helsinki, 1983.

59. R. Kuhn, J.-C. Junqua, and P.D. Martzen. Rescoring multiple pronunciations generated from spelled words. In *Proceedings of the 5th Int'l Conference on Spoken Language Processing (ICSLP-98)*, Sydney, Austrailia, 1998.

60. P. Ladefoged. *A Course in Phonetics*. Harcourt Brace Jovanovich, Inc., third edition, 1993.

61. L. Lamel and G. Adda. On designing pronunciation lexicons for large vocabulary, continuous speech recognition. In *Proceedings of the 4th Int'l Conference on Spoken Language Processing (ICSLP-96)*, 1996.

62. V. I. Levenshtein. Binary codes capable of correcting deletions, insertions, and reverslal. *Cybernetics and Control Theory*, 10(8):707–710, 1966.

63. Linguistic Data Consortium (LDC). The PRONLEX pronunciation dictionary. Available from the LDC, ldc@unagi.cis.upenn.edu, 1996. Part of the COMLEX distribution.

64. K. Livescu and J. Glass. Lexical modeling of non-native speech for automatic speech recognition. In *Proceedings of the 5th Int'l Conference on Spoken Language Processing (ICSLP-2000)*, Istanbul, Turkey, 2000.

65. B. Lowerre and R. Reddy. The HARPY speech recognition system. In W. A. Lea, editor, *Trends in Speech Recognition*, chapter 15, pages 340–360. Prentice Hall, 1980.

66. J.M. Lucassen and R.L. Mercer. An information theoretic approach to the automatic determination of phonemic baseforms. In *Proceedings IEEE Int'l Conference on Acoustics, Speech, & Signal Processing (ICASSP-84)*, 1984.

67. K. Ma, G. Zavaliagkos, and R. Iyer. Pronunciaion modeling for large vocabulary conversational speech recognition. In *Proceedings of the 5th Int'l Conference on Spoken Language Processing (ICSLP-98)*, Sydney, Australia, December 1998.

68. D. McAllaster, L. Gillick, F. Scattone, and M. Newman. Fabricating conversational speech data with acoustic models: A program to examine model-data mismatch. In *Proceedings of the 5th Int'l Conference on Spoken Language Processing (ICSLP-98)*, pages 1847–1850, Sydney, Australia, December 1998.

69. M.K. McCandless and J.R. Glass. Empirical acquisition of word and phrase classes in the ATIS domain. In *3rd European Conference on Speech Communication and Technology (Eurospeech-93)*, volume 2, pages 981–984, Berlin, Germany, 1993.

70. Nikki Mirghafori, Eric Fosler, and Nelson Morgan. Fast speakers in large vocabulary continuous speech recognition: Analysis & antidotes. In *4th European Conference on Speech Communication and Technology (Eurospeech-95)*, 1995.

71. M. Mohri and M. Riley. Integrated context-dependent networks in very large vocabulary speech recognition. In *6th European Conference on Speech Communication and Technology (Eurospeech-99)*, Budapest, Hungary, 1999.

72. M. Mohri, M. Riley, D. Hindle, A. Ljolje, and F. Pereira. Full expansion of context-dependent networks in large vocabulary speech recognition. In *Proceedings of the 5th Int'l Conference on Spoken Language Processing (ICSLP-98)*, Sydney, Austrailia, December 1998.

73. H. Mokbel and D. Jouvet. Derivation of the optimal phonetic transcription set for a word from its acoustic realisations. In *ESCA Tutorial and Research Workshop on Modeling Pronunciation Variation for Automatic Speech Recognition*, pages 73–78, Kerkrade, Netherlands, 1998.

74. X. Mou, S. Seneff, and V. Zue. Context-dependent pobabilistic hierarchical sub-lexical modelling using finite state transducers. In *7th European Conference on Speech Communication and Technology (Eurospeech-2001)*, Aalborg, Denmark, 2001.

75. H.J. Nock and S.J. Young. Detecting and correcting poor pronunciations for multiword units. In H. Strik, J.M. Kessens, and M. Wester, editors, *ESCA Tutorial and Research Workshop on Modeling Pronunciation Variation for Automatic Speech Recognition*, pages 85–90, Kerkrade, Netherlands, April 1998.

76. J. J. Odell. The use of decision trees with context sensitive phoneme modeling. Master's thesis, Cambridge University, Cambridge, England, 1992.

77. J. J. Ohala. There is no interface between phonetics and phonology: A personal view. *Journal of Phonetics*, 18:153–171, 1990.

78. J. Oncina, P. García, and E. Vidal. Learning subsequential transducers for pattern recognition tasks. *IEEE Transcations on Pattern Analysis and Machine Intelligence*, 15:448–458, May 1993.

79. B. Oshika, V. Zue, R. V. Weeks, H. Neu, and J. Aurbach. The role of phonological rules in speech understanding research. *IEEE Transactions on Acoustics, Speech, and Signal Processing*, ASSP-23(1):104–112, February 1975.

80. M. Ostendorf. Moving beyound the 'beads-on-a-string' model of speech. In *1999 IEEE Workshop on Automatic Speech Recognition and Understanding*, Keystone, Colorado, December 1999.

81. M. Ostendorf, B. Byrne, M. Bacchiani, M. Finke, A Gunawardana, K. Ross, S. Roweis, E. Shriberg, D. Talkin, A. Waibel, B. Wheatley, and T. Zeppenfeld. Modeling systematic variations in pronunciation via a language-dependent hidden speaking mode. In F. Jelinek, editor, *1996 LVCSR Summer Research Workshop Technical Reports*, chapter 4. Center for Language and Speech Processing, Johns Hopkins University, April 1997.

82. S. Della Pietra, V. Della Pietra, R. K. Mercer, and S. Roukos. Adaptive language modeling using minimum discriminant estimation. In *Proceeding of the Speech and Natural Language DARPA Workshop*, February 1992.

83. P. Placeway, S. Chen, M. Eskenazi, U. Jain, V. Parikh, B. Raj, M. Ravishankar, R. Rosenfeld, K. Seymore, M. Siegler, R. Stern, and E. Thayer. The 1996 Hub-4 Sphinx-3 system. In *DARPA Speech Recognition Workshop*, Chantilly, VA, February 1997.

84. P. Price, W. Fisher, J. Bernstein, and D. Pallet. The DARPA 1000-word Resource Management database for continuous speech recognition. In *Proceedings IEEE Intl. Conf. on Acoustics, Speech, and Signal Processing*, volume 1, pages 651–654, New York, 1988. IEEE.

85. L. Rabiner and B.-H. Juang. *Fundamentals of Speech Recognition*. Prentice Hall Signal Processing Series. Prentice Hall, Englewood Cliffs, NJ, 1993.

86. M. A. Randolph. A data-driven method for discovering and predicting allophonic variation. In *Proceedings IEEE Int'l Conference on Acoustics, Speech, & Signal Processing (ICASSP-90)*, volume 2, pages 1177–1180, Albuquerque, New Mexico, 1990.

87. K. Ries, F.D. Buø, and Y.-Y. Wang. Towards better language modeling in spontaneous speech. In *Proceedings IEEE Int'l Conference on Acoustics, Speech, & Signal Processing (ICASSP-95)*, Yokohama, Japan, 1995.

88. M. Riley. A statistical model for generating pronunciation networks. In *Proceedings IEEE Int'l Conference on Acoustics, Speech, & Signal Processing (ICASSP-91)*, pages 737–740, 1991.

89. M. Riley, W. Byrne, M. Finke, S. Khudanpur, A. Ljolje, J. McDonough, H. Nock, M. Saraclar, C. Wooters, and G. Zavaliagkos. Stochastic pronunciation modelling from hand-labelled phonetic corpora. In *ESCA Tutorial and Research Workshop on Modeling Pronunciation Variation for Automatic Speech Recognition*, pages 109–116, Kerkrade, Netherlands, April 1998.

90. M.D. Riley and A. Ljolje. Automatic generation of detailed pronunciation lexicons. In *Automatic Speech and Speaker Recognition: Advanced Topics*. Kluwer Academic Publishers, 1995.

91. Anthony Robinson. The British English Example Pronunciation Dictionary, v0.1. Cambridge University, 1994.

92. S. Russell and P. Norvig. *Artificial Intelligence: A Modern Approach*. Prentice Hall, 1995.

93. D. Sankoff and J. Kruskal. *Time warps, string edits and macromolecules*. CSLI Publications, reissue edition edition, 1999.

94. M. Saraçlar and S. Khudanpur. Pronunciation ambiguity vs. pronunciation variability in speech recognition. In *Proceedings IEEE Int'l Conference on Acoustics, Speech, & Signal Processing (ICASSP-2000)*, Istanbul, Turkey, 2000.

95. M. Saraçlar, H. Nock, and S. Khudanpur. Pronunciation modeling by sharing Gaussian densities across phonetic models. *Computer Speech and Language*, 14:137–160, 2000.

96. F. Schiel. A new approach to speaker adaptation by modelling pronunciation in automatic speech recognition. *Speech Communication*, 13:281–286, 1993.

97. F. Schiel, A. Kipp, and H. G. Tillmann. Statistical modelling of pronunciation: it's not the model, it's the data. In H. Strik, J.M. Kessens, and M. Wester, editors, *ESCA Tutorial and Research Workshop on Modeling Pronunciation Variation for Automatic Speech Recognition*, pages 131–136, Kerkrade, Netherlands, April 1998.

98. P. Schmid, R. Cole, and M. Fanty. Automatically generated word pronunciations from phoneme classifier output. In *Proceedings IEEE Int'l Conference on Acoustics, Speech, & Signal Processing (ICASSP-93)*, volume 2, pages 223–226, 1987.

99. H. Schramm and X. Aubert. Efficient intregration of multiple pronunciations in a large vocabulary decoder. In *Proceedings IEEE Int'l Conference on Acoustics, Speech, & Signal Processing (ICASSP-2000)*, Istanbul, Turkey, 2000.

100. T.J. Sejnowski and C.R. Rosenberg. Parallel networks that learn to pronounce English text. *Complex Systems*, 1:145–168, 1987.

101. M. A. Siegler and R. M. Stern. On the effects of speech rate in large vocabulary speech recognition systems. In *Proceedings IEEE Int'l Conference on Acoustics, Speech, & Signal Processing (ICASSP-95)*, 1995.

102. T. Sloboda and A. Waibel. Dictionary learning for spontaneous speech recognition. In *Proceedings of the 4th Int'l Conference on Spoken Language Processing (ICSLP-96)*, 1996.

103. R. Sproat and M. Riley. Compilation of weighted finite-state transducers from decision trees. In *Proceedings of the 34th Meeting of the Association for Computational Linguistics*, pages 215–222, Santa Cruz, CA, 1996.

104. A. Stolcke, H. Bratt, J. Butzberger, J. Franco, C. R. Rao Gadde, M. Plauché, C. Richey, E. Shriberg, K. Sönmez, F. Weng, and J. Zheng. The SRI March 2000 Hub-5 conversational speech transcription system. In *Proc. NIST Speech Transcription Workshop*, College Park, Maryland, 2000.

105. H. Strik. Pronunciation adaptation at the lexical level. In J-C. Juncqua and C. Wellekens, editors, *ISCA Tutorial and Research Workshop on Adaptation Methods For Speech Recognition*, pages 123–131, Sophia-Antipolis, France, August 2001.

106. H. Strik and C. Cucchiarini. Modeling pronunciation variation for ASR: A survey of the literature. *Speech Communication*, 29:225–246, 1999.

107. Gary Tajchman, Eric Fosler, and Daniel Jurafsky. Building multiple pronunciation models for novel words using exploratory computational phonology. In *4th European Conference on Speech Communication and Technology (Eurospeech-95)*, Madrid, Spain, September 1995.

108. Gary Tajchman, Daniel Jurafsky, and Eric Fosler. Learning phonological rule probabilities from speech corpora with exploratory computational phonology. In *Proceedings of the 33rd Meeting of the Association for Computational Linguistics*, 1995.

109. L. Mayfield Tomokiyo. Lexical and acoustic modeling of non-native speech in lvcsr. In *Proceedings of the 5th Int'l Conference on Spoken Language Processing (ICSLP-2000)*, Bejing, China, 2000.

110. M. Weintraub, E. Fosler, C. Galles, Y.-H. Kao, S. Khudanpur, M. Saraclar, and S. Wegmann. WS96 project report: Automatic learning of word pronunciation from data. In F. Jelinek, editor, *1996 LVCSR Summer Research Workshop Technical Reports*, chapter 3. Center for Language and Speech Processing, Johns Hopkins University, April 1997.

111. M. Weintraub, H. Murveit, M. Cohen, P. Price, J. Bernstein, G. Baldwin, and D. Bell. Linguistic constraints in hidden Markov model based speech recognition. In *Proceedings IEEE Int'l Conference on Acoustics, Speech, & Signal Processing (ICASSP-89)*, pages 651–654, 1988.

112. J. Wells et al. Sampa computer readable phonetic alphabet. http://www.phon.ucl.ac.uk/home/sampa/home.htm, 2002.

113. C.-M. Westendorf and J. Jelitto. Learning pronunciation dictionary from speech data. In *Proceedings of the 4th Int'l Conference on Spoken Language Processing (ICSLP-96)*, 1996.

114. M. Wester and E. Fosler-Lussier. A comparison of data-derived and knowledge-based modeling of pronunciation variation. In *Proceedings of the 5th Int'l Conference on Spoken Language Processing (ICSLP-2000)*, Bejing, China, 2000.

115. M. Wester, J. Kessens, and H. Strik. Modeling pronunciation variation for a Dutch CSR: Testing three methods. In *Proceedings of the 5th Int'l Conference on Spoken Language Processing (ICSLP-98)*, Sydney, Australia, December 1998.

116. David Arthur Gethin Williams. *Knowing what you don't know: roles for confidence measures in automatic speech recognition*. PhD thesis, University of Sheffield, Sheffield, England, 1999.

117. J. J. Wolf and W. A. Woods. The HWIM speech understanding system. In W. A. Lea, editor, *Trends in Speech Recognition*, chapter 14, pages 316–339. Prentice Hall, 1980.

118. C. Wooters and A. Stolcke. Multiple-pronunciation lexical modeling in a speaker independent speech understanding system. In *Proceedings of the 3rd Int'l Conference on Spoken Language Processing (ICSLP-94)*, 1994.

119. C. C. Wooters. *Lexical modeling in a speaker independent speech understanding system*. PhD thesis, University of California, Berkeley, 1993. International Computer Science Institute Technical Report TR-93-068.

120. Q. Yang and J.-P. Martens. Data-driven lexical modeling of pronunciation variations for ASR. In *Proceedings of the 5th Int'l Conference on Spoken Language Processing (ICSLP-2000)*, Bejing, China, 2000.

121. S. J. Young, J. J. Odell, and P. C. Woodland. Tree-based state tying for high accuracy acoustic modelling. In *Proceedings IEEE Int'l Conference on Acoustics, Speech, & Signal Processing (ICASSP-94)*, pages 307–312, 1994.
122. J. Zheng, H. Franco, F. Weng, A. Sankar, and H. Bratt. Word-level rate of speech modeling using rate-specific phones and pronunciations. In *Proceedings IEEE Int'l Conference on Acoustics, Speech, & Signal Processing (ICASSP-2000)*, Istanbul, Turkey, 2000.
123. A. Zwicky. Auxiliary Reduction in English. *Linguistic Inquiry*, 1(3):323–336, July 1970.
124. A. Zwicky. Note on a phonological hierarchy in English. In R. Stockwell and R. Macaulay, editors, *Linguistic Change and Generative Theory*. Indiana University Press, 1972.
125. A. Zwicky. On Casual Speech. In *Eighth Regional Meeting of the Chicago Linguistic Society*, pages 607–615, April 1972.

Statistical Language Modelling

Yoshihiko Gotoh and Steve Renals

University of Sheffield, Department of Computer Science

1 Introduction

Grammar-based natural language processing has reached a level where it can 'understand' language to a limited degree in restricted domains. For example, it is possible to parse textual material very accurately and assign semantic relations to parts of sentences. An alternative approach originates from the work of Shannon over half a century ago [41], [42]. This approach assigns probabilities to linguistic events, where mathematical models are used to represent statistical knowledge. Once models are built, we decide which event is more likely than the others according to their probabilities. Although statistical methods currently use a very impoverished representation of speech and language (typically finite state), it is possible to train the underlying models from large amounts of data. Importantly, such statistical approaches often produce useful results. Statistical approaches seem especially well-suited to spoken language which is often spontaneous or conversational and not readily amenable to standard grammar-based approaches.

This chapter concerns statistical language modelling. In a speech recognition system the role of the language model is to assign probabilities to word sequences. Recently, similar models to speech recognition language models have been employed to perform higher level tasks, such as structuring and extracting information from spoken language. In this chapter, we first outline the basic framework of n-gram language models (section 2), which form the core of current statistical approaches. A crucial technical consideration here is how to estimate n-gram statistics from sparse training data. We go on to describe two approaches—based on n-gram models—to encapsulate varying contents and styles: section 3 is concerned with mixture language models and section 4 builds on the observation that the occurrence rate of a word is not uniform, but varies between documents. Finally we describe a statistical finite state model for the extraction of information, such as proper names and dates from spoken language.

2 n-gram Language Modelling

2.1 The Basics of n-gram Modelling

The standard formulation of a statistical speech recognition system may be written as:

$$p(w \mid x) \propto \underbrace{p(x \mid w)}_{\substack{\text{acoustic}\\\text{model}}} \cdot \underbrace{p(w)}_{\substack{\text{language}\\\text{model}}} \quad . \tag{1}$$

S. Renals, G. Grefenstette (Eds.): Text- and Speech-Triggered Info. Access, LNAI 2705, pp. 78-105, 2003.
© Springer-Verlag Berlin Heidelberg 2003

The generation of the acoustic data $x = \{x_1, x_2, \ldots, x_t\}$ from a word sequence $w = \{w_1, w_2, \ldots, w_m\}$ is described by the acoustic model, $p(x \mid w)$. This often takes the form of a hidden Markov model (HMM). The language model, $p(w)$, is a prior probability distribution over word sequences, and is typically an n-gram model (discussed below). Since $p(w)$ does not depend on acoustics, it is usual to estimate the language model from textual data. Although this can introduce some distortion to the model, the amount of reliable speech transcription is generally not sufficient for statistical estimation.

Building n-grams. First we consider the following sentence:

> later the prime minister tony blair telephoned mr. yeltsin

taken from the *THISL data collection*[1]. An n-gram is simply a sequence of successive n words, *e.g.*,

unigram	yeltsin
bigram	mr. yeltsin
trigram	telephoned mr. yeltsin
four-gram	blair telephoned mr. yeltsin

An n-gram model is statistical because it builds on the 'counts' (*i.e.*, the number of occurrences) of such events. Indeed, counting may be thought of as the simplest form of statistical learning. Shown below are the most frequently occurring words in the collection:

the	394 481 occurrences
to	240 001
a	225 506
in	177 997
and	133 962
is	109 217
be	84 020
that	69 265

Given that there were 7 488 445 words in the collection, we can make some simple statistical guesses: for example the word 'the' appears once in every 20 words on average.

Fig. 1. A finite state machine builds an n-gram language model.

---

[1] The *THISL data collection* [36] consists of a large amount of programme scripts, audio data, and some human generated reference transcriptions from a variety of TV and radio news and current affairs programmes broadcast by the BBC since 1997.

More formally, we can specify a finite state machine that generates a sequence of words using a probabilistic model[2] (figure 1). For computational reasons, we apply the Markov assumption; that is to say the model has a limited horizon, and is time invariant. The former implies that the current word does not depend on the entire history, but at most on the last few words. The latter asserts that an n-gram model is roughly stationary. Assuming a dependency on the two previous words results in a trigram model:

$$p_{\text{trigram}}(w) = p(w_1)\, p(w_2 \mid w_1)\, p(w_3 \mid w_1, w_2)\, \ldots\, p(w_m \mid w_{m-2}, w_{m-1})\ . \qquad (2)$$

Although crude in appearance, it has proven difficult to develop more sophisticated language models that consistently outperform trigrams in large vocabulary speech recognition tasks [21].

In practice, the text is *normalized* before counting n-gram occurrences. Text normalization includes the removal of most punctuation and case information, the verbalization of numbers (*e.g.*, \$12.8bn becomes 'twelve point eight billion dollars'), the setting of relevant markers such as sentence breaks, and the correction of spelling errors. The vocabulary size may be restricted to a certain number (say, 65 536 words). In this case, out-of-vocabulary (OOV) words may be mapped to a single unknown word symbol (<unk>) when counting n-grams.

The value of n is an important question for n-gram modelling. A small value of n leads to more reliable parameter estimation. Larger values of n lead to a more detailed context. The total number of potential n-grams scales exponentially with n, so most higher order n-grams do not occur in the training data[3]. Consequently, bigram or trigram models are most widely used for n-gram modelling of large vocabularies.

Sparseness of Training Data. Maximum likelihood (ML) estimation maximizes the probability of the model generating the training data. For example, the ML estimate for a bigram (v, w)—word v, followed by word w—is given by the conditional form:

$$p(w \mid v) = \frac{c(v, w)}{c(v)}\ , \qquad (3)$$

where $c(v, w)$ and $c(v)$ imply unigram and bigram frequencies observed in the training data[4].

ML estimation of n-gram language models can be seriously affected by training data sparsity. For example, the *THISL data collection* contains about 7.5 million words;

---

[2] This is equivalent to saying that we play a Shannon game ('what is the next word?') using a probabilistic model [42].

[3] Suppose the vocabulary size is 65 536 words, the number of parameters for bigram, trigram, and four-gram models are up to 4.3×10^9, 2.8×10^{14}, and 1.8×10^{19}, respectively. On the other hand, a typical corpus size is on the order of 10^5 to 10^9.

[4] The ML estimate is also given by the joint probability form, $p(v, w) = \dfrac{c(v, w)}{N}$, where N denotes the total number of training instances. However, it is more natural to use the conditional form because most calculations for language modelling are carried out by exploiting conditional relations. Thus for the rest of this chapter, we show conditional forms only.

if we estimate a trigram language models using a 65 536 word vocabulary, the number of possible trigrams is about 37 million times greater than the size of the training data. Hence simple ML estimation will result in many 'zero probabilities'; any word sequence, whose n-gram component was not present in the training data, will not be processed properly using the ML formulation (2).

In order to address this problem, a variety of smoothing techniques have been developed. They are designed to 'smooth' the probability estimates for n-gram models so that any n-gram component is given a non-zero probability. Smoothing techniques may be divided into two main classes: discounting schemes for re-distributing frequencies to unseen events; and approaches to combine different level models (*e.g.*, interpolation, back-off).

2.2   Discounting Techniques

ML estimation of n-gram language models results in over-estimates of the probabilities of those n-grams that are observed in the training data. The probabilities of unobserved n-grams are under-estimated (set to zero). This is sometimes called the *zero probability problem* . Discounting schemes, such as Good-Turing and absolute discounting, address this problem by reducing, or *discounting*, the ML probability estimates, and re-distributing the 'freed' probability mass to previously unseen events (figure 2).

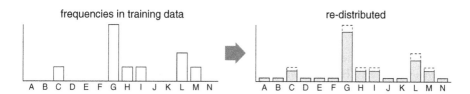

Fig. 2. 'Discounted mass' is re-distributed to events not observed in the training data.

Table 1 shows discounted bigram frequency estimates, calculated from the *THISL data collection*. The details of each approach are given below.

Empirical Estimation. An empirical approach (sometimes referred to as held-out estimation) may be based on the question 'how often do bigrams that appear r times in the training data tend to occur in new data?', using a held-out data set to empirically validate an estimated model. Let u_r denote the number of n-grams that occur exactly r times in the training data, and $c_t(\,\cdot\,)$ and $c_h(\,\cdot\,)$ represent frequencies in the training and the held-out data, respectively. A discounted frequency for a bigram (v,w) is calculated as follows [8], [28]:

$$\hat{r}_{emp} = \frac{1}{u_r} \cdot \sum_{\substack{(v,w): \\ c_t(v,w)=r}} c_h(v,w) \ . \tag{4}$$

Table 1. This table summarizes discounted bigram frequency estimates for the *THISL data collection*. u_r denotes the number of bigrams that occurred r times in the training data. $\hat{r}_{emp}$ is an empirical estimate derived from the test data for bigrams that occurred r times in the training data. $\hat{r}_{ml}(=r)$ is a simple ML estimate. $\hat{r}_{cv}$, $\hat{r}_{gt}$, and $\hat{r}_{abs}$ are the cross validation, the Good-Turing, and the absolute discounting estimates. They were obtained from the training data only, without looking at the test data, but they are closer to $\hat{r}_{emp}$ than the ML estimate.

r	u_r	$\hat{r}_{emp}$	$\hat{r}_{ml}$	$\hat{r}_{cv}$	$\hat{r}_{gt}$	$\hat{r}_{abs}$
0	–	0.0019	0	0.0015	0.0021	0.0023
1	839 300	0.47	1	0.45	0.53	0.34
2	220 490	1.22	2	1.25	1.23	1.34
3	90 077	2.21	3	2.23	2.26	2.34
4	50 826	3.24	4	3.21	3.23	3.34
5	32 882	4.10	5	4.20	4.18	4.34
6	22 928	5.14	6	5.15	5.21	5.34
7	17 053	6.10	7	6.13	6.23	6.34
8	13 290	7.23	8	7.11	7.24	7.34
9	10 693	8.13	9	8.18	8.19	8.34

If the amounts of training and held-out data are different, they should be normalized. The conditional relative bigram frequency is:

$$\hat{f}_{emp}(w \mid v) = \frac{\hat{r}_{emp}}{c(v)} \; .$$

Table 1 contains a column showing the empirical estimation of discounted bigram frequencies for the *THISL data collection*, using program scripts (7 488 445 words, 1 394 406 bigrams) as the training data and reference transcriptions (487 027 words, 182 441 bigrams) as the held-out data.

Cross Validation. Cross validation is a related approach to the held-out estimation. It may be carried out by the following steps [28]:

1. Separate the entire training data into $K > 1$ sections.
2. For each $k = 1 \ldots K$, hold out section k and
   (a) from the remaining $K - 1$ sections (referred to as 'development data'), collect statistics $u_r(k)$: the number of n-grams that occur exactly r times;
   (b) from the held-out section k, collect the number of total occurrences $t_r(k)$ of bigrams that appear exactly r times in the development data; normalize $t_r(k)$ according to the development data and the held-out data sizes.
3. Calculate the average:

$$\hat{r}_{cv} = \frac{\sum\limits_{k=1 \ldots K} t_r(k)}{\sum\limits_{k=1 \ldots K} u_r(k)} \; . \tag{5}$$

Table 1 also shows estimates by cross validation, where program scripts were split into two parts (one with 3 755 764 words, 906 100 bigrams, and the other with 3 732 681 words, 903 811 bigrams).

Good-Turing Discounting. The Good-Turing estimate of discounted frequencies does not rely on a held-out data set. Originally attributed to Turing, it may be derived as a special case of cross validation in which a single training instance is held out at each time of iteration [8], [14], [22], [30]. The Good-Turing discounted frequency $\hat{r}_{gt}$ (for $r > 0$) has the form:

$$\hat{r}_{gt} = (r+1)\frac{u_{r+1}}{u_r} \quad , \tag{6}$$

where u_r is the number of n-grams that occur exactly r times in the training data.

Suppose we denote the number of the training instances by $N = \sum_r r \cdot u_r$, then the total discounted mass from cases for $r > 0$ is given by

$$N - \sum_r \hat{r} \cdot u_r = N - \sum_r (r+1) \cdot u_{r+1} = u_1 \quad .$$

which is then redistributed to all unobserved events. For a vocabulary of size $\mathcal{V}$, the number of n-grams not observed in the training data is $u_0 = |\mathcal{V}|^n - \sum_r u_r$. In this case the Good-Turing estimate for $r = 0$ is $\hat{r}_{gt} = \frac{u_1}{u_0}$.

For the *THISL data collection* with 19 959 vocabulary words, the number of zero frequency bigrams is $u_0 = 19959^2 - 1393940 = 396967741$, among which the discounted mass was thinly distributed. The zero frequency estimate is in fact not zero but $\hat{r}_{gt} = 0.0021$ as indicated in table 1.

If we define the discounting factor as $d_r = \frac{\hat{r}_{gt}}{r}$, then we can write the conditional relative frequency for discounted bigrams as:

$$\hat{f}_{gt}(w \mid v) = d_{c(v,w)} \cdot f_{ml}(w \mid v) \quad , \tag{7}$$

for $c(v, w) = r > 0$, using the ML estimate $f_{ml}(w \mid v) = \frac{c(v, w)}{c(v)}$.

Absolute Discounting. Absolute discounting [14], [30] is an alternative scheme that does not require a held out set, in which a constant e is subtracted from each non-zero count, and redistributed over unseen events:

$$\hat{r}_{abs} = \begin{cases} r - e & \text{if } r > 0 \\ \dfrac{e}{u_0} \times \sum_r u_r & \text{if } r = 0 \end{cases} \quad , \tag{8}$$

where r and u_r are defined as before. The discounting constant e may be estimated from the held-out data. Alternatively, Ney *et al.* [30] suggested $e \sim \dfrac{u_1}{u_1 + 2u_2}$; using

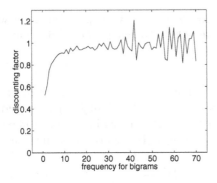

r	d_r	d_r^*
0	-	-
1	0.53	0.46
2	0.61	0.56
3	0.75	0.72
4	0.81	0.78
5	0.84	0.81
6	0.87	0.85
7	0.89	0.87
8	0.91	1.00
9	0.91	1.00

Fig. 3. The Good-Turing estimate may not be very accurate for large r. The graph on the left indicates it is no longer reliable for the *THISL data collection*. Instead Katz [23] suggested an alternative approach that discounts for $1 \leq r \leq k$ only, using $d_r^* = \dfrac{\frac{\hat{r}_{gt}}{r} - \xi_k}{1 - \xi_k}$ where $\xi_k = \dfrac{(k+1)u_{k+1}}{u_1}$, and $d_r^* = 1$ for $r > k$. For example, suppose we wish to discount d_r^* between $1 \leq r \leq 7$, then $\xi_7 = \dfrac{8 \cdot u_8}{u_1} = 0.127$. The table on the right shows discounted frequencies by the Good-Turing (6) and by Katz's formulation.

this approximation, we have calculated $e = 0.656$, and thus the zero frequency estimate $\hat{r}_{abs} = 0.0023$, for the *THISL data collection* (table 1).

The conditional relative frequency for discounted bigrams is given by

$$\hat{f}_{abs}(w \mid v) = \frac{\hat{r}_{abs}}{c(v)} = f_{ml}(w \mid v) - \frac{e}{c(v)} \quad , \tag{9}$$

for $c(v, w) = r > 0$, using the ML estimate $f_{ml}(w \mid v)$.

2.3   Smoothing with Lower Level n-grams

In the previous section we discussed discounting techniques that freed some probability mass to take account of unseen events. We now consider two approaches that enable a redistribution of the discounted mass by combining different levels of n-gram models (unigram, bigram, trigram, ...) in such a way that the most precise model available is used. We consider *interpolation* and *back-off* smoothing: each approach recursively redistributes discounted mass from each level of an n-gram model to lower level n-gram models.

Interpolation. The interpolation method is based on a linear combination of n-gram models. For example, the probability for a trigram (u, v, w)—word 'u', followed by word 'v', then 'w'—may be smoothly estimated as:

$$p_{int}(w \mid u, v) = \lambda_3 p(w \mid u, v) + \lambda_2 p(w \mid v) + \lambda_1 p(w) + \lambda_0 \cdot \mathcal{A} \quad , \tag{10}$$

with some constant $\mathcal{A}$ and constraints $\sum_j \lambda_j = 1$ for $0 \leq \lambda_j \leq 1$ [20]. Generally, λ can be a function of the history (*i.e.*, '$\ldots, u, v$') that satisfies the total probability constraints, $\sum p_{int} = 1$.

Combining different levels of n-gram models is beneficial because the discounted probability estimate of a lower level n-gram (observed in the training data) is more reliable than probability estimates of unseen higher level n-grams. The following recursive formulation is based on that by Federico *et al.* [14].

Consider the estimation of a conditional trigram probability $p(w \mid u,v)$. This may be calculated using a discounted relative frequency $\hat{f}(w \mid u,v)$ and a bigram probability $p(w \mid v)$:

$$p(w \mid u,v) = \hat{f}(w \mid u,v) + \{1 - \alpha(u,v)\} \cdot p(w \mid v)$$
$$\text{where} \quad \alpha(u,v) = \sum_{w \in \mathcal{E}(u,v,w)} \hat{f}(w \mid u,v) \ . \tag{11}$$

$\alpha(u,v)$ is a non-zero estimate of the marginal probability that a trigram with context (u,v) exists in the model, where $\mathcal{E}(u,v,w)$ implies the trigram entry in the model.

The bigram and unigram probabilities are estimated in a similar fashion:

$$p(w \mid v) = \hat{f}(w \mid v) + \{1 - \alpha(v)\} \cdot p(w)$$
$$\text{where} \quad \alpha(v) = \sum_{w \in \mathcal{E}(v,w)} \hat{f}(w \mid v) \ ; \tag{12}$$

$$p(w) = \hat{f}(w) + \{1 - \alpha\} \cdot \mathcal{A}$$
$$\text{where} \quad \alpha = \sum_{w} \hat{f}(w) \ . \tag{13}$$

One possible choice of the constant may be $\mathcal{A} = \dfrac{1}{|\mathcal{W}|}$ with sufficiently large $|\mathcal{W}|$ (say, $|\mathcal{V}| \ll |\mathcal{W}|$). Finally, to verify the total probability constraints for the conditional trigram probability, suppose that $\sum_{w \in \mathcal{E}(v,w)} p(w \mid v) = 1$,

$$\sum_{w \in \mathcal{E}(u,v,w)} p(w \mid u,v) = \sum_{w \in \mathcal{E}(u,v,w)} \hat{f}(w \mid u,v) + \{1 - \alpha(u,v)\} \cdot \sum_{w \in \mathcal{E}(v,w)} p(w \mid v) = 1 \ .$$

Similar calculations may be done for bigram and unigram probabilities as well.

Back-Off. Rather than combining different level n-gram models, the back-off method chooses the most appropriate n-gram level to use when estimating conditional probabilities. The back-off method partitions the mass between n-grams which are backed off from higher level models. An analogous recursive formulation to that used for interpolation-based smoothing may be employed.

The conditional trigram probability $p(w \mid u,v)$ is estimated using a discounted relative frequency $\hat{f}(w \mid u,v)$ if the trigram is observed in the training data, otherwise the model *backs off* to a bigram probability estimate $p(w \mid v)$:

$$p(w \mid u,v) = \begin{cases} \hat{f}(w \mid u,v) & \text{if } \mathcal{E}(u,v,w) \text{ exists} \\ \beta(u,v) \cdot p(w \mid v) & \text{otherwise} \end{cases}$$

$$\text{where} \quad \beta(u,v) = \frac{1 - \alpha(u,v)}{1 - \displaystyle\sum_{w \in \mathcal{E}(u,v,w)} \hat{f}(w \mid v)} \quad . \tag{14}$$

$\beta(u,v)$ is the back-off factor, $\alpha(u,v)$ is the non-zero marginal probability estimate, and $\mathcal{E}(u,v,w)$ implies the trigram entry in the model.

The bigram and unigram estimates again take a similar form:

$$p(w \mid v) = \begin{cases} \hat{f}(w \mid v) & \text{if } \mathcal{E}(v,w) \text{ exists} \\ \beta(v) \cdot p(w) & \text{otherwise} \end{cases}$$

$$\text{where} \quad \beta(v) = \frac{1 - \alpha(v)}{1 - \displaystyle\sum_{w \in \mathcal{E}(v,w)} \hat{f}(w)} \quad ; \tag{15}$$

$$p(w) = \begin{cases} \hat{f}(w) & \text{if } \mathcal{E}(w) \text{ exists} \\ \beta \cdot \mathcal{A} & \text{otherwise} \end{cases}$$

$$\text{where} \quad \beta = \frac{1 - \alpha}{1 - \sum_w \mathcal{A}} \quad . \tag{16}$$

We note that $\sum_w \mathcal{A} = |\mathcal{V}| \cdot \mathcal{A}$, where $\mathcal{A} = \dfrac{1}{|\mathcal{W}|}$ is again a possible choice. To verify the total probability constraints, suppose $\mathcal{E}(u,v,w)$ does not exist,

$$\sum_{\mathcal{E}(u,v,w)=\phi} p(w \mid v) = 1 - \sum_{w \in \mathcal{E}(u,v,w)} p(w \mid v) = 1 - \sum_{w \in \mathcal{E}(u,v,w)} \hat{f}(w \mid v) \quad .$$

Thus,

$$\sum_w p(w \mid u,v) = \sum_{w \in \mathcal{E}(u,v,w)} \hat{f}(w \mid u,v) + \beta(u,v) \cdot \sum_{\mathcal{E}(u,v,w)=\phi} p(w \mid v) = 1 \quad .$$

Evaluating Language Models. In order to evaluate language models, an average log probability is often used. Suppose the test data contain N words:

$$LP = \frac{1}{N} \sum_{i=1...N} \log_2 p(w_i \mid w_{i-n+1}, \ldots, w_{i-1}) \quad ;$$

and the *perplexity* is the average branching factor defined by $PP = 2^{-LP}$. The best language model will average the fewest guesses over the text data. For the example sentence at the beginning of this chapter, table 2 shows individual trigram probabilities using the Good-Turing discounted and backed off model. From the table, we can immediately calculate the average log probability, $LP = -7.55$, and the perplexity, $PP = 187.6$.

Table 2. This table shows probabilities for individual trigram components from the test sentence 'later the prime minister tony blair telephoned mr. yeltsin', using Good-Turing discounting and back-off modelling, derived from the *THISL data collection*. All numbers are in log domain (base 2). For example, this table indicates that a trigram entry for 'the prime minister' exists in the model, thus the probability estimate is simply the discounted relative frequency for the trigram. However, the trigram entry for 'tony blair telephoned' is not found in the model, so we need to back-off to a bigram 'blair telephoned', which again does not exist and we further back-off to a unigram 'telephoned'. The trigram probability estimate for 'tony blair telephoned' is thus a product (a sum in the log domain) of back-off factors and the discounted relative frequency for the unigram 'telephoned'.

(u,v,w)	$p(w \mid u,v)$	$\hat{f}(w \mid u,v)$	$\beta(u,v)$	$\hat{f}(w \mid v)$	$\beta(v)$	$\hat{f}(w)$
later	-10.86					-10.86
later the	-4.08			-4.08		
later the prime	-8.27	-8.27				
the prime minister	-0.31	-0.31				
prime minister tony	-6.10	-6.10				
minister tony blair	-1.29	-1.29				
tony blair telephoned	-20.88	$\rightarrow$	-0.22		$\rightarrow$ -2.15	-18.51
blair telephoned mr.	-10.03	$\rightarrow$	0		$\rightarrow$ -0.80	-9.23
telephoned mr. yeltsin	-6.15	$\rightarrow$	0	-6.15		

3 Adaptive Language Modelling: Topic Coherence

The *n*-gram model is syntactic and locally constrained, based on a Markov chain of a word sequence whose parameters are derived from word frequency counts given a training corpus. Because the *n*-gram is a statistical model, a fundamental assumption is that the task domain is similar to that for the training corpus. Consequently, a relatively large amount of training data is required to accommodate the great number of variations that may occur in spoken language. The *n*-gram approach works well when these underlying assumptions of static task domain and sufficient training data hold, while it does not when the application domain varies from the training conditions.

To address this problem, several adaptive language modelling schemes have been proposed. Since the *n*-gram model has a constrained context (typically the previous two or three words) most adaptive language modelling schemes attempt to exploit longer distance dependencies. In this section we develop a mixture language modelling approach, in which the component models display a degree of topic coherence. We decompose the task into two problems: document classification (employing techniques first developed for text retrieval) and mixture modelling.

3.1 Document Classification

Topic dependent language models may be obtained by the automatic derivation of topic information from text, followed by the combination of global and topic dependent text statistics. A 'bag-of-words' model, which is based on a histogram of weighted unigram frequencies, is used to estimate the topic of a document[5]. This approach—frequently adopted in text retrieval—assumes that the similarity between documents can be measured from word (or term) co-occurrence statistics. The similarity operation may be regarded as being carried out in a high dimensional space whose dimension is given by the vocabulary size. One advantage of using such a measure is that local constraints that might have an adverse global effect, such as word order, may be discarded. We present a brief overview of some relevant text retrieval concepts; a more thorough discussion is available elsewhere (*e.g.*, [44], [45], or chapter 4 of this book).

Term Weighting. A focal point of document classification is the calculation of weights for words according to their importance in documents. For example, unigram frequencies of vocabulary items may be used. As the total word counts often vary in orders of magnitude between documents, estimates of unigram probabilities can be used instead in order to avoid possible effects of document size. It would also be beneficial to weight the more important words in order to avoid distortions occurring due to common non-content words.

Term weighting schemes combine global and local factors to produce weighting factors for the within-document unigram probabilities[6]. Suppose that g_i implies a global weight for a word w_i in a collection of documents and that l_{ij} is a local value within a document d_j. The global weight is designed to enhance words which are not widely distributed across many documents, whereas the local weight is usually related to term frequency within the document. There exist a number of approaches to evaluate g_i and l_{ij}, such as $tf \cdot idf$ [48], and Okapi term weighting [37]. In general, a term weight a_{ij} has the form:

$$a_{ij} = g_i \cdot l_{ij} \ , \tag{17}$$

and a document vector for d_j is defined as a collection of term weights $d_j = \{a_{ij}\}$ (which is usually very sparse). Documents can be classified according to their vector representations. A consistent distance measure is the angle between two document vectors.

Dimension Reduction. So far the distance between two documents has been defined in a $|\mathcal{V}|$-dimensional space. One text retrieval approach, known as *latent semantic indexing*, estimates document similarity in a reduced dimension space by calculating the principal components (eigenvectors) of the $|\mathcal{V}|$-dimensional document vectors [11]. It is based on the *singular value decomposition* of a very large, sparse, word by document matrix [3]. Let $A = \{d_j\}$ denote an $m \times n$ matrix whose rank is r; each column describes a document vector d_j, with the entries being some measure associated with vocabulary items in that document. A can be decomposed as

$$A = U\Sigma V^T \ , \tag{18}$$

---

[5] We use the term 'document' loosely; in spoken language applications it may refer to an entire story, paragraph, or even a fixed size window of, say, 500 words.

[6] More generally stopping and stemming algorithms may be used before term weighting schemes [15].

where V^T is the transpose of V. Σ is an $r \times r$ diagonal matrix whose non-zero elements correspond to the singular values, or the non-negative square roots of r eigenvalues for AA^T. U and V are $m \times r$ and $n \times r$ matrices whose rows may be referred to as word and document singular vectors. They define the orthonormal eigenvectors associated with the r eigenvalues of AA^T and $A^T A$, respectively.

The singular vectors corresponding to the s ($s \leq r$) largest singular values are then used to define an s-dimensional document space. Using these vectors, $m \times s$ and $n \times s$ matrices U_s and V_s can be redefined along with $s \times s$ singular value diagonal matrix Σ_s. It is known that $\hat{A}_s = U_s \Sigma_s V_s^T$ is the closest matrix (in a least square sense) of rank s to the original matrix A [3]. As a consequence, given an m-dimensional vector d that describes a document, it is warranted that an s-dimensional projection $\hat{d}_s$ computed by

$$\hat{d}_s = d^T U_s \Sigma_s^{-1} \ , \tag{19}$$

lies in the closest s-dimensional document subspace with respect to the original m-dimensional space. The projection $\hat{d}_s$ represents principal components that capture the largest variation of words and documents without sacrificing much information. s is typically of the order of 100, many times smaller than the original document dimension.

3.2 Mixture Language Modelling

Once documents have been classified into topics, topic-dependent n-gram models may be derived. We now outline a scheme to combine these component language models into a *mixture language model*.

Formulation. A mixture model, denoted by $\mathcal{M}$, is built as the weighted sum of J components, $< \mathcal{M}_1, \ldots, \mathcal{M}_J >$, derived from a partitioned corpus; this is a similar approach to the dynamic cache models discussed in section 4. Let $f(w_t \mid w_1^{t-1}; \mathcal{M})$ and $f(w_t \mid w_1^{t-1}; \mathcal{M}_j)$ imply n-gram type parameters for a mixture and its jth component, respectively. A mixture is defined as

$$p(w_t \mid w_1^{t-1}; \mathcal{M}) = \sum_{j=1}^{J} c_j p(w_t \mid w_1^{t-1}; \mathcal{M}_j) \ . \tag{20}$$

Given this form and the constraints $\sum_{j=1}^{J} c_j = 1$, we wish to find mixing factors, c_j, that maximize the likelihood for a document (sequence of words). The expectation maximization (EM) algorithm [13] is an iterative procedure that is suitable for this purpose; we start from an appropriate initial guess $c_j^{[0]}$. If there are T words in the document, then the pth estimate is given by

$$c_j^{[p]} = \frac{1}{T} \sum_{\tau=1}^{T} \frac{c_j^{[p-1]} p(w_\tau \mid w_1^{\tau-1}; \mathcal{M}_j)}{\sum_{k=1}^{J} c_k^{[p-1]} p(w_\tau \mid w_1^{\tau-1}; \mathcal{M}_k)} \ . \tag{21}$$

The procedure is similar to other mixture density parameter estimation problems [35].

Formula (21) produces updated estimates of the mixing factors only after the entire document is processed. This is not very useful because a major objective is to flexibly adjust to the varying style of documents. Suppose that $t - 1$ words $\{w_1, \ldots, w_{t-1}\}$ have been processed so far; a new word w_t is given. Then the tth incremental estimate is obtained recursively by

$$c_j^{[t]} = \frac{t-1}{t} c_j^{[t-1]} + \frac{1}{t} \gamma_j^{[t]} \quad \text{where} \quad \gamma_j^{[t]} = \frac{c_j^{[t-1]} p(w_t \mid w_1^{t-1}; \mathcal{M}_j)}{\sum_{k=1}^{J} c_k^{[t-1]} p(w_t \mid w_1^{t-1}; \mathcal{M}_k)}. \quad (22)$$

Using this form, the mixing factors are adjusted automatically to maximize the likelihood of the document, thus indirectly incorporating topic information.

3.3   Evaluation

There is a large body of work in the general area of document classification (see chapter 4 and [28]). The Text Retrieval Conference (TREC) has been a forum for the evaluation of text retrieval systems for a variety of tasks including routing, filtering and spoken document retrieval. Recent evaluations have consistently indicated that many of the best performing systems use Okapi term weighting [37] (or a closely related approach) and do not employ dimension reduction. Our own experiments in mixture language modelling have indicated that Okapi term-weighting performs best and that SVD dimension reduction causes a degradation in performance [16].

Table 3 indicates that the mixture model improves the perplexity over the conventional model, even though the trigram hit rate declines. A lower hit rate is unavoidable when a corpus is partitioned to smaller subsets: despite this handicap, the mixture model has shown improved perplexities compared with the conventional approach.

Table 3. Perplexities and trigram hit rates for a baseline model (a single trigram derived from the complete training data), and a mixture of 10 component models (derived using Okapi term weighting). The experiment was performed using the *British National Corpus* [5].

model	perplexity	trigram hit (%)
single model	180.0	62.4
mixture of 10 class models	164.2	42.8

4   Adaptive Language Modelling: Word Level Correlation

In both spoken and written language, word occurrences are not random but vary greatly from document to document. Indeed, modern text retrieval relies on the degree of departure from randomness as a discriminative indicator [44], [45]. In this section we discuss ways to mathematically realize the intuition that an occurrence of a certain word may increase the chance for the same word being observed later. Dynamic language models aim to incorporate longer distance correlations between words, either through an explicit probabilistic model or by blending statistics for recent words with a global model. An alternative approach uses a statistical model of word occurrence based on the use of the Poisson distribution [18], [38].

4.1 Dynamic Language Models

Although a constant word rate is an unlikely premise, it is nevertheless assumed in n-gram language modelling. The notion of adaptive modelling by a mixture of topic-dependent language models (section 3) is one proposed solution to this problem. Alternatively, Rosenfeld incorporated trigger pairs (longer distance word-level dependencies) into a model structure using maximum entropy [22], [40].

The *dynamic cache model* is a simpler approach, based on an observation that recently appearing words are more likely to re-appear than would be predicted by a static n-gram model [10], [25]. This model blends the global n-gram model with a local model:

$$\hat{p}(w_t|w_a^{t-1}) = p_{\text{global}}(w_t|w_a^{t-1}) + p_{\text{local}}(w_t|w_a^{t-1}) \ . \tag{23}$$

$p_{\text{local}}(w_t|w_a^{t-1})$ is usually estimated using a *cache* of the last K words. In the simplest form, dynamic cache models blend a locally estimated unigram model with the globally estimated n-gram (typically trigram). Such models have been reported to lower perplexity by around 10% [10], [25], but to have minimal effects on the word error rate in large vocabulary speech recognition (*e.g.*, [47]).

4.2 Variable Word Rates

A variant of the dynamic cache model incorporates recency into the cache by using an exponential decaying weight on the contribution of words in the cache. However, rather than relying on such *ad hoc* devices to model variable word occurrences, it is possible to use an explicit probabilistic model of word rate, such as a Poisson mixture. Church and Gale [9] have demonstrated that a continuous mixture of Poisson distributions can produce accurate estimates of variable word rate. In related work Lowe [26] applied a beta-binomial mixture model to topic tracking and detection.

If we consider that occurrences of each word are the result of an underlying Poisson process, then the word rate is no longer uniform. Consider a set of documents[7] and a word w. We assume that each document produces w independently according to a Poisson process with a single parameter $\lambda > 0$:

$$\theta^{[poiss]}(x) = \mathcal{P}(X = x; \lambda) = \frac{e^{-\lambda}\lambda^x}{x!} \ , \tag{24}$$

where X is a discrete, non-negative random variable representing the number of occurrences of w, with expected value $E[X] = \lambda$ and variance $V[X] = \lambda$.

---

[7] Recall our loose definition of a document; basically it is a unit of spoken (or written) data of a certain length that contains some topic(s), or content(s).

A less constrained model of variable word rate is offered by a *mixture of Poissons*. Suppose the parameter λ of the pdf (24) is distributed according to some function $\phi(\lambda)$, then we define a continuous mixture of Poisson distributions by

$$\theta(x) = \int_0^\infty \theta^{[poiss]}(x)\phi(\lambda)d\lambda \ . \tag{25}$$

In particular, if $\phi(\lambda)$ is a gamma distribution, *i.e.*, $\phi(\lambda) = \mathcal{G}(\lambda;\ \alpha,\beta) = \dfrac{\lambda^{\alpha-1}e^{-\frac{\lambda}{\beta}}}{\beta^\alpha\Gamma(\alpha)}$, for $\alpha > 0$ and $\beta > 0$, then the integral (25) is reduced to a discrete distribution for $x = 0, 1, \ldots$ such that

$$\theta^{[nb]}(x) = \mathcal{NB}(X = x;\ \alpha,\beta) = \binom{\alpha+x-1}{x}\frac{\beta^x}{(1+\beta)^{\alpha+x}} \ . \tag{26}$$

This $\theta^{[nb]}(x)$ is a *negative binomial distribution*[8] and its expected value and variance are given by $E[X] = \alpha\beta$ and $V[X] = \alpha\beta(\beta+1)$, respectively.

The histograms in figure 4 show the number of word (unigram) and bigram occurrences in news broadcast. 'for' and 'you' appeared approximately the same number of times across all the transcripts. Using the constant word rate assumption, they would have been assigned a probability of around 0.0086. However their occurrence rates varied between documents; about 11% and 33% of all documents did not contain 'for' and 'you' (respectively), while 1% and 3% contained these words more than 30 times. This seems to indicate that occurrences of 'for' is less dependent on the content (or the style) of a document. A negative binomial distribution was used to model the variable word rate in each case.

The negative binomial seems to model word occurrence rate relatively well for most vocabulary items, regardless of frequency. Figure 4 illustrates this for one of the most frequent words 'of' (probability of 0.023 according to the constant word rate assumption) and the less frequently occurring 'church' (less than 0.00029). In particular, 'church' appeared only in 93 out of 2583 documents, but 28 of them contained more than 10 instances, suggesting strong correlation with the document content. We also collected statistics of bigrams. They are very sparse; for example, 'for you' and 'of church' appeared in 127 and 6 documents. The negative binomial model fits bigrams as well, indicating that variable bigram rate can also be modelled using a continuous mixture of Poissons.

4.3   Variable Word Rate Language Models

Taking word occurrence rate into account changes a probabilistic language model from a situation akin to playing a lottery, to something closer to betting on a horse race:

---

[8] Let $\phi(\lambda) = \mathcal{G}(\lambda;\ \alpha,\beta)$. Integration (25) is straightforward using the definition of the gamma function, $\Gamma(\alpha) = \int_0^\infty t^{\alpha-1}e^{-t}dt$, and the recursion, $\Gamma(\alpha+1) = \alpha\Gamma(\alpha)$. The resultant pdf (26) has a slightly unconventional form in comparison to that in most of standard textbooks (*e.g.*, [12]), but is identical by setting a new parameter $\gamma = \dfrac{1}{1+\beta}$ with $0 < \gamma < 1$.

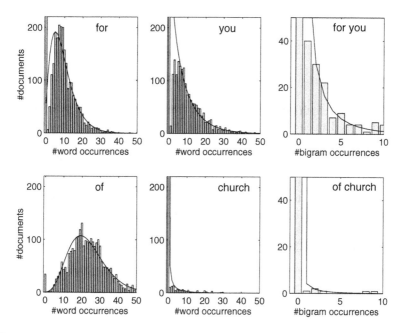

Fig. 4. Word and bigram occurrences vary between documents. Histograms show the number of occurrences taken from transcripts of the *Hub–4* Broadcast News acoustic training data (1996–97 — not free, but available from http://www.ldc.upenn.edu/). These transcripts were separated into documents according to section markers and those with less than 100 words were removed, resulting 2583 documents containing slightly less than 1.3 million words in total. The number of occurrences were then normalized to 1000-word length documents. A negative binomial distribution (solid line) was used to approximate each histogram.

the odds for a certain word improve if it has come up in the past. We eliminate the constant word rate assumption and present a variable word rate *n*-gram language model. Discounting and smoothing schemes are also considered.

Relative Frequencies with Prior Word Occurrences. An expected value for a random variable X, given a condition $X \geq a$ for a certain value a, is calculated by replacing the pdf $\theta(X = x)$ with the conditional pdf $\theta(X = x; X \geq a)$:

$$E[X; X \geq a] = \int_{-\infty}^{\infty} x\theta(X = x; X \geq a)dx = \frac{\int_{a}^{\infty} x\theta(x)dx}{\int_{a}^{\infty} \theta(x)dx} \tag{27}$$

(*e.g.*, see page 105 of [33]). Now in discrete space, let $c(w)$ imply the frequency of word w in the training data. We denote by $f(w; c(w) \geq r_w)$ a conditional relative frequency after observing r_w occurrences of word w, which is given by

$$f(w; c(w) \geq r_w) = \frac{1}{N} E[w; c(w) \geq r_w] = \frac{1}{N} \frac{\sum_{j=r_w}^{N} j \cdot \theta_w(j)}{\sum_{j=r_w}^{N} \theta_w(j)} . \qquad (28)$$

N is a document length (*e.g.*, for histograms in figure 4, N is normalized to 1000) and function (28) is defined for $r_w = 0, 1, \ldots, N$. $\theta_w(j)$ is the occurrence rate for word w in an N-length document (*e.g.*, Poisson, negative binomial), satisfying $\sum_{j=0}^{N} \theta_w(j) = 1$.

The conditional relative frequency formula satisfies our intuition as well; the value of (28) increases monotonically as the number of observation r_w accumulates (easy to verify), and it reaches '1' when $r_w = N$. To the other end,

$$f(w; c(w) \geq 0) = \frac{1}{N} \sum_{j=0}^{N} j \cdot \theta_w(j) , \qquad (29)$$

and this corresponds to the case with no prior information of word occurrence. For the conventional approach with the constant word rate assumption, this $f(w; c(w) \geq 0)$ is used regardless of any word occurrences.

Figure 5 illustrates how conditional expected values change after observing word occurrences. Figure 6 demonstrates conditional relative frequencies derived by function (28). The graph on the right indicates that the first few instances do not increase the relative frequency very much for frequent words (*e.g.*, 'of'), but have a substantial effect for the less common word (*e.g.*, 'church'). As the number of observations increases, the former is caught up by the latter.

Variable bigram rate relative frequencies can be calculated in a similar fashion. In the following we use short hand notations $f(r_w)$ and $f(r_{w|v})$ for indicating $f(w; c(w) \geq r_w)$ and $f(w \mid v; c(v,w) \geq r_{w|v})$, respectively. The same notations are used for $p(r_w)$ and $p(r_{w|v})$, *i.e.*, probabilities by variable rate models.

Discounting and Smoothing Techniques. Recall that, for any practical application, smoothing of the probability estimates is essential to avoid zero probabilities for events that were not observed in the training data. As before, let $\mathcal{E}(v, w)$ denote a bigram entry in the model. A bigram probability $p(r_{w|v})$ can be smoothed with a unigram probability $p(r_w)$ using the interpolation [14]:

$$p(r_{w|v}) = \hat{f}(r_{w|v}) + \{1 - \alpha(v)\} \cdot p(r_w)$$
$$\text{where} \quad \alpha(v) = \sum_{w \in \mathcal{E}(v,w)} \hat{f}(r_{w|v} , \qquad (30)$$

where $\hat{f}(r_{w|v})$ implies a 'discounted' relative frequency of variable bigram rate (described later) and $\alpha(v)$ is a non-zero probability estimate as introduced in section 2.

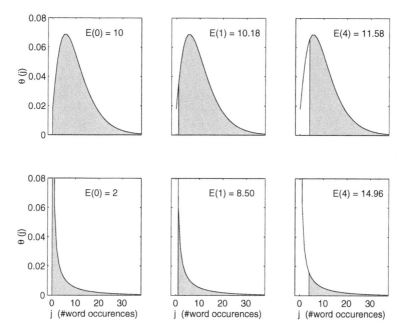

Fig. 5. These graphs illustrates the modelled occurrence rates typically observed for frequent function words (top three, *e.g.*, 'of') and for words that bear strong content information (bottom three, *e.g.*, 'church'). Conditional expected values $E(r_w) \equiv E[w; c(w) \geq r_w]$ are calculated from the shaded areas and shown together. Two graphs in the most left indicate the cases with no prior knowledge of word occurrence (constant word rate assumption). Once a word is observed, the expected value changes very little for a function word, but increases dramatically for a content words (graphs in the middle). Graphs in the right show the cases when each word has occurred four times; now we expect to see this content word more often than some function words.

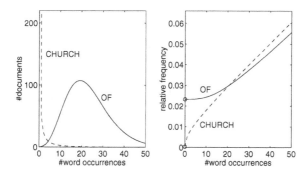

Fig. 6. The left graph shows word occurrence rates for a function word, 'of', and a content word, 'church', observed in documents of 1000-word length (normalized), modelled by negative binomial distributions (identical to those in figure 4). The right graph indicates conditional relative frequencies after a certain number of word occurrences. Circles ('o') correspond to relative frequencies under the constant word rate assumption (0.023 for 'of' and 0.00029 for 'church').

The alternative is to apply a back-off smoothing [23]. Let $\beta(v)$ denote a back-off factor, then

$$p(r_{w|v}) = \begin{cases} \hat{f}(r_{w|v}) & \text{if } \mathcal{E}(v,w) \text{ exists} \\ \beta(v) \cdot p(r_w) & \text{otherwise} \end{cases}$$

$$\text{where} \quad \beta(v) = \frac{1 - \alpha(v)}{1 - \sum\limits_{w \in \mathcal{E}(v,w)} \hat{f}(r_w)} \quad . \tag{31}$$

A variable rate unigram probability $p(r_w)$ can be obtained in a similar fashion by smoothing with some constant value.

Finally, discounting functions for variable word rate models, analogous to those described in section 2, may be

$$\hat{f}_{gt}(r_{w|v}) = d_r \cdot f(r_{w|v}) \tag{32}$$

for the Good-Turing discounting and

$$\hat{f}_{abs}(r_{w|v}) = f(r_{w|v}) - \frac{e}{N} \tag{33}$$

for the absolute discounting. We note that zero prior information case (*i.e.*, $f(0)$'s) may be used to calculate discounting factors, d_r and e.

Table 4 shows the improvement achieved by variable word rate modelling. The document size was set to 1000 words for the unigram case, however, in order to obtain substantial improvement using bigram models, we need to handle the larger size of document (say, over 10 000 words). It is predictable because bigrams are orders of magnitude more sparse than unigrams.

Table 4. This table shows unigram perplexities using the constant (baseline) and the variable word rate models, using conditions described in figure 4. Perplexities were calculated for the reference transcription of the 1997 *Hub–4* evaluation data, containing three hours of speech (approximately 32 000 words). For the variable word rate model, parameters were adjusted 'on-line' — for each occurrence of a word in the evaluation data, a histogram of the past 1000 words was collected and relative frequencies were calculated using the Poisson estimates. Appropriate normalization, discounting and smoothing techniques were applied.

model	perplexity
constant word rate model	936.5
variable word rate model	845.8

5   Information Extraction

Simple statistical models underlie many successful applications of speech and language processing. The language model component of state-of-the-art large vocabulary speech recognition systems uses the n-gram approaches described in this chapter. The most accurate document retrieval systems are typically based on unigram statistics. Although these models are limited representationally, they are trainable and can be scaled to large corpora containing 10^9 words or more.

More recently, similar statistical finite state models have been developed for spoken language processing applications beyond direct transcription to enable, for example, a production of structured transcriptions [4], [17], [24], [31], [43]. This section discusses the development of trainable statistical models for *information extraction* from spoken language. In particular we concentrate on statistical finite state models for identifying proper names and other *named entities* (NE) in television and radio broadcast news.

Named Entities. Proper names account for around 9% of broadcast news output, and their successful identification would be useful for structuring the output of a speech recognizer (through punctuation, capitalization and tokenization), and as an aid to other spoken language processing tasks, such as summarization and database creation. The task of NE identification involves identifying and classifying those words or word sequences that may be classified as proper names, or as certain other classes such as monetary expressions, dates and times. This is not a straightforward problem. While 'Wednesday 1 September' is clearly a date, and 'Alan Turing' is a personal name, other strings, such as 'the day after tomorrow', 'Sheffield Linux Users' Group' and 'Nobel Prize' are more ambiguous. Here we consider seven classes of named entity (<location>, <person>, <organization>, <date>, <time>, <money> and <percentage>) which were defined for a recent *Hub–4* broadcast news evaluation [7]. According to this definition the following NE tags would be correct:

<date>Wednesday 1 September</date>
<person>Alan Turing</person>
the day after tomorrow
<organization>Sheffield Linux Users' Group</organization>
Nobel Prize

In this case 'The day after tomorrow' is not tagged as a date, since only 'absolute' time or date expressions are recognized; 'Nobel' is not tagged as a personal name, since it is part of a larger construct that refers to the prize. Similarly, 'Sheffield' is not tagged as a location since it is part of a larger construct tagged as an organization.

Both rule-based [19], [46] and statistical approaches have been used for NE identification, with some grammar-based systems employing probabilistic or trainable components [1], [29]. Bikel *et al.* introduced a trainable,. statistical system for NE identification [4] based on an ergodic HMM, in which the hidden states corresponded to NE classes, and the observed symbols corresponded to words.

A straightforward approach to identifying named entities in speech is to transcribe the speech automatically using a recognizer, then to apply a text-based NE identification method to the transcription. It is more difficult to identify NEs from automatically transcribed speech compared with text, since speech recognition output is missing features that may be exploited by 'hard-wired' grammar rules or by attachment to vocabulary items, such as punctuation, capitalization and numeric characters. More importantly, no speech recognizer is perfect, and spoken language is rather different from written language. Although planned, low-noise speech (such as dictation, or a news bulletin read from a script) can be recognized with a word error rate (*WER*) of less than 10%, speech which is conversational, in a noisy (or otherwise cluttered) acoustic environment or from a different domain may suffer a *WER* in excess of 40%. Additionally, the natural unit seems to be the phrase, rather than the sentence, and phenomena such as disfluencies, corrections and repetitions are common. It could thus be argued that statistical approaches, that typically operate with limited context and very little notion of grammatical constructs, are more robust than grammar-based approaches. Spoken NE identification was first demonstrated by Kubala *et al.* [24], who applied the model of [4] to the output of a broadcast news speech recognizer. An important conclusion of that work was that the error of an NE identifier degraded linearly with *WER*, with the largest errors due to missing and spuriously tagged names.

5.1   Finite State Model

In this section we outline a statistical framework for NE identification [17], which is closely related to that of Bikel *et al.* [4] and Palmer *et al.* [31].

Formulation. First, let $\mathcal{V}$ denote a vocabulary and C be a set of name classes. We consider that $\mathcal{V}$ is similar to a vocabulary for conventional speech recognition systems (*i.e.*, typically containing tens of thousands of words, and no case information or other characteristics). When there is no ambiguity, these named entities are referred to as 'name(s)'. As a convention here, a class <other> is included in C for those words not belonging to any of the specified names. Because each name may consist of one word or a sequence of words, we also include a marker <+> in C, implying that the corresponding word is a part of the same name as the previous word. The following example is taken from a human-generated reference transcription for the 1997 *Hub–4* evaluation data:

$$\text{at the } \underbrace{\text{ronald reagan center}}_{\text{<organization>}} \text{ in } \underbrace{\text{simi valley}}_{\text{<location>}} \underbrace{\text{california}}_{\text{<location>}}$$

The corresponding class sequence is

   <other> <+> <organization> <+> <+> <other> <location> <+> <location>

because 'simi valley' and 'california' are considered two different names.

   Class information may be interpreted as a word attribute (the left model of figure 7). Formally, we define a class-word token $<c,w> \in C \times \mathcal{V}$ and consider a joint probability model

$$p(<c,w>_1,\ldots,<c,w>_m) = \prod_{i=1\ldots m} p(<c,w>_i \mid <c,w>_1,\ldots,<c,w>_{i-1}) \qquad (34)$$

that generates a sequence of class-word tokens $\{<c,w>_1,\ldots,<c,w>_m\}$. This formulation is best viewed as a straightforward extension to standard *n*-gram language modelling having implicit class transition[9].

---

[9] Denoting $e = <c,w>$, formulation (34) is identical to *n*-gram language models.

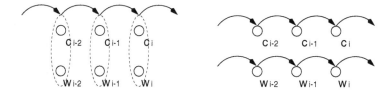

Fig. 7. Topologies for NE models. The left model assumes that class information is a word attribute. The right model explicitly models word-word and class-class transitions.

Unfortunately, this approach would not work as well as other statistical approaches can do. This is an example of a data sparsity problem that is observed in almost every aspect of spoken language processing. Although NE models cannot accommodate a complete set of parameters, a successful recovery of name expressions is heavily dependent on an existence of higher order n-grams. The implicit class transition approach contributes adversely to the data sparsity problem because it causes the set of possible tokens to increase in size from $|\mathcal{V}|$ to $|C \times \mathcal{V}|$.

Alternatively, word-word and class-class transitions may be explicitly formulated (the right model of figure 7). Then we consider a probability model

$$p(c_1, w_1, \ldots, c_m, w_m) = \prod_{i=1\ldots m} p(c_i, w_i \mid c_1, w_1, \ldots, c_{i-1}, w_{i-1}) \qquad (35)$$

that generates a sequences of words $\{w_1, \ldots, w_m\}$ and a corresponding sequence of NE classes $\{c_1, \ldots, c_m\}$. It is a state machine, but it cannot be considered as an HMM, as the probabilities are conditioned both on the previous word and on the previous class. It compensates for the fundamental sparseness of n-gram tokens in a vocabulary set; a bigram level modelling of form (35) outperforms a trigram model of form (34) [17].

Formulation (35) treats class and word tokens independently. Using bigram level constraints, it is reduced to

$$p(c_1, w_1, \ldots, c_m, w_m) = \prod_{i=1\ldots m} p(c_i, w_i \mid c_{i-1}, w_{i-1}) . \qquad (36)$$

The right side of (36) may be decomposed as

$$p(c_i, w_i \mid c_{i-1}, w_{i-1}) = p(w_i \mid c_i, c_{i-1}, w_{i-1}) \cdot p(c_i \mid c_{i-1}, w_{i-1}) . \qquad (37)$$

The conditioned current word probability $p(w_i \mid c_i, c_{i-1}, w_{i-1})$ and the current class probability $p(c_i \mid c_{i-1}, w_{i-1})$ are in the same form as a conventional n-gram, hence can be estimated from annotated text data[10].

---

[10] There exists an alternative approach to decomposing the right side of (36):

$$p(c_i, w_i \mid c_{i-1}, w_{i-1}) = p(c_i \mid w_i, c_{i-1}, w_{i-1}) \cdot p(w_i \mid c_{i-1}, w_{i-1}) .$$

Theoretically, if the 'true' conditional probability can be estimated, decompositions by (37) and above should produce identical results. This ideal case does not occur, and various discounting and smoothing techniques will cause further differences between two decompositions.

Smoothing Techniques. The amount of annotated data available is orders of magnitude smaller than the amount of text data typically used to estimate n-gram models for large vocabulary speech recognition. Smoothing the ML probability estimates is therefore essential to avoid zero probabilities, in which more specific models are smoothed with progressively less specific models. The following smoothing path can be chosen for the first term on the right side of (37):

$$p(w_i \mid c_i, c_{i-1}, w_{i-1}) \longrightarrow p(w_i \mid c_i, c_{i-1}) \longrightarrow p(w_i \mid c_i) \longrightarrow p(w_i) \longrightarrow \frac{1}{|\mathcal{W}|} .$$

$|\mathcal{W}|$ is the size of the possible vocabulary that includes both observed and unobserved words from the training text data (*i.e.*, $|\mathcal{W}|$ is sufficiently greater than $|\mathcal{V}|)^{11}$. Similarly, the smoothing path for the current class probability (the final term in (37)) may be

$$p(c_i \mid c_{i-1}, w_{i-1}) \longrightarrow p(c_i \mid c_{i-1}) \longrightarrow p(c_i) .$$

This assumes that each class occurs sufficiently in training text data; otherwise, further smoothing to some constant probability may be required.

Given the smoothing path, the current word probability may be computed using an interpolation method described in section 2:

$$p(w_i|c_i,c_{i-1},w_{i-1}) = \hat{f}(w_i|c_i,c_{i-1},w_{i-1}) + \{1-\alpha(c_i,c_{i-1},w_{i-1})\}\cdot p(w_i|c_i,c_{i-1})$$
$$\text{where} \quad \alpha(c_i,c_{i-1},w_{i-1}) = \sum_{w_i \in \mathcal{E}(c_{i-1},w_{i-1},c_i,w_i)} \hat{f}(w_i \mid c_i,c_{i-1},w_{i-1})$$

$$(38)$$

where $\hat{f}(w_i \mid c_i,c_{i-1},w_{i-1})$ is a discounted relative frequency, $\alpha(c_i,c_{i-1},w_{i-1})$ is a non-zero probability estimate and $\mathcal{E}(c_{i-1},w_{i-1},c_i,w_i)$ implies the event such that current class c_i and word w_i occur after previous class c_{i-1} and word w_{i-1}.

Alternatively, the back-off smoothing method of [23] could be applied:

$$p(w_i \mid c_i,c_{i-1},w_{i-1}) = \begin{cases} \hat{f}(w_i \mid c_i,c_{i-1},w_{i-1}) & \text{if } \mathcal{E}(c_{i-1},w_{i-1},c_i,w_i) \text{ exists} \\ \beta(c_i,c_{i-1},w_{i-1})\cdot p(w_i \mid c_i,c_{i-1}) & \text{otherwise} \end{cases}$$
$$\text{where} \quad \beta(c_i,c_{i-1},w_{i-1}) = \frac{1-\alpha(c_i,c_{i-1},w_{i-1})}{1-\sum_{w_i \in \mathcal{E}(c_{i-1},w_{i-1},c_i,w_i)} \hat{f}(w_i \mid c_i,c_{i-1})}$$

$$(39)$$

This second decomposition alone would not work as well as the initial decomposition. Crudely speaking, it calculates the distribution over classes for each word; consequently it would reduce accuracy for uncommon words with less reliable probability estimates. Decomposition by (37) makes a more balanced decision because it relies on the distribution over words for each class, and usually there are orders of magnitude fewer classes than words.

[11] Smoothing to $p(w_i \mid c_i,c_{i-1})$ would probably produce a better results than smoothing to $p(w_i \mid c_i,w_{i-1})$, since the former could be more accurately estimated from the annotated training data.

where $\beta(c_i, c_{i-1}, w_{i-1})$ is a back-off factor. Using standard discounting techniques described in section 2, discounted relative frequencies and non-zero probability estimates can be obtained from the training data[12].

Given a sequence of words $\{w_1, \ldots, w_m\}$, named entities can be identified by searching the Viterbi path such that

$$<\hat{c}_1 \ldots \hat{c}_m> = \underset{c_1 \ldots c_m}{\text{argmax}}\, p(c_1, w_1, \ldots, c_m, w_m) \ . \tag{40}$$

Although the smoothing scheme should handle novel words well, the introduction of conditional probabilities for <unk> (which represents those words not included in the vocabulary $\mathcal{V}$) may be used to model unknown words directly. In practice, this is achieved by setting a certain cutoff threshold when estimating discounting probabilities. Those words that occur less than this threshold are treated as <unk> tokens. This does not imply that smoothing is no longer needed, but that conditional probabilities containing the <unk> token may occasionally pick up the context correctly without smoothing with weaker models. The drawback is that some uncommon words are lost from the vocabulary.

5.2   Experiment

NE identification systems are evaluated using an unseen set of evaluation data; the hypothesized NEs are compared with human annotated NE tags in a reference transcription[13]. In this situation there are two possible types of error: *type*, where an item is tagged as the wrong kind of entity and *extent*, where the wrong number of word tokens are tagged. A third error type *content* arises from speech recognition errors. These three error types each contribute $1/3$ to the overall error count, and precision (P) and recall (R) can be calculated in a usual way. A weighted harmonic mean ($P\&R$), sometimes referred to as the F-measure [45], is often calculated as a single summary statistic:

$$P\&R = \frac{2RP}{R+P} \ .$$

$P\&R$ has the disadvantage of deweighting missing and spurious identification errors compared with incorrect identification errors [27]. The slot error rate (SER) is an alternative measure that weights the three types of identification error equally. Analogous to WER, SER may be obtained by:

$$SER = \frac{I+M+S}{C+I+M}$$

where C, I, M, and S denote the numbers of correct, incorrect, missing, and spurious identifications. Using this notation, precision and recall scores may be calculated as $R = C/(C+I+M)$ and $P = C/(C+I+S)$, respectively.

---

[12] The weaker models—$p(w_i \mid c_i, c_{i-1})$, $p(w_i \mid c_i)$, and $p(w_i)$—may be smoothed in a way analogous to that used for $p(w_i \mid c_i, c_{i-1}, w_{i-1})$. Approaches to discounting and combining with different level models are similar when handling the conditioned current class probabilities, i.e., $p(c_i \mid c_{i-1}, w_{i-1})$, $p(c_i \mid c_{i-1})$, and $p(c_i)$.

[13] Inter-annotator agreement for reference transcriptions is around 97–98% [39].

Table 5 shows NE identification scores by the statistical finite state machine approach. The model parameters with explicit class-class and word-word transitions were derived from the relatively small amount of training data (one million words). Like other language modelling problems, a simple way to improve the performance is to increase the amount of training data. As a final note, it should not be under-stated that an appropriate choice and implementation of discounting/smoothing strategies is very important, particularly because a more complex model structure is being trained with less data, compared with conventional language models for speech recognition systems.

Table 5. The table compares NE identification scores on hand transcription (no word error) and speech recognizer output (21% *WER*). A finite state model was derived from the *Hub–4* training data, consisting of about one million words of transcripts having manual NE annotation. It selected 17,560 words (from those occurring more than once in the training data) as a vocabulary and the rest (those occurring exactly once — nearly 10,000 words) were replaced by the <unk> token. The combined Good-Turing/absolute discounting scheme was applied, followed by back-off smoothing. Further detail may be found in [17].

	WER	R	P	P&R	SER
hand transcription	.000	.863	.922	.892	.187
recognizer output	.210	.729	.823	.773	.381

6   Summary

This chapter first outlined the basics of statistical language models (*e.g.*, estimating from sparse training data, encapsulating varying contents and styles of spoken language), then discussed a more recent area for applying n-gram based approaches such as named entity extraction.

Constraints by the Markov assumption, that enforces the local structure of (spoken) language, achieve success only to some extent, but their fundamental brittleness may be alleviated by incorporating richer, and more linguistically motivated models. Chelba and Jelinek have addressed the use of probabilistic dependency grammar [6], where the probability of each word is estimated from several other words that, unlike conventional n-gram models, are not necessarily those immediately preceeding the word.

Another area, that is not discussed in this chapter but worth noting, is the maximum entropy approach. It is a conceptually clean way to model information from multiple sources. It is recently applied to areas such as parsing [34], statistical machine translation [2], [32], and the incorporation of trigger word pair constraints into an n-gram language model [40]. Although computationally challenging, series of successful applications seem to indicate the potential of the framework.

References

1. J. Aberdeen, J. Burger, D. Day, L. Hirschman, P. Robinson, and M. Vilain. MITRE: Description of the Alembic system used for MUC-6. In *Proceedings of the 6th Message Understanding Conference (MUC-6)*, pages 141–1552, November 1995.

2. Adam L. Berger, Stephen A. Della Pietra, , and Vincent J. Della Pietra. A maximum entropy approach to natural language processing. *Computational Linguistics*, 22(1):39–71, March 1996.

3. Michael W. Berry, Susan T. Dumais, and Gavin W. O'Brien. Using linear algebra for intelligent information retrieval. *SIAM Review*, 37(4):573–595, 1995.

4. Daniel M. Bikel, Richard Schwartz, and Ralph M. Weischedel. An algorithm that learns what's in a name. *Machine Learning*, 211–231:1999, 34.

5. Lou Burnard. Users reference guide, British National Corpus version 1.0. Oxford University Computing Service, May 1995.

6. Ciprian Chelba and Frederick Jelinek. Structured language modeling. *Computer Speech and Language*, 14:283–332, 2000.

7. Nancy Chinchor, Patty Robinson, and Erica Brown. Hub-4 named entity task definition (version 4.8). SAIC - http://www.nist.gov/speech/hub4_98/hub4_98.htm, August 1998.

8. Kenneth W. Church and William A. Gale. A comparison of the enhanced Good-Turing and deleted estimation methods for estimating probabilities of English bigrams. *Computer Speech and Language*, 5:19–54, 1991.

9. Kenneth W. Church and William A. Gale. Poisson mixtures. *Natural Language Engineering*, 1(2):163–190, June 1995.

10. P. R. Clarkson and A. J. Robinson. Language model adaptation using mixtures and an exponentially decaying cache. In *Proceedings of ICASSP-97*, volume 2, pages 799–802, April 1997.

11. Scott Deerwester, Susan T. Dumais, George W. Furnas, Thomas K. Landauer, and Richard Harshman. Indexing by latent semantic analysis. *Journal of the Society for Information Science*, 41(6):391–407, 1990.

12. Morris H. DeGroot. *Optimal Statistical Decisions*. McGraw Hill, New York, NY, 1970.

13. A. P. Dempster, N. M. Laird, and D. B. Rubin. Maximum likelihood from incomplete data via the EM algorithm. *Journal of the Royal Statistical Society, series B*, 39(1):1–38, 1977.

14. Marcello Federico, Mauro Cettolo, Fabio Brugnara, and Giuliano Antoniol. Language modelling for efficient beam-search. *Computer Speech and Language*, 9:353–379, 1995.

15. W. B. Frakes and R. Baeza-Yates. *Information Retrieval: Data Structures and Algorithms*. Prentice Hall, Englewood Cliffs, NJ, 1992.

16. Yoshihiko Gotoh and Steve Renals. Topic-based mixture language modelling. *Natural Language Engineering*, 5(4):355–375, December 1999.

17. Yoshihiko Gotoh and Steve Renals. Information extraction from broadcast news. *Philosophical Transactions of the Royal Society, series A*, 358:1295–1310, April 2000.

18. Stephen P. Harter. A probabilistic approach to automatic keyword indexing (part 1). *Journal of the American Society for Information Sceince*, 26(4):197–206, July 1975.

19. J. Hobbs, D. Appelt, J. Bear, D. Israel, M. Kameyama, M. Stickel, and M. Tyson. FASTUS: A cascaded finite state transducer for extracting information from natural language text. In *Finite State Language Processing*, pages 381–406. MIT Press, 1997.

20. F. Jelinek and R. L. Mercer. Interpolated estimation of Markov source parameters from sparse data. In *Proceedings of the Workshop: Pattern Recognition in Practice*, pages 381–397, May 1980.

21. Frederick Jelinek. Up from trigrams! The struggle for improved language models. In *Proceedings of Eurospeech-91*, volume 3, pages 1037–1040, September 1991.

22. Frederick Jelinek. *Statistical Methods for Speech Recognition.* MIT Press, Cambridge, MA, 1997.

23. Slava M. Katz. Estimation of probabilities from sparse data for the language model component of a speech recognizer. *IEEE Transactions on Acoustics, Speech and Signal Processing*, 35(3):400–401, March 1987.

24. Francis Kubala, Richard Schwartz, Rebecca Stone, and Ralph Weischedel. Named entity extraction from speech. In *Proceedings of DARPA Broadcast News Transcription and Understanding Workshop*, 1998.

25. R. Kuhn and R. De Mori. A cache-based natural language model for speech recognition. *IEEE Transactions on Pattern Analysis and Machine Intelligence*, 12(6):570–583, June 1990.

26. Stephen A. Lowe. The beta-binomial mixture model for word frequencies in documents with applications to information retrieval. In *Proceedings of Eurospeech-99*, volume 6, pages 2443–2446, September 1999.

27. John Makhoul, Francis Kubala, Richard Schwartz, and Ralph Weischedel. Performance measures for information extraction. In *Proceedings of DARPA Broadcast News Workshop*, pages 249–252, February 1999.

28. Christopher D. Manning and Hinrich Schütze. *Foundation of Statistical Natural Language Processing.* MIT Press, Cambridge, MA, 1999.

29. A. Mikheev, C. Grover, and M. Moens. Description of the LTG system used for MUC-7. In *Proceedings of the 7th Message Understanding Conference (MUC-7)*, 1998.

30. Hermann Ney, Ute Essen, and Reinhard Kneser. On the estimation of 'small' probabilities by leaving-one-out. *IEEE Transactions on Pattern Analysis and Machine Intelligence*, 17(12):1202–1212, December 1995.

31. David D. Palmer, Mari Ostendorf, and John D. Burger. Robust information extraction from automatically generated speech transcriptions. *Speech Communication*, 32(1/2):95–109, September 2000.

32. K. A. Papineni, S. Roukos, and R. T. Ward. Maximum likelihood and discriminative training of direct translation models. In *Proc. IEEE ICASSP*, pages 189–192, 1998.

33. Athanasios Papoulis. *Probability, Random Variables, and Stochastic Processes.* McGraw Hill, New York, NY, 2nd edition, 1984.

34. Adwait Ratnaparkhi. Learning to parse natural language with maximum entropy models. *Machine Learning*, 34, 1999.

35. Richard A. Redner and Homer F. Walker. Mixture densities, maximum likelihood and the EM algorithm. *SIAM Review*, 26(2):195–239, April 1984.

36. S. Renals, D. Abberley, D. Kirby, and T. Robinson. Indexing and retrieval of broadcast news. *Speech Communication*, 32(1/2):5–20, September 2000.

37. S. E. Robertson and K. Spärck Jones. Simple, proven approaches to text retrieval. Technical Report TR356, University of Cambridge, Computer Laboratory, 1997. http://www.ftp.cl.cam.ac.uk/ftp/papers/reports/.

38. S. E. Robertson and S. Walker. Some simple effective approximations to the 2-Poisson model for probabilistic weighted retrieval. In *Proceedings of SIGIR-94*, pages 232–241, 1994.

39. Patricia Robinson, Erica Brown, John Burger, Nancy Chinchor, Aaron Douthat, Lisa Ferro, and Lynette Hirschman. Overview: Information extraction from broadcast news. In *Proceedings of DARPA Broadcast News Workshop - Herndon, VA*, pages 27–30, February 1999.

40. Ronald Rosenfeld. A maximum entropy approach to adaptive statistical language modeling. *Computer Speech and Language*, 10:187–228, 1996.

41. C. E. Shannon. A mathematical theory of communication. *Bell System Technical Journal*, 27(3,4):379–423 and 623–656, 1948.

42. C. E. Shannon. Prediction and entropy of printed English. *Bell System Technical Journal*, 30(1):50–64, January 1951.

43. Elizabeth Shriberg, Andreas Stolcke, Dilek Hakkani Tür, and GükhanTür. Prosody modeling for automatic sentence and topic segmentation from speech. *Speech Communication*, 32(1/2):127–154, September 2000.

44. K. Spärck Jones, S. Walker, , and S. E. Robertson. A probabilistic model of information retrieval: Development and status. Technical report, Technical Report TR446, University of Cambridge, Computer Laboratory - Available from
http://www.ftp.cl.cam.ac.uk/ftp/papers/reports/, 1998.

45. C. J. van Rijsbergen. *Information Retrieval*. Butterworths, London, 2nd edition, 1979.

46. T. Wakao, R. Gaizauskas, , and Y. Wilks. Evaluation of an algorithm for the recognition and classification of proper names. In *Proceedings of COLING-96*, pages 418–423, 1996.

47. P. C. Woodland, T. Hain, G. L. Moore, T. R. Niesler, D. Povey, A. Tuerk, and E. W. D. Whittaker. The 1998 HTK broadcast news transcription system: Development and results. In *Proceedings of DARPA Broadcast News Workshop*, pages 265–270, February 1999.

48. C. T. Yu and G Salton. Effective information retrieval using term accuracy. *Communications of the ACM*, 20:135–142, 1977.

Very Large Scale Information Retrieval

David Hawking

CSIRO Mathematical and Information Sciences, Canberra, Australia

Abstract. This chapter is based on a series of five lectures presented at the EL-SNET TesTia Summer School held in Chios, Greece in July, 2000. The material has been updated in August 2001 and, at the suggestion of the students, some explanatory diagrams which were at the time drawn on the whiteboard have been included in more polished form.

The scale of electronic document collections has grown dramatically in recent decades. Test collections of the 1960s and 70s (such as Cranfield [9]) contained thousands of documents; the initial TREC collection of 1991 [21] reached almost a million; and the collections indexed by current Web search engines contain approximately a billion.

Information Retrieval (IR) has been associated from its beginning with the analogy of "looking for a needle in a haystack." Extending this metaphor to very large scale, we see that the haystack is now big enough to cover Australia! Furthermore, enthusiastic farmers have filled it with every possible type of item, including many which are very similar to needles but which are not what the searcher wanted. Most items include instructions on how to go directly to other items, but often the instructions are misleading or out of date.

Now there are not only needles but sewing machines, business cards for tailors, needle exchange services, needle-sharpening services, a sewing technology futures exchange, catalogues of needles available for sale or hire and directories of where to find needles within the haystack.

Unfortunately, cunning businesspeople have inserted items which look identical to needles but which turn out to be pictures of naked women or advertisements for get-rich-quick schemes.

Millions of searchers arrive each day to search and they do so with the expectation that they will find what they want within less than two seconds. Some of them are very demanding; they are looking for a particular individual needle and they will not be satisfied unless they find it first. Others want to find as many different needles as they can. Some just want to get an overview of the types of needles which are "out there". A few start looking for needles but when they find one, realise that what they really wanted was a can-opener or an air-ticket to Hawaii!

This chapter attempts to cover the changes which occur when document collections and searcher populations become very large. It addresses the major engineering challenges imposed by very large scale search (particularly on the World Wide Web), outlines parallel and distributed models and canvasses the problem of how to evaluate the effectiveness of very large scale retrieval.

S. Renals, G. Grefenstette (Eds.): Text- and Speech-Triggered Info. Access, LNAI 2705, pp. 106-144, 2003.

Table 1. Examples of different types of Information Retrieval (IR) application.

Category	Description	Example Task
Ad hoc retrieval	Find "relevant" documents in a fixed collection.	*Find documents which tell me about investment strategies.*
Question answering	Extracting answers from retrieved documents.	*Who is the prime minister of Australia?*
Directory lookup	Navigating to a specific Web page.	*Where is the ELSNET home page?*
Selective dissemination of information.	Monitor an incoming stream of documents for ones which match a stored profile.	*Send me any new information on high-tech companies.*
Document Clustering	Automatically grouping similar documents.	*Find the natural groupings in this set of scientific publications.*
Document Categorisation	Assigning pre-defined category labels to a set of documents	*Classify incoming books according to their Dewey decimal category.*
Document Synthesis	Extracting information from multiple retrieved documents	*Construct a personalised travel guide for my visit to Athens in July, 2000.*
Database Lookup	Extracting records from a structured database.	*Find books where author = Hawking and year = 2001*

1   Introduction to Information Retrieval (IR)

Before considering the special issues associated with very large scale, it is important to have an understanding of the fundamentals of IR. A recent text book in the area is [3].

1.1   Types of IR Application

Table 1 lists a number of different types of electronic information processing activity which may be considered to fall under the IR umbrella. Among these applications, the inclusion of database lookup may be considered a little controversial, because the database and information retrieval fields of research are traditionally distinct.

Database research generally deals with highly structured data and with issues of simultaneous update, transaction logging, access authorisation and recovery after failure. The types of queries which can be supported by a given relational database are determined by the database schema and queries have a precisely defined, certain answer set[1]. Any uncertainty which may have been present in the original data has been removed during data entry.

---

[1] For simplicity of exposition, let us ignore the fact that many modern database systems include text retrieval facilities such as free text fields, relevance ranking and approximate textual matching.

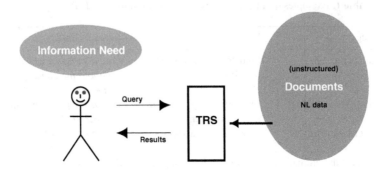

Fig. 1. The ad hoc text retrieval model. A searcher with a particular information need submits a query to a Text Retrieval System. The query is processed against a document collection, whose contents may be considered to be static, and a set of results is returned to the searcher.

Topic A fully-detailed written description of a searcher's information need. (As an researcher might write down for a research assistant.)
Query What the searcher actually types to the retrieval system in order to try to satisfy their information need. Queries are usually very much shorter than the topics to which they correspond.
Search term The textual elements of a query, such as words, phrases, word prefixes etc. The list of acceptable search types depends upon the particular retrieval system.
Boolean retrieval system One which takes a query containing logical operators such as AND, NOT and OR and produces an unranked answer set containing all documents which match the query expression.
Ranked retrieval system One which takes a query and ranks documents on the basis of a computed similarity or relevance score.

Fig. 2. Terminology. Definitions of some jargon used in the text.

By contrast, IR research generally deals with unstructured (or semi-structured) text or multimedia documents and often considers collections to be read-only, thereby avoiding the need to consider updates. However, this simplification is compensated for by uncertainty as to what constitutes the set of right answers. Modern retrieval systems tend to rank documents in decreasing order of estimated likelihood of relevance. Whether or not a document is actually relevant can only be determined subjectively, by a human judge. Judgments vary from person to person and may also depend upon the judge's state of mind at the time.

Space prevents treatment of all the Table 1 IR applications here. Accordingly, this chapter concentrates entirely on the ad hoc retrieval application, particularly in the context of Web[2] search. There are important issues of scale in other IR applications such as

---
[2] Here, the capitalised W is used to mean the World Wide Web as opposed to an arbitrary hyperlinked web of documents.

clustering but ad hoc retrieval on the Web reaches very large scales indeed and is used daily by millions of people.

1.2   Ad Hoc Retrieval

Figure 1 shows the basic model of ad hoc document retrieval. In its purest form, a stream of incoming queries is processed against a fixed set of documents, the inverse of the *selective dissemination of information* case, where a stream of incoming documents is processed against a fixed set of queries (see Table 1). Figure 2 defines some expressions which will be used in the following discussion.

Web search engines are now the most heavily used ad hoc retrieval service but ad hoc retrieval systems are also found on individual websites, in commercial information services such as Dialog and Lexis-Nexis and on informational CD-ROMs such as encyclopaedias.

Results from some ad hoc retrieval systems are in the form of an unranked set comprising all documents matching a specified criterion. Queries to such a system are usually Boolean (eg. ELSNet AND "Summer School" AND (Chios OR Greece) and the systems are often described as *Boolean retrieval systems*. Unskilled searchers often have trouble understanding Boolean queries. (Does the query cat AND dog mean "I want documents which mention both words", or does it mean, "I want documents that contain cat AND I want documents that contain dog"?)

The recent trend has been in favour of *ranked retrieval systems* in which queries are treated as *bags of words*. This means that there are no operators and that the order of query words isn't important. For example, Summer Chios School. In a ranked retrieval system, the result set is sorted in order of decreasing estimated relevance to the query. Relevance estimates are made by combining weights of the query features in a document. In the simplest case the query features are the query words and the weight assigned to a query word in a document may depend upon the number of occurrences in this document, the length of the document and the number of other documents containing this word.

The basic elements of a query, such as words, phrases and part words are usually referred to as *terms*.

In reality, ranked retrieval systems often have Boolean aspects. Often, only documents which are members of the set which would result from the dysjunction of all the query terms (Summer OR Chios OR School) are eligible to be ranked. In fact, some popular search engines restrict rankings to documents which are members of the set which would result from the conjunction of all the query terms (i.e. Summer AND Chios AND School). From here on, only ranked retrieval systems will be considered.

Searchers in an ad hoc retrieval system are concerned with various important dimensions of a ranked retrieval service:

1. Does it present results in a useful way?
2. Does it respond quickly enough?
3. Does it rank documents in sensible order?

The first of these questions is largely independent of the scale of the retrieval problem, and comes under the area of Human-Computer Interaction (HCI), but questions two and three are particularly important in the area of very large scale retrieval. Past IR research has mostly focused on question 3.

A series of collaborative experiments in ad hoc retrieval has been carried out since 1991 under the auspices of the Text REtrieval Conference, TREC [41]. The TREC ad hoc test collections now comprise about two million government and newspaper documents, along with 500 topics and corresponding relevance judgments.

```
<num> Number: 261
<title> Topic: Threat posed by Fissionable Material

<desc> Description:
Does the availability of fissionable material in the
former states of the Soviet Union and its susceptibility
to theft, pose a real and growing threat that terrorist
groups/terrorist states will acquire such
material and be able to construct nuclear weapons?

<narr> Narrative:
Under the terms of the strategic disarmament treaty with
the U.S., the states of the former Soviet Union have been
dismantling 2000 warheads each year.  From each warhead a
shiny sphere of plutonium is extracted.  These spheres,
called ''pits'', are the elemental cores of a bomb.  In addition,
other forms of plutonium are scattered over the former Soviet
Union in institutes, laboratories, plants, shipyards and
power stations.  Disgruntled employees, who are often underpaid
or paid irregularly have access to the plutonium.  This worries
leaders in other countries.  Enriched uranium, an alternate fuel,
is harder to come by because it is stored in well-guarded military
facilities, but it is easier to turn into a bomb.  The Russians
have denied that it came through or from their country, but German
authorities believe that it did.  Any item which speaks to failures
in the safeguarding of nuclear material or to black-market operations
in nuclear material, or to efforts of terrorist groups or terrorist
states to acquire such material would be relevant.
</top>
```

Fig. 3. An example of a TREC topic. The narrative in this case is longer than average.

TREC distinguishes between *topics*, which are structured, detailed, English language statements of a searcher's information need and *queries*, possibly expressed in a system-specific query language, which are sent to the retrieval system in an attempt to find documents matching the underlying information need. Figures 3 and 4 show a sample TREC topic and queries which might correspond to the same information need.

Figure 5 illustrates the test collection approach to information retrieval evaluation. A realistic information need is recorded, e.g. as a TREC topic, and a corresponding

A. Threat posed by Fissionable Material

B. [threat* danger*] [fissionable plutonium uranium U238]
   [USSR Soviet]

C. (threat OR danger) AND (plutonium OR uranium OR fissionable OR U238)
   AND (USSR OR Soviet)

Fig. 4. Examples of different queries derived from the example topic in the preceding figure.

query is fed to the IRS (Information Retrieval System). The query may be generated by automatic processing of the topic description or it may be manually generated by either the originator of the search or by a search intermediary.

The IRS processes the query with respect to a collection of documents and generates a list of results. On the right hand side of the diagram a group of relevance assessors takes the specified information need and assesses whether documents from the collection are relevant to the topic or not. These judgments are then used by an *evaluation package* to evaluate the quality of the ranked results returned by the IRS and to generate performance measurements by which this IRS can be compared with others. For such comparisons to be meaningful, a large number of topics (usually 50 or more) must be used to average out topic-specific variations.

Judging Issues. If the document collection contains more than a few thousand documents, it is not feasible to judge each document in the collection. TREC addresses this issue by using a technique known as *pooling* in which the union of the sets of documents retrieved by a broad and diverse range of retrieval systems forms the pool of documents to be judged. Documents not in the pool are assumed to be irrelevant. Zobel [61] has shown that although the TREC collections do include unjudged relevant documents, these have a very small effect on system comparisons made using TREC.

Voorhees [57] has shown that although agreement between different assessors is far from perfect, that system comparisons are remarkably stable across judgment sets prepared by different assessors.

Measures. The measures used to compare systems are almost always variants of precision and recall. Looking at the documents retrieved at a particular point in the ranking, *precision* is the proportion of retrieved documents which are relevant and *recall* is the proportion of all relevant documents in the collection which have been retrieved. In Web search, searchers are typically more concerned with the precision of the results on the first one or two result pages than with recall. Consequently, *precision at n documents retrieved* or P@n, where n is typically 10 or 20, is a useful measure.

It is usual in TREC to plot precision against recall to give a full picture of the performance characteristics of the retrieval system. Example precision-recall curves are shown in Figure 6. In TREC, systems are often compared using the single number

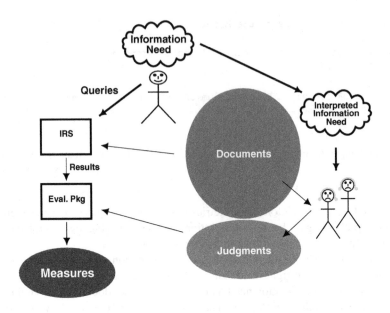

Fig. 5. The TREC retrieval evaluation paradigm.

measure *mean average precision* which takes into account aspects of both precision and recall. *Average precision* corresponds to the area under the precision recall curve and can be computed by summing the precisions at each point in the ranking where a relevant document was retrieved[3] and dividing by the number of known relevant documents for the topic. A mean is then taken of the average precisions recorded across a large number of topics[4].

1.3   Multi-media Retrieval

Ideally, a retrieval system would not be restricted to the text domain and would be able to retrieve documents containing information in the form of images, sounds, video, music and perhaps even tastes and smells. Many fascinating issues arise in non-textual retrieval, such as how to express queries and how to match queries against documents.

However, retrieval in the textual domain is quite fascinating in itself and more than sufficient to fill five lectures! Please note that documents in non-textual media may often be retrieved effectively by applying text retrieval techniques to captions, transcripts, catalogue entries, metadata records and in other descriptive information. For example, a GIF or JPEG image referenced in a Web document may include useful descriptive information in the name of the file, and in the alternate-text field which many Web authors provide for the benefit of blind people or people with non-graphical browsers. For example:

---

[3] Note that recall only changes when a relevant document is retrieved.

[4] Please note that other authors sometimes use different definitions of the term average precision.

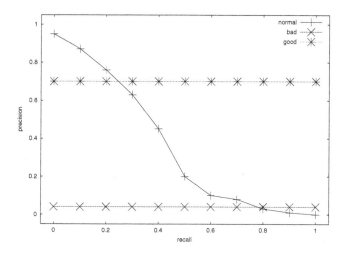

Fig. 6. Precision-recall curves. The horizontal line at the top shows the performance of an unrealistically good retrieval system and the horizontal line at the bottom shows the performance of a very poor system. The third line is more typical of real ad hoc retrieval, showing that discrimination between relevant and irrelevant is initially very good but falls with increasing recall, becoming almost random at very high recall levels.

'`<img src="keystaff.gif" alt="Key Asian studies staff at the ANU">`'.
Some search engines provide "image search" services based on this type of information.

Some also allow retrieval of multi-media web pages on the basis of the *anchor text* of hyper links which refer to them. The following example shows an HTML link whose target is a JPEG file and whose anchor text is "The Mayor welcomes students to Chios." The anchor text is highlighed when displayed by a Web browser and you click on it to make the browser display the target.

```
<a href="x.y.z/Welcome-to-Chios.jpg">The Mayor welcomes students
to Chios.</a>
```

1.4   Cross-Language Retrieval

Given the very wide range of linguistic backgrounds represented at the Summer School, I am very sorry that only a tiny part of this chapter can relate to the topic of cross-language or multi-lingual retrieval. Cross-language retrieval means that queries phrased in one language may retrieve documents written in another.

In the past, the TREC conference has included special interest tracks on Chinese and Spanish retrieval and also spawned a cross-language track involving English, French, German and Italian, which has now gained its independence as the European based CLEF initiative [8].

There are many challenging issues in cross-language retrieval and also in retrieval of documents in the searcher's native language from within a multi-lingual collection. These problems are rapidly becoming more important as the once-supreme dominance of English as the language of the Web is eroded.

The lowest level problem is that of the character set. The ASCII character-set is inadequate for even European languages. The ISO 8859 series of standards extends 8-bit character sets to permit the representation of European accented letters and additional letters. However, 8 bits are insufficient to accommodate the additional characters needed in languages such as Arabic, Thai, Japanese and Chinese. Unicode standards [54] encompass 16 and 32 bit character formats to address this problem, however, Unicode has been by no means universally adopted. My understanding is that most Japanese electronic text is actually encoded in EUC, JIS, or Shift-JIS formats.

Another problem is cross language polysemy. The word *sale* means "reduced-price selling" in English, "dirty" in French and, I think, "salt" in Italian. Even a sequence of words may have meaning in multiple languages. For example, *la chair sale* might mean "dirty flesh" in French whereas *LA chair sale* could refer to a discount furniture sale in Los Angeles.

Text retrieval systems operating in a multi-lingual environment must recognise the use of different character sets and detect the language being used. To complicate matters, more than one character set and more than one language may be used in the same document [31]. Systems performing cross-language retrieval need to incorporate translation facilities for queries.

1.5   How Do Text Retrieval Systems Work?

Text retrieval systems based solely on statistical analysis of patterns of term occurrences within documents consistently perform well on TREC ad hoc tasks. A *term* is the basic indexable unit, such as a word, word-stem or phrase, from which queries and documents are constructed. For retrieval purposes, both documents and queries can be considered to be sequences of terms. In what follows, *term* can usually be interpreted as *word*.

Surprisingly, on TREC ad hoc tasks, systems using natural language processing (NLP) techniques such as word-sense disambiguation and part of speech tagging have not managed to outperform the best statistical systems[5].

Text Retrieval Models. Over the years, a number of information retrieval models have been proposed to estimate document relevance based on the statistics of term occurrences. The most prominent are the Vector Space Model, exemplified in the SMART retrieval system from Cornell University [47] and the Probabilistic Models , exemplified in the Okapi retrieval system [45] from City University, London and the Inquery system [1] from the University of Massachussets.

In practice, when implemented, there is relatively little difference between these models. All are based on the following simple heuristics:

1. The more occurrences of a query term in a document, the more likely it is that the document is relevant.

---

[5] However, NLP processing has come into its own in the TREC question-answering track. [56]

2. A long document containing the same number of occurrences of a query term as a short one is less likely to be relevant.
3. The more documents in the collection which contain a query term, the less weight should be attached to it in determining relevance.

The Okapi BM25 weighting function [45] is a very well known mathematical formulation of these heuristics:

$$w_t = q_t \times tf_d \times \frac{\log(\frac{N-n+0.5}{n+0.5})}{2 \times (0.25 + 0.75 \times \frac{dl}{avdl}) + tf_d} \ . \tag{1}$$

where w_t is the relevance weight assigned to a document due to query term t, q_t is the weight attached to the term by the query, tf_d is the number of times t occurs in the document, N is the total number of documents, n is the number of documents containing at least one occurrence of t, dl is the length of the document and $avdl$ is the average document length.

Retrieval models based on lexical proximity of term occurrences have been proposed ([26] [7] [14] but have not been widely adopted. They arise from an additional heuristic:

4 Occurrences of multiple query words within close lexical proximity are more significant than isolated occurrences.

```
1. Foreach document
       Set document score to zero.
2. Foreach query term
       Foreach document containing the query term
          Compute the relevance contribution.
          Add the contribution to this document's score.
3. Sort documents into descending order of score.
```

Fig. 7. The basic IR ranking algorithm.

A Simple Ranking Algorithm. Figure 7 shows a very simple algorithm for producing a ranked list of documents using a relevance formula like Okapi BM25. In order to actually implement it, there are a number of lexical issues to resolve:

1. Should *stopwords* such as of, the and and be considered as words?
2. Should words be represented in the form in which they appear, or should they be *stemmed*? Stemming means that different forms of the same word are represented as a common stem or root. For example run, running, ran, runs, runner and so on might all be represented as run.

3. Should letters be *case folded*? i.e. should upper case letters be converted to lower case, so that The and the are treated as the same?
4. What exactly should constitute a term? Is 2001 a word? What about B52 or anti-social?
5. Are there areas of text which should be excluded from consideration? For example, HTML comments and tags?

Stemming and case folding generally increase recall and may sometimes improve precision. However, they can also dramatically reduce precision. For example, the query word Hawking would be stemmed and case-folded to hawk and is likely to match other English family names such as Hawke, Hawker, Hawkins and Hawkes as well as ordinary words such as hawk (a bird) and hawker (a door-to-door salesperson). Similarly, the acronym IT would be case-folded so as to be indistinguishable from a common pronoun.

Retrieval systems differ in the way they handle these lexical issues.

Data Structures for Text Retrieval. A *full text scanning* implementation of the algorithm shown in Figure 7 can be written very quickly and easily in a language like perl provided that the document collection is not too large and there is no requirement for query processing speed. Full text scanning means that the full text of each document in the collection is scanned for query terms, once for each query term (inner loop in Step 2.)

However, query processing speed is usually very important and the collections discussed in this chapter are very large. The data structure most commonly used to speed up Step 2 of the algorithm is the *inverted file index*, diagrammed in Figure 8.

An inverted file speeds up processing by keeping lists of the documents in which each term occurs. These lists are called *postings lists* for reasons which will be explained in Section 1.5. In the inverted file shown in Figure 8, each posting in the postings list contains both a document number and the corresponding *tf* value (how many times the term occurred in the document) for use in the Okapi formula.

¿From the example we can see that the word oboe occurs three times in document 2, once in document 7, twice in document 11 and so on. The document table shown in the bottom right allows us to match up document numbers to real documents and also records information about the document such as length (for use in the Okapi formula), a checksum (CRC) of the content and a snippet (small sample) of text to be displayed when presenting query results.

Efficient lookup of the term dictionary is essential to achieve fast query processing. The term dictionary shown in the figure is sorted into lexicographic order to permit binary searching.

Building an Inverted File – The Old Way. The first step of the original method for building inverted files was to scan the text of the documents and to append a *posting* to the end of the postings file each time a term was encountered. Each posting consists of a (*document – id, term – id*) pair. Understanding what postings are and how to generate the postings file is important to make sense of what follows. Readers are advised to work through the example documents in Figure 9 and be sure they understand.

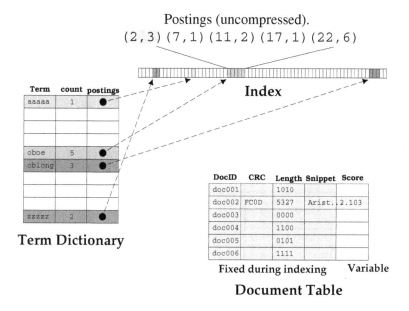

Fig. 8. Key IR data structures: Term dictionary, document table and inverted file index.

It should be obvious that the postings generated as described in the preceding paragraph must initially be emitted in document order. The postings file can subsequently be *inverted* by sorting the postings using *term − id* as the primary key and *document − id* as the secondary. Study the inverted file shown in Figure 9 to be sure you understand what it represents. The first posting relates to term 0 (a) which occurs only in document 2. This is the complete postings list for that term. Next there are two postings for term 1 (ate) and they appear in order of the documents in which they occur.

A post-processing step is needed to convert the sorted postings into the form shown in Figure 8. First, note that it is not necessary to record the term number in each posting – that information is implicitly recorded in the term dictionary. Second, note that whenever the same term occurs *tf* > 1 times in the same document, the sort described in the preceding paragraph will produce a consecutive sequence of *tf* identical postings. The post-processing step replaces every sequence of *tf* identical postings with a single (docid,*tf*) posting and fills in the offset field in the document table.

The final result is the document table and inverted file as shown in Figure 9.

Processing Queries Using an Inverted File. To confirm your understanding of inverted files, work through the query processing example in Figure 10. Don't bother to compute Okapi scores, just count how many query terms are present in each document. Look up each query term in the term dictionary and use the offset (entry in the third column) to find where the postings for the term start in the inverted file. Then add one to the score of each document mentioned in the postings for the term.

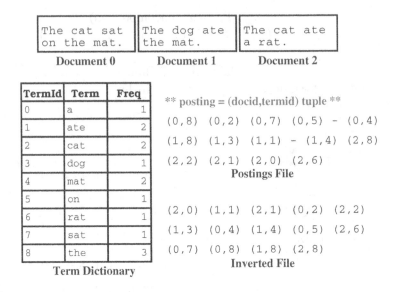

Fig. 9. Raw postings and inverted file index for a collection of three tiny documents.

More Sophisticated Inverted Files. The primitive form of inverted file shown in Figure 9 contains considerable redundancy due to the encoding (often repeated) of the *term − id*. This information doesn't need to be stored, as it may easily be deduced from the term dictionary. If phrases or proximity operators must be supported, it is usual to replace the *term − id* with the position of the term occurrences within the document. On the other hand, if position information is not needed, multiple postings for the same (*document − id, term − id*) pair can be replaced with a single (*document − id, tf*) pair.

Section 4 describes more efficient ways of building an inverted file and also covers another type of posting which can reduce query processing time.

1.6   Relevance Feedback

When searching for documents relevant to a topic, the initial query generated by the searcher is usually far from optimal. A widely used technique for improving it is based on *relevance feedback*, which works as follows: The initial query is processed and documents returned high in the ranking are judged by the searcher. The retrieval system then attempts to identify terms which usefully discriminate between the known relevant documents and the rest of the collection. These new terms are added to the query with appropriate weights and the augmented query is run to produce the final result list.

Interestingly, the same process can also be made to work in the absence of human judgments by assuming that the top 10 or so documents are relevant whether they actually are or not. This technique is often called *pseudo relevance feedback* and, in TREC ad hoc tasks, it has been shown to significantly boost average retrieval effec-

Query: "the cat ate"

The cat sat on the mat.	The dog ate the mat.	The cat ate a rat.
Document 0	**Document 1**	**Document 2**

Term	Freq	Offset
a	1	0
ate	2	1
cat	2	3
dog	1	5
mat	2	6
on	1	8
rat	1	9
sat	1	10
the	3	11

Term Dictionary

** scoring by simple coordination level **

Docid	Score
0	2
1	2
2	3

Doc. Table

(2,0) (1,1) (2,1) (0,2) (2,2)
(1,3) (0,4) (1,4) (0,5) (2,6)
(0,7) (0,8) (1,8) (2,8)

Inverted File

Fig. 10. A query processing example using the document collection and inverted file from the previous figure. For simplicity, relevance scores are simply a count of how many of the query terms were present in the document.

tiveness. Sometimes it causes harm but usually there is an improvement of some kind. The question for us, is whether it works on a very large question and whether it can be implemented efficiently.

1.7 Scaling Up over the Last Two Decades

The reason that it is important to consider very large scale information retrieval is that over the last 20 years there has been stupendous growth both in the scale of text document collections and in the cost-effectiveness of computing resources. At the time of the Summer School I calculated that the "bang-per-buck" ratio for computer CPUs had increased by a factor of about 200,000 or 5.3 orders of magnitude over that period. The comparable figures for random-access memory (RAM) and disk were 4.7 and 4.3 orders of magnitude respectively. Even more dramatic has been the growth in computer networks which were almost non-existent in 1980.

In 1980, IR researchers were still working with test collections comprising only a couple of megabytes, i.e. a few thousand documents. By comparison the VLC2 collection [25] first distributed in 1998 contains 100 gigabytes of data (18.5 million documents) and represents an increase of 4.7 orders of magnitude.

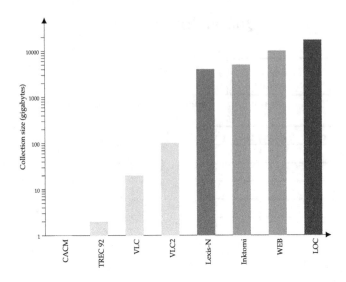

Fig. 11. Approximate sizes (in gigabytes. One gigabyte is approximately the amount of text in one thousand books) of various text collections. The barely discernable bar at the extreme left represents the collection of Communications of the ACM abstracts which was a commonly used test collection. At the far right, the 17 million volumes held by the U.S. Library of Congress represent slightly more data than indexed by Web search engines in 2000. Lexis-Nexis is a commercial document service.

At the time of the summer school, several public Web search engines were indexing of the order of 500 million pages or about 5 terabytes of text.

2   Introduction to the World Wide Web

The dramatic increase in importance of very large scale text retrieval has been almost entirely due to the advent and growth of the Web. In 2001 millions of ordinary people each day submit queries to be processed over "the entire Web"[6]. Web search is very large scale both in terms of the collection size and in terms of query volume. Engines like Alta Vista, Inktomi, FAST and Google are believed to handle loads in excess of one thousand queries per second.

Figure 12 shows a number of ways in which the Web differs from traditional electronic document collections. In some cases, the differences provide opportunities to improve retrieval effectiveness. In others, they represent additional hurdles to be overcome.

Figure 13 shows the components of a typical web search system. The indexer and query processor components may correspond quite closely to a traditional text retrieval

---

[6] In reality it makes little sense to talk of the entire Web, as the size of the Web is made boundless by the presence of automatic page generators.

Hyperlinks. Web pages are routinely hyperlinked. Sometimes this is to provide access from a stand-alone Web page to other Web resources but in other cases Web pages are merely components of a hyperdocument and the links are used to define its structure. Traditional documents sometimes contain links (e.g. citations from within a scientific article) but on the Web, these links can be followed instantaneously.

Dynamic nature. The document collection represented by the Web changes with time. Web pages are frequently created and destroyed and often change their content.

Viewpoint dependence. Discovery of Web pages is normally done by recursively following links from a set of starting points. Consequently, the set of Web pages which are visible depends upon the access rights of the observer, the set of start points and the range of page formats from which the observer can extract and follow links.

Multimedia. It is common for Web pages to include or to link to images, sound clips and videos.

Multiple languages. Very many languages are represented among the documents of the Web.

Multiple formats. Text documents published via the Web are seldom in plain text format. The majority use HTML (HyperText Markup Language) but many use PDF (Portable Document Format), PostScript, or Microsoft Word.

Duplicate documents. The Web provides mechanisms by which duplicate documents are systematically created. Due to hostname, directory name and filename aliasing, the same Web page may have many different URLs. (A URL, [55] or Uniform Resource Locator is the standard way of referencing a web page. For example, the URL http://www.youruni.edu.au/physics/PH2040/index.html might be equivalent to http://youruni.edu.au/subjects/PH2040/index.html. Another means by which duplicate documents are created is through the technique of *mirroring*. To save download cost and time and to reduce server load, the content of a popular Web site may be replicated or mirrored on other web servers around the world.

SPAM. The Web is heavily used for commercial purposes and many commercial operators attempt to increase traffic to their sites by fooling Web search engines. The most naive SPAM merely inserts large numbers of deceptive keywords which are invisible to the user. For example, inserting "Who wants to be a millionaire" many times into a pornographic Web page, but in white text on a white background.

Fig. 12. Features which distinguish the Web from conventional document collections.

system. In web search, the spider (sometimes called a crawler or robot) is necessary in order to identify the documents which form part of the "collection". The decrypter might be part of either kind of system, depending upon goals or requirements.

Spidering or crawling is the process of discovering Web pages to index by recursively following links from a set of seed pages. Spiders must be programmed to adhere to the following etiquette:

1. Respect the robots.txt protocol [36]. Web publishers may place a robots.txt in the root of their Web directory to specify which pages should and should not be accessed.

2. Ensure that individual Web servers are not overloaded. A typical rule of thumb is that requests to a particular server should not be sent more than once per second. However, Web servers vary greatly in their ability to handle load and their responsiveness to requests depends upon the amount of load from other sources.

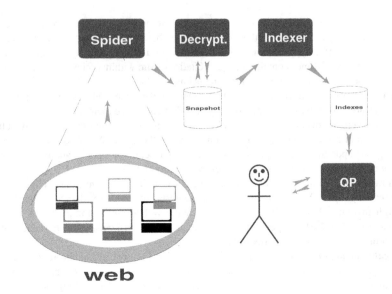

Fig. 13. The components of a simple web search engine. The spider discovers Web pages to index by recursively following links from a set of seed pages. The output of the spider is a kind of snapshot of the visible part of the Web. Note that the snapshot may take weeks or months to build up. Not all search engines include a decrypter, but if included its job is to extract indexable text from binary or compressed formats such as Microsoft Word and PDF. The indexer builds an inverted file index from the documents in the decrypted snapshot. Finally, the index is used by the query processor to process incoming queries.

Consequently some spiders vary the length of delay they insert between successive requests based on observed response times from the server.

3. Ensure that elements of the Internet infrastructure are not overloaded. Even if the spider shows appropriate politeness to each individual server, it can still overload a network link if it simultaneously accesses many servers in the same region of the network. Andrei Broder, Chief Scientist at Alta Vista reports that the Alta Vista spider is easily capable of soaking up the entire bandwidth of the network connection to countries as large as Spain.

Spiders implement various policy decisions about which types of web resource will be fetched. For example, one spider may decide to fetch HTML and plaintext pages only whereas another may also fetch XML and PDF pages as well as JPEG and GIF images. File types may be determined using MIME-type information supplied by the Web server or by the URL suffix (eg. .htm). Unfortunately, both sources of information are frequently inaccurate. Consequently, it is advisable to confirm the file type by looking at the head of the file.

Other Spidering Issues. Implementers of Web spiders face a range of major challenges caused by the pathological nature of large parts of the Web. Web servers are frequently guilty of supplying misleading or inaccurate information. Many Web site constructors deliberately or inadvertently set up spider traps. Others set up automatic scripts which generate infinite sequences of pages with trivially different content. Some Web authors include unprintable characters, spaces and newlines in the URLs of their Web pages.

Readers are referred to [29] for further discussion of spidering issues and information on how to build a spider.

3   Properties of Very Large Collections

The major impacts of very large collection size are on efficiency rather than effectiveness.

3.1   Collection Size and Speed/Efficiency

A larger collection obviously requires more disk space for the documents themselves and for associated data structures.

Vocabulary size   A large English dictionary contains of the order of 100,000 entries. A naive person might assume that the vocabulary size for a collection would stop growing once this number had been reached. However, a profusion of typographical errors, acronyms, codes (such as message identifiers and car registration numbers), new words, headword variants, proper nouns and foreign words mean that, even after 100,000 different words have been found, the vocabulary size continues to grow at a rate of something like one new word per thousand words of additional text. Depending upon the definition of a word, the number of distinct indexable words in the VLC2 collection is something like ten million! In other words, 99% of distinct words in the collection are not dictionary headwords.

A very large vocabulary increases the time taken to look up a word both during indexing and while processing queries. It also increases the size of the term dictionary and consequently the demands on memory space.

Increased number of occurrences of common terms. As a document collection grows, the number of occurrences of common words is likely to increase in proportion. This means that postings lists for common terms will be longer, increasing processing time during both indexing and query processing. The inverted file also grows in proportion to the size of the collection. File size limits imposed by the operating system may be exceeded, increasing implementation complexity.

Increased number of documents. An increase in the number of documents in the collection results in an increase in the size of the document table. If the Okapi BM25 scoring function shown in Equation 1 were used and the document table were represented as shown in Figure 8 a serious memory residency issue might arise from pattern of accesses to the document length information.

Many more matches for a query. A larger collection is likely to result in proportionately more documents containing each of the query terms. This raises memory residency issues when recording document scores and may non-linearly increase the cost of the final sort.

3.2   Effectiveness and Collection Size

It is fairly intuitive that a very narrowly specified query is more likely to find an answer within a large collection than within a much smaller one. This would obviously be true if the small collection were a subset of the big one. In general, when looking for a particular document, that document is more likely to be a member of a large collection than a small one.

When the query is broad enough that there are many answers within a small collection, would you expect retrieval effectiveness to be greater within a small collection or within a superset of it? You might think that retrieval would be easier because there are more right answers. Alternatively, you might expect it to be harder because there are also an increased number of documents which share features with the relevant documents but which are not actually relevant.

Signal detection theory [52] predicts that precision at fixed cutoff (e.g. precision at n documents retrieved) will be lower in a sample collection. It predicts that there will be a smaller number of documents in the high-scoring range where the difference between the signal distribution and the noise distribution, and consequently the probability of relevance, is greatest. These predictions have been borne out empirically in the TREC Very Large Collection track, where all participants observed a decline in precision at 20 documents retrieved when processing a set of queries over a 10% sample of the 20 gigabyte VLC collection[28]. See Table 2.

Table 2.

Group	Baseline	VLC	Ratio
City	0.320	0.515	1.61
ATT	0.348	0.530	1.52
ACSys	0.356	0.509	1.43
UMass	0.387	0.505	1.31
IBMg	0.275	0.361	1.31
Waterloo	0.498	0.643	1.29
IBMs	0.271	0.348	1.28

The expected increase in early precision when querying a very large collection of documents could form the basis of an optimisation technique in which only part of a large collection were actually processed. This might achieve acceptable effectiveness for a large proportion of queries but would seriously harm others. It is unclear whether this optimisation is used in practical Web search.

3.3   Exercise 1 – Characterising Search Engines

Take a comparative look at three or four of the following search engines:
www.metacrawler.com, www.google.com, www.euroseek.com, www.altavista.com

www.thunderstone.com, www.fast.com, www.teoma.com, www.northernlight.com
www.hotbot.com, www.LookSmart.com, www.go.com.

Try to answer the following questions:

```
1. How good is the result presentation:
 - How many answers are displayed on first screen?
 - How good are the displayed summaries?
 - How easy is it to find help?

2. Does the engine use stemming?
3. Does the engine eliminate stopwords?
4. Is the engine case sensitive?
5. Does the engine support phrases?
6. Does the engine assume term conjunction? (AND)
```

For the following queries:

```
1. Chios
2. ELSNet Summer Courses 2000
3. Aareschlucht
4. who is the current Greek prime minister?
5. the The
6. "to be or not to be"
7. "David Hawking"
```

look at the result lists and determine the rank of the first useful answer. (Give up after ten results.)

This is not a very good evaluation experiment because assessment is not blind, there aren't enough test queries and the measure employed may not be sufficiently stable. In Section 7 more rigorous evaluations are presented.

4   Efficiency Techniques

Efficiency differs from *speed* or *throughput* in that it is expressed relative to the resources employed. It is an imprecise measure of the amount of work achieved by a retrieval system, using a given amount of hardware. Efficiency is increased if queries are processed or text is indexed faster, without upgrading the hardware. Alternatively, efficiency has increased if the same throughput is achieved by a smaller machine configuration.

Two classes of technique are used to improve the efficiency of a retrieval system. Techniques of the first kind are *lossy* in that they may materially affect the quality of results obtained by taking shortcuts in the query evaluation or indexing process. Computational optimisations and engineering improvements which increase the speed of indexing or query processing without changing the results make up the second class.

This section proposes some general efficiency advice and then covers efficiency aspects of each of the spider, indexer and query processor components of the Web search system diagrammed in Figure 13 on page 122.

To give an idea of the relative time required for each of the processes, the intranet search engine at the Australian National University takes about two days to spider the whole site, a few hours to decrypt non-HTML documents, and about an hour to index the snapshot. It processes typical queries in a fraction of a second.

4.1 General Advice

It is important to choose efficient algorithms and data structures. For example, an $O(n^2)$ sorting algorithm applied to a list of one million search results may require 50,000 times as many comparisons as an $O(n \log n)$ one.

It is also crucially important to implement algorithms and data structures in a way which makes minimises the number of accesses to slower levels of memory. In certain circumstances, it may be advantageous to use an algorithm with a slower theoretical running time in order to make better use of faster memory.

To illustrate how enormous are the speed differences between different levels of memory, consider a 1.5 gHz Intel Pentium IV CPU with 512 megabytes of RAM and a 7200 r.p.m disk. A disk like this has an average rotational latency of 4.2 ms (milliseconds) and a typical seek latency of 5 ms. Consequently, when a disk read request is issued which cannot be satisfied from buffers or caches, a delay of about 9ms ensues. During this period of time, something like 180 megabytes could be transferred from (RAMBUS) RAM to the CPU and the CPU could execute about 13.5 million instructions from its on-chip cache. It is clearly of crucial importance to ensure high cache hit rates and to minimize disk accesses.

Most modern operating systems run programs in *virtual memory*. In other words, program code and data structures are assigned to addresses in an imaginary address space without regard to the limited size of primary memory (RAM) and the need to share it with other programs or processes. The operating system divides the virtual address space into *pages* (often about 4 kilobytes in size). At a particular point in the execution of a program, some of the pages will be represented in primary memory, others will be represented only on disk and some may not yet have been created. As execution proceeds, reference may be made to an address in a page which is not resident in primary memory, causing a *page fault*. When this happens some pages in primary memory may be written out to disk and replaced by others from the disk which are known or predicted to be needed by the computation.

Virtual memory operates efficiently provided that page faults occur infrequently. It can degenerate into extreme inefficiency (known as *page thrashing*)if this is not the case. During page thrashing the retrieval process is forced to operate at disk speed rather than primary memory or CPU speed. Frequent page faults will occur when the pattern of memory references is not localised. In indexing or query processing this could occur if random accesses were made into a file or data structure which is larger than the available primary memory.

An example of where a data structure re-organisation could improve memory reference locality is the document table in Figure 8 on 117. Consider the memory access pattern caused by processing queries using the simple algorithm shown in Figure 7. In Step 1, the score field only of every row in the table is accessed sequentially. In Step 2, each successive query term is associated with a sweep through the table which accesses the document length of each document which contains the term and updates the score. Step 3 accesses all the scores.

It is not until the results are prepared for display to the searcher that the docid, crc and snippet fields are accessed at all. Furthermore, during result display only a small number of the rows in the table are accessed.

The presence of docid, crc and snippet in amongst the score and length information reduces the locality of memory references in Steps 1, 2 and 3. It increases the number of virtual memory pages which must be loaded to perform these steps. Reference locality could be significantly improved by splitting the table such that scores and lengths were in one table and docids, crcs and snippets in another.

4.2 Compression

Compressing data structures is another way to improve locality of reference, during spidering, index building and query processing. For example, rather than representing a document length as a 32-bit integer, it could be represented in a smaller number of bits. Compression of URLs during spidering is discussed in [29]. Very effective methods exist for compressing lists of postings and you are referred to *Managing Gigabytes* [60] for a detailed treatment.

In addition to improving memory reference locality, compression may significantly reduce the amount of disk space required to store the raw text and the various index files. It also reduces I/O transfer times from disk at the expense of additional CPU time to decompress postings.

4.3 Spidering

Section 2 explained the basic operation of a spider and outlined the politeness constraints under which spiders should operate.

Network Costs. A major motivation for efficiency in spidering is the cost of network traffic. If a billion pages, averaging 12.5 kbytes each, are spidered from Australia, where network traffic charges are of the order of 80 euros per gigabyte, the total cost will be one million euros!

Network traffic can be reduced by ensuring that excessively large files are truncated or not fetched at all and that binary files are detected and truncated.

Further reductions in cost can be achieved by detecting infrequently updated or infrequently accessed parts of the Web and spidering them less frequently.

Incremental Spidering. A basic spider fetches every page it encounters. An incremental spider tries to fetch only those pages which have changed since they were last fetched. Potentially, a great deal of network traffic can be eliminated by this means but the technique only works if Web servers supply accurate information such as last modified date, size, or checksum.

Another issue to deal with is how to detect pages in the snapshot which have been removed from the Web.

Multi-threading. It is not feasible for a spider to scan the entire Web if, due to requirements of etiquette, it accesses only one page per second. At that rate, at most 86,400
pages can be fetched per day and it would take more than 31 years to collect a billion.

An obvious solution is multi-threading. A hashing function can be used to assign
each distinct Web server to a particular parallel thread. Each thread inserts the appropriate politeness delay between successive requests, and each can operate independently
of the others without risking etiquette violations. Large scale spiders may make use of
thousands of parallel threads, possibly spread across multiple systems.

URL Storage. A spider must maintain two lists of URLs: a) a *frontier* of URLs still to
be fetched, and b) a *cache* of URLs already encountered. In simplest form, the frontier
can be a straight-forward queue but it may be priority-ordered to enable the most useful
pages to be fetched first [32]. To save memory, it can reference URLs in the cache rather
than repeating the strings.

The cache must be capable of very rapid lookup and insertion. Every URL encountered in every page scanned must be looked up in the cache. If found, no action is
required. Otherwise, a new entry must be made in both the cache and the frontier. When
a URL from the frontier is selected for fetching, it is removed from the frontier.

In a multi-threaded spiderer, there should be a frontier for each thread to avoid the
need for scanning to find the next URL to be processed by a thread. The cache may also
be divided across threads.

The amount of memory required to store all the URLs in the cache is potentially
huge. If there are a billion URLs and the average length of a URL is 50 characters, the
amount of space required in a naive implementation exceeds 50 gigabytes! This is too
large to fit in memory and careful organisation is needed to ensure that most lookups
can be satisfied with few or no disk accesses. Compression techniques can be used to
reduce the storage required for URLs.

Detection of Duplicate Pages and Mirror Sites. The Web provides two ways by
which duplicate content or near-duplicate content can be created. The first is aliasing of
hostnames, directory names and files in which there multiple URLs refer to exactly the
same page on the same machine. The second is mirroring, where a popular Web site is
replicated on other hosts to improve responsiveness and cut network traffic costs. The
content of pages on a mirror site may be slightly different to those on the original due
to the addition of a site label or date or to version differences.

Exact duplicates can be detected with very small error rate using checksums, but
checksums must be efficiently computed and another efficient lookup structure with up
to a billion entries must be created. Detection of mirror sites (and deciding what to do
about them) is less straight forward and the reader is referred to [4] for details.

4.4 Indexing

Some systems impose a limit, say 64 kilobytes, on how much of a document they will
index. Words occurring after that limit will not be indexed. This reduces not only index
size but also indexing time and eventually the processing time for some queries. Some

important information will be lost, but often there is enough information in the head of a document to accurately characterise it.

Inverted File Postprocessing. Considerable computational savings can be effected if the postings in an inverted file index contain relevance-contribution information rather than raw term frequencies. To understand this, consider the Okapi BM25 formula in Equation 1 and notice that the only query dependent variable is q_t. For every possible (term, document) pair, the values of all other variables are known once the indexer has finished scanning the collection. Either during indexing or, more simply, in a post-processing step, the tf_d values in the inverted file (as in e.g. 8) can be replaced by the values obtained by pre-evaluating the bulk of Equation 1. These values would normally be computed as floating point numbers but, if desired, they can be quantised and represented in a more space-efficient way with a small cost in accuracy.

The benefit at query time of pre-computed relevance contributions is considerable. Not only is the number of arithmetic operations, including a logarithm, reduced, but the need to randomly access the table of document lengths is averted. If physical memeory is small, the effect of the latter may be dramatic.

Index Pruning. Having pre-computed relevance contributions for each (term, document) pair as described in the immediately preceding section, it is possible to sort the postings for a term into order of decreasing contribution and to truncate the tail of the postings list at the point where the contribution becomes so small to be unlikely to significantly affect the final ranking. The truncation condition can be tuned to achieve the desired balance between speed and effectiveness.

This is a lossy technique because information is being discarded. There may be rare cases where effectiveness is harmed, but there is evidence [2, 33] that usually it is not.

More Efficient Index Building. In Web search, fast query processing is much more important than fast indexing because hundreds of millions of queries may be processed in the interval between successive index builds.

However, use of efficient indexing algorithms and appropriate data structures is worthwhile: a) to increase the amount of text which can be indexed on a given hardware configuration, and b) to allow rapid response to changes in the collection.

The traditional method for building inverted files was described in Section 1.5 and Figure 9. The major flaw of this algorithm is the potentially very time consuming and disk-space intensive external (i.e. disk based) sort of the postings.

Moffat et al [40] have proposed various efficient schemes for sorting postings including methods which require no additional disk space. However, the following method avoids sorting altogether and is quite fast in practice. Similar ideas are presented in [15, chapter 3].

The basic idea is that multiple passes are made over the text collection. The first pass does not write postings but merely builds up a term dictionary including occurrence counts for each term. Subsequent passes are responsible for re-scanning the input and writing the inverted file.

At the end of the first pass, it is possible to compute the size of the inverted file and the offset within the file of the postings list for each term. After this has been done a file of the necessary size is created.

If disk space is not excessively tight, the first pass can also write a tokenised version of the input, to avoid the relatively expensive lexical scanning of the raw text.

For convenience and efficiency during the output passes, the inverted file, or part of it, is memory mapped using the virtual memory capabilities available in most modern operating systems[7]. Once the file is mapped, it can be treated as an array and accessed using normal array subscripting.

As each virtual memory page of the inverted file is accessed, it will be read into memory. Depending upon how much memory is available, this may result in a less recently accessed page being written out to disk and removed from memory.

If sufficient primary memory is available to accommodate the entire inverted file, only one additional pass is needed because there will be no unnecessary virtual memory activity. The tokenised input is rescanned and a posting for each indexable term encountered is written in the appropriate spot in the postings file. Then a pointer associated with this term's entry in the term dictionary is incremented to indicate where the next posting for this term should be placed.

As you can probably see, the pattern of accesses to the inverted file is highly random. If the inverted file is significantly larger than the available primary memory, there will be a high probability that each access will generate a page fault. This would cause the speed of the process to drop from memory speed to disk speed, possibly causing indexing time to grow from hours to days or weeks!

A solution presented in [22] is to divide the inverted file into a number of equal sized *windows* where each window is approximately the size of available physical memory, and to write each window in a separate pass through the tokenised text. During each pass the entire tokenised file is read but term references corresponding to postings lying outside the currently memory mapped window are ignored. Consequently, accesses to the inverted file are restricted to the memory-resident window and speed is restored. A large amount of additional disk i/o is generated by the need to repeatedly rescan the tokenised input but: a) sequential access to the disk is far more efficient than random access, and b) the tokenised form of the input can be a lot smaller than the original text.

Compression of postings can also have a highly beneficial effect on writing of the inverted file by significantly reducing the number of output passes required.

Efficient Lexical Scanning. During the first indexing pass, attention to a number of engineering issues can make a large difference to the amount of time required for the first pass and also beneficially affect subsequent passes and query processing.

Choosing a data structure for the term dictionary which supports rapid insertions as well as rapid lookups is essential. The best choices are probably a hash table or a trie [35]. For a large collection, the memory space occupied by the term dictionary will be considerable. It must be kept memory resident because accesses will be random. A hash table should be designed to minimise the frequency and cost of collisions.

---

[7] e.g. the mmap() call in Unix or Linux.

Stemming can be applied either during indexing or at query processing time. In my opinion, it is not a good idea to stem words during indexing, because stemming actually discards information which could be useful during query processing. However, stemming does reduce the size of the term dictionary and many retrieval systems create stemmed indexes. If stemming is performed during indexing, a great deal of time may be saved by using a second trie or hash table to translate words to their corresponding stems rather than calling a stemming function. For example, the public domain Porter stemming function [15] takes 17 microseconds per call on a Sun Ultra-1 machine. In a 100 gigabyte collection, approximately 7 billion word occurrences need to be stemmed, adding about 33 hours to (i.e. more or less doubling) the indexing time.

The actual lexical scanning code needs careful attention. It should be implementable as a finite state machine [17, 30] (coded by hand or using a lexical scanner generator like flex). Its running time should be linear with the length of the input text. It is important to design the finite state machine in such a way as to reject parts of the text which do not need to be indexed. Doing so will reduce the size of the term dictionary, the tokenised input file and the inverted file.

Examples of parts of documents which should normally be rejected include random message-identifiers, HTML or XML tags, HTTP headers, binary data or text written in languages the system is not designed to accept. If non-textual data is not rejected, accidental sequences of letters will be recognized as words, increasing data structure sizes and possibly reducing precision for certain queries.

4.5 Query Processing

One of the best ways to speed up query processing is to avoid processing the query at all. Many current search engines do this by caching the results of queries, sometimes on a machine dedicated to the task. However, although some queries are repeated very often a large percentage are submitted only once [49]. Consequently, it is necessary to optimize the query processing machinery.

Early Termination of Query Processing. Another lossy optimisation technique involves processing the query terms in order of decreasing importance, until some stopping condition is satisfied. The importance of a query term must take into account both the weight assigned to it by the query (through repetition or explicit weight setting) and its discrimination power within the collection. The latter could be estimated by the highest relevance score contribution found in its postings list or more simply by its inverse document frequency (i.e. the reciprocal of the number of documents in which it occurs.)..

The stopping condition could be expressed in terms of a fixed number of terms to process, a fixed time limit (CPU or elapsed), or a more sophisticated dynamic termination condition.

Whether or not the index has been pruned as described in Section 4.4, processing of postings in a contribution-sorted postings list can be terminated early, when it is determined that subsequent postings are unlikely to have any effect.

Optimisation of Document Scoring. In the document table shown in Figure 8 there is a score accumulator for every document in the collection. An alternative scheme is to limit the number of document score accumulators to some arbitrary number, thus reducing: a) memory usage, b) time taken to zero scores, and c) time taken to sort results. On the other side of the ledger, an additional computation is required to locate the accumulator assigned to a particular document. This can be done using a hash table.

Used in conjunction with both query term re-ordering and ordering of term postings by relevance score contribution, this scheme can save time with negligible harm to effectiveness.

```
1. Foreach document accumulator
      Set accumulator to zero.
2. Sort query terms into order of decreasing importance
3. Foreach query term
      Foreach posting for the query term
         a. find the accumulator allocated to the document
         b. if no accumulator has been allocated, try to allocate a new one
         c. if an accumulator is now assigned, add the relevance contribution
         d. Exit inner loop if next posting may be neglected
      Exit outer loop if the stopping condition is satisfied.
4. Sort document accumulators into descending order of score.
```

Fig. 14. An optimised IR ranking algorithm. It is assumed that postings contain pre-computed relevance contributions and that postings lists have been sorted in decreasing order of contribution.

A more efficient query processing algorithm based on pre-computed relevance contributions, sorted postings lists and limited score accumulators is shown in Figure 14. Note that because of the ordering of query terms and the ordering of postings for a query term, document accumulators are allocated preferentially to the best terms and to the best documents for those terms. Once the limit on the number of accumulators is reached, postings referencing documents which have no accumulator assigned are simply ignored.

Efficient Ranking. Once document scores have been calculated in response to a query, the task of ranking involves sorting all the non-zero document accumulators and keeping track of the associated documents.

A very widely used sorting algorithm is quicksort [35] whose average running time is $O(n \log(n))$, but $O(n^2)$ in the worst case. If there are a million numbers to sort, $n^2 = 10^{12}$, a factor of 5×10^4 slower than $n \log(n) = 2 \times 10^7$. Unix qsort() exhibits worst case behaviour when values are equal, which could happen with certain relevance scoring functions or when relevance scores are quantised to a small number of distinct values.

Three options are available to avoid this problem:

1. Avoid the need for a final sort by maintaining a *heap* [60, 35] of top scores during score update.
2. Introduce a secondary sorting key, such as document number, to ensure that the comparison function used by qsort() never signals equality.
3. Use *radix sort* [35] rather than quicksort. Radix sort can potentially sort a million numbers in less than two passes, but requires that the numbers to be sorted be quantised into a small number of distinct values (typically between 1000 and 1,000,000).

Efficient Result Presentation. Once a ranking has been generated internally, it must be presented to the searcher in a useful format. This typically involves looking up the document table to find the document identifier and snippet (or canned summary). Accesses into the document table are of course random and, in the worst case, presenting n results could require n disk accesses, another case where memory residency is important and compression could help.

Better quality result listings replace the snippet or canned summary with a *query-biased* summary [53] showing the context of query words within the document. It is possible to generate query biased summaries on the fly, opening files and running a summariser program for each document. However, under heavy query load, this would be unacceptably slow and it would be more efficient to make use of the tokenised input file created during indexing to identify the context of query term occurrences.

4.6   Processing Phrases and Proximity Operators

If the query language supports proximity operators such as near or followed by, for example ELSNet near summer, postings in the inverted file must specify the word position within the document where the term occurred. One way is to leave the primary inverted file in the format shown in Figure 8 and to use an additional file to record the term positions. For efficiency, this file can include skip records which allow positions which cannot possibly form part of the desired proximity relation to be skipped over rather than examined one by one.

Computing the proximity relation for two terms requires intersecting the two postings lists. This can be done efficiently by examining the positions for the term with the lowest *df* occurrence by occurrence and then skipping through the position list for the second term to find the occurrences which form part of the desired relation. Note that the position lists can be compressed even though the skip records consume some additional information.

In this model, phrases can be computed as followed by relations with a one-word proximity limit. Common two-word phrases can be processed even more efficiently by building a phrase cache. The first time a phrase is encountered it is entered into a phrase dictionary associated with the cache, possibly replacing a phrase which hasn't been accessed recently. Then, a postings list created by evaluating the phrase using the proximity operation, is associated with the new entry. Subsequent references to the same phrase will be served from the cache.

A further alternative for phrases is to record the term identifier for the following term with each term position in the positions file, as proposed by Williams [59].

4.7   Relevance Feedback

Pseudo relevance feedback has proven quite effective in the context of TREC ad hoc retrieval. However, very few large scale text retrieval systems implement it. This is probably because of the computational expense entailed in doing so. Moreover, recent evidence [50] suggests that less benefit may arise from relevance feedback in a Web context.

Assuming that relevance feedback is to be used, the Vector Space model of retrieval allows for cheaper relevance feedback, using the Rocchio [46] than does Okapi. In the Okapi model of relevance feedback it may be necessary to return to the raw text of the top ranked documents, build term tables for those documents and to thereby identify terms whose occurrence densities in the relevant text is higher than for the text as a whole. The Robertson term selection value [44] is used to pick the best terms to add to the query.

5   Use of Parallelism in IR

Parallel computing hardware has been used extensively to increase the data handling and/or query handling capacity of text retrieval systems.

5.1   Types of Parallelism

Stanfill and colleagues [51] and Reddaway [43] have described the use of *SIMD* (Single Instruction Multiple Data, or data parallel) machines in text retrieval applications. However, these machines are no longer common.

A number of early search engines made use of *SMP* (Symmetric Multi-Processing) machines such as up-market DEC (later Compaq) Alpha machines. In these machines, a number of processors share a single large memory. However, systems of this type are quite expensive.

In the last few years, the *MIMD* (Multiple Instruction Multiple Data) model of parallelism, implemented as a cluster of PCs (COP), has become the dominant search engine architecture. Inktomi, FAST and Google are all understood to use it. Figure 15 shows a typical arrangement. Usually, each node in an n node cluster is responsible for $1/n$ of the collection. This is called document-id partitioning. [39] Each query is broadcast to all nodes in the cluster and each of them processes the query over the index for the piece of the collection for which they are responsible. The nodes may need to communicate with each other to exchange global statistical information such as df values. They definitely need to communicate with each other to form a merged ranking of the top t documents.

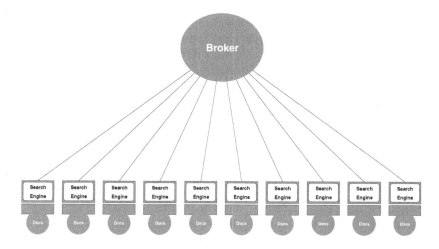

Fig. 15. The cluster of PCs (COP) model.

5.2   Parallel Efficiency and Scalability

The *parallel efficiency* of a retrieval system on a COP can be computed as $\frac{t_{one-node} \times 100}{t_{n-nodes} \times n}\%$. An ideal system in which there is no penalty for a parallel as opposed to a sequential algorithm will show a parallel efficiency of 100%. The parallel efficiency of a real system will fall short of perfection due to three possible causes: a) sequential parts of the algorithm, b) communication overhead, and c) load imbalance.

It is easy to obtain high parallel efficiency for text search on a COP provided that: a) there is sufficient data to ensure that the (parallelisable) work of actually processing the query dominates the sequential parts of broadcasting the query and merging results, b) care is taken to minimize the amount of communication, c) each node has a similar amount of similar data.

Another term often used in the context of parallel computing is that of *scalability*. A search system can be considered to be scalable either if the time taken to process a query is directly proportional to the number of nodes in the cluster. i.e. doubling the number of nodes halves the time taken to process queries. An alternative definition of a scalable system is a system where query processing time remains constant despite growth in data, provided that the number of nodes in the cluster is proportionately increased.

5.3   Replication to Increase Throughput

If a given retrieval system, be it a single PC, an SMP server or a COP, can process q queries per second, it is possible to increase query handling to mq queries per second, for arbitrary m, by replicating the system m times.

Vendors such as CISCO and Layer Four sell network devices to which all m query processing systems can be connected and made to look like a single very fast system with a single network address. The network device allows for systems being added or taken off-line and automatically bypasses systems which crash.

Provided that the capacity of the network device is not exceeded, the parallel efficiency of this type of parallelism is effectively 100%.

5.4   Real Web Search Hardware

If a single PC can efficiently process queries over a collection of 10 million Web pages, a cluster of 100 PCs will be needed to deal with a collection of one billion pages. This represents a large investment in hardware. Search engine companies have a strong motivation to try to avoid using a cluster of this size to evaluate every single incoming query. One obvious solution is to cache the results of the most commonly submitted queries and to dedicate a single PC to intercepting these queries and supplying canned answers. (See Section 4.5.) Something like one third of incoming queries can be handled in this way, resulting in large scale savings in hardware required.

A considerable investment in hardware is needed to operate a large-scale Web search engine. Google, whose indexes cover nearly a billion Web pages, and whose query rate is of the order of 140 million queries per day, is understood to use cheap Intel Celeron PCs. However, at last count around 12,000 such PCs were deployed!

5.5   Exercise 2 – Search Engine Economics

The InfoGurgle company operates a search engine which is funded entirely by advertising revenue. InfoGurgle technology is based on low cost PC hardware. One InfoGurgle PC is capable of processing queries over only 10 million web pages, but PCs may be clustered to handle larger amounts of data. In addition to the search PCs, there are a number of PCs dedicated to serving cached answers to common queries. The InfoGurgle spider works by completely respidering the entire Web each time.

The following are the budget and operating estimates for the forthcoming year.

```
Size of index: 1 billion pages
Average Web page size: 10 kbytes
Average size of InfoGurgle results page: 15 kbytes
Revenue per query: 0.25 cents
Number of queries per day: 20 million average, 50 million peak.
Time taken to fully process a query:  0.2 sec average.
Time taken to process a cached query: 0.001 sec.
Proportion of query load processed from cache: 35\%
Cost per standard PC: 300 Euro (annual lease cost)
Network charges: 30 Euro per gigabyte
Budget for spidering: 1.2 million Euros
Fixed costs (eg. salaries, rent, Ferrari lease): 2 million Euros.
```

Q1: How much does it cost (in network charges) to re-spider once?

Q2: What interval must there be between spider runs to stay within budget?

Q3: How many search PCs are needed to cope with the uncached query portion of peak load?

Q4: How many cached-query PCs are needed to cope with the cached query portion of peak load?

Q5: What is the cost of the query processing hardware?

Q6: What is the expected total revenue?

Q7: What will be InfoGurgle's profit or loss this year?

Q8: What would be InfoGurgle's profit/loss if the following measures were adopted?

    a. Use larger and more expensive (3000 Euro p.a.) cached query PCs to increase the percentage of queries handled from cache to 50%, while retaining current response time.

    b. Introducing a query optimisation which speeds query processing to 0.15 sec.

Q9: If the spidering budget were reduced to the point necessary for financial break-even, how often would spidering occur?

Q10: What motivation is there for InfoGurgle to:
    a. Improve the quality of its search results?
    b. Update its index more frequently?

6 Distributed Information Retrieval

Centralised web search engines which operate purely as shown in Figure 13 and as described above, are unable to index all the information published via the Web. Apart from the fact that the Web is infinite due to the presence of automatic content generators, spiders are unable to index Web *dark matter*.

Dark matter is content which is published via the HTTP protocol from a server on the Internet but which can't be fetched by a particular spider due to password protection, IP-address or DNS-domain restriction, robots.txt exclusion, or because the page is not reachable by that spider by following links.

An alternative model of search which can potentially avoid these problems is *meta-search* or distributed information retrieval, shown in Figure 17. Most current meta-searchers such as MetaCrawler, ProFusion and SavvySearch address the alleged problem [38] that centralised search engines only index a small fraction of the Web by broadcasting queries to a selection (often ten or twelve) of centralised search engines and merge the results into a single list.

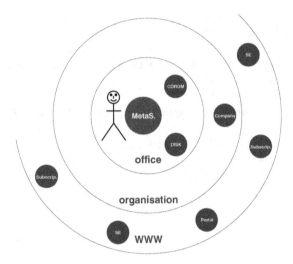

Fig. 16. The range of different information sources available to a modern information worker.

An alternative model uses the search broker to aggregate results obtained from a large number of local search engines operating on individual sites or groups of sites across the Web. Local search engines are potentially able to index more, or all, of the local content and may not have to obey `robots.txt`. Interesting examples of sites operating local search services include current news sites (such as www.msnbc.com), and the PubMed index of medical abstracts.

Figure 16 shows that a modern worker in their office has access to a large number of different information sources. An ideal distributed information retrieval system might provide a unified search service over all of them.

To do so, it would need to solve four key problems:

Server identification and characterisation It is a non-trivial matter to identify all the potentially useful search services available and to gather useful information about them – what types of documents they index, how many documents, how effective is the search algorithm they employ.

Server selection Using knowledge of the available servers, what would constitute an appropriate server subset for processing this query. It may be undesirable to forward the query to all servers because of network and computational costs and because some servers may charge money for each query processed. There is also a possibility that search quality may be improved by restricting the search to the most appropriate servers.

Query Translation Different search engines support different query syntax and implement different semantics. Consequently, queries submitted to the broker must be translated for some engines.

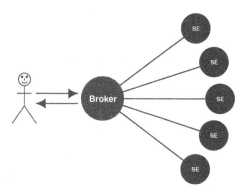

Fig. 17. The architecture of a metasearcher.

Result Merging Combining several results lists into a single merged list is more difficult than it sounds. Merging based on reported relevance scores is problematic because scores returned by different algorithms (or even the same algorithm working on different collections) are not in general comparable. Even worse, scores are often not reported. It is usually possible to merge on the basis of ranks but the highest ranked document from one search server may be inferior to the lowest supplied by another. In general, best results are obtained by downloading all the documents and running a high quality relevance scoring function over the resulting pool of documents.

6.1   Further Reading

Space does not permit a full treatment of the field of distributed information retrieval. As a substitute you may wish to read research papers in the following areas:

- **Combining centralised Web search engines:** [48, 16]
- **Fusion of partitioned collections** [6, 58, 20, 13, 42]
- **Metasearching using cooperating servers** [19, 27, 34]
- **Metasearching by downloading** [5, 37, 10]

7   Evaluation of Web Search Quality

Figure 5 shows an evaluation paradigm for standard retrieval systems. This paradigm must be interpreted and refined if it is to be applied to the evaluation of public Web search engines. When evaluating Web search engines from across the Web, it is not possible to isolate the indexing/ranking process from spidering (and decrypting). The quality of results returned must depend upon all of these components. If one or more of the desired answers to a search failed to be found by the spider, they will not be in the collection and cannot be returned as a search result. Similarly, if a required answer document is in PDF format, the spider must be able to find it and the decrypter must be able to extract its text content for the search to have any chance of success.

Furthermore, there is no standardised, stable test collection. Rather, it is necessary to treat the whole Web as the test collection. Because the Web is dynamic, relevance or quality judgments are not re-usable. Two detailed studies of search engine performance discuss in detail the various methodological questions associated with public search engine evaluation. [18, 23]

One of the key issues in Web search evaluation is that there are in fact many different types of search. Was the searcher trying to buy something on the Web? Were they looking for the homepage of a person or organisation? Did they need background information for a newspaper article they were writing? Did they need up-to-date information about the latest terrorist attack? Were they trying to find the most popular fan sites for the latest pop culture hero? Were they instead conducting an exhaustive search for every Web page that mentions their name?

Evaluation of each different mode of search potentially may require mode-specific: a) judging criteria, b) number of results judged, and c) measures to be reported. Not only that, but it is fairly clear that optimal ranking algorithms are search-mode dependent. [12, 50]

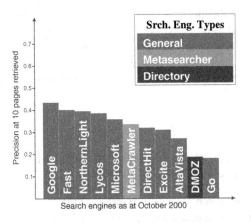

Fig. 18. Comparison of public search engines on the basis of their ability to find documents relevant to a topic. Judges were asked to judge result pages were as either relevant or irrelevant. A relevant page was required to a) be on the topic and b) to contribute some additional information not supplied by the question. Judging was blind and results from all engines were pooled prior to judging. Fifty-four queries were used, taken from search engine query logs. An example is: 'thalidomide and multiple sclerosis'.

Figures 18 - 20 show the results of more recent evaluations I have conducted with my colleagues for: a) topic relevance, b) online service location and c) homepage finding modes of search. More detailed reports of these studies are to be found in [24] and [11].

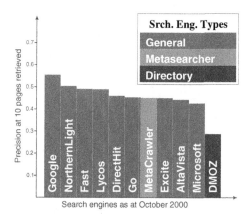

Search engines as at October 2000

Fig. 19. Comparison of public search engines on the basis of their ability to find online services. Judges were asked to judge whether result pages were useful. A useful page was required to provide direct access to the desired service. Judging was blind and results from all engines were pooled prior to judging. One hundred and six queries were used, taken from search engine query logs. An example is: 'where can i buy power tools online?'

References

1. J. Allan, J. Callan, M. Sanderson, J. Xu, and S.Wegmann. INQUERY and TREC-7. In *Proceedings of TREC-7*, November 1998. NIST special publication 500-242, trec.nist.gov/pubs/trec7/t7_proceedings.html.

2. Vo Ngoc Anh, Owen de Kretser, and Alistair Moffat. Vector-space ranking with effective early termination. In *Proceedings of ACM SIGIR'01*, pages 35–42, New Orleans, LA, 2001.

3. Ricardo Baeza-Yates and Berthier Ribeiro-Neto. *Modern Information Retrieval*. ACM Press/Addison-Wesley, New York, 1999.

4. Krishna Bharat and Andrei Broder. Mirror, mirror on the web: a study of host pairs with replicated content, 1999. www8.org/w8-papers/4c-server/mirror/mirror.html.

5. J. Callan, M. Connell, and A. Du. Automatic discovery of language models for text databases. In *Proceedings of ACM SIGMOD'99*, pages 479–490, New York, 1999.

6. James P. Callan, Zihong Lu, and W. Bruce Croft. Searching distributed collections with inference networks. In *Proceedings of ACM SIGIR'95*, pages 12–20, 1995.

7. Charles L.A. Clarke and Gordon V. Cormack. Shortest-substring retrieval and ranking. *ACM Transactions on Information Systems*, 18(1), 44-78 2000.

8. Cross Language Evaluation Forum webpage. www.iei.pi.cnr.it/DELOS/CLEF/. accessed 25 Sep 2001.

9. Cyril Cleverdon. The Cranfield tests on index language devices. In Karen Sparck Jones and Peter Willett, editors, *Readings in Information Retrieval*, pages 47–59. Morgan Kauffman, San Francisco, 1997. (Reprinted from Aslib Proceedings, 19, 173-192).

10. Nick Craswell, Peter Bailey, and David Hawking. Server selection on the world wide web. In *Proceedings of the ACM Digital Libraries Conference, San Antonio, Texas*, pages 37–46. ACM Press, New York, June 2000.

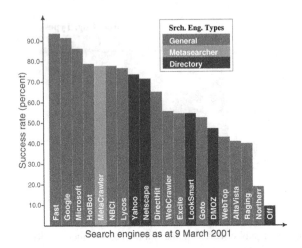

Search engines as at 9 March 2001

Fig. 20. Comparison of public search engines on the basis of their ability to find airline home pages. Queries were 100 names of airlines listed in the IATA (International Air Transport Association) member list. The correct answer for each query was the official homepage as listed in the members page. Manual judging of results was only necessary to identify aliases of the correct answer. For example www.qantas.com and www.qantas.com.au/index.html may reference the same page. The measure used was *success rate* – the proportion of cases in which the right answer (or an alias) was found in the top ten results.

11. Nick Craswell, David Hawking, and Kathleen Griffiths. Which search engine is best at finding airline site home pages? Technical Report 2001/45, CSIRO Mathematical and Information Sciences, 2001. www.ted.cmis.csiro.au/ nickc/pubs/airlines.pdf.

12. Nick Craswell, David Hawking, and Stephen Robertson. Effective site finding using link anchor information. In *Proceedings of ACM SIGIR 2001*, pages 250–257, New Orleans, 2001. www.ted.cmis.csiro.au/nickc/pubs/sigir01.pdf.

13. Nick Craswell, David Hawking, and Paul Thistlewaite. Merging results from isolated search engines. In John Roddick, editor, *Proceedings of the 10th Australasian Database Conference, Auckland, NZ*, pages 189–200. Springer-Verlag, January 1999. www.ted.vic.cmis.csiro.au/ nickc/pubs/adc99.ps.gz.

14. Owen de Kretser and Alistair Moffat. Effective document presentation with a locality based similarity heuristic. In *Proceedings of ACM SIGIR'99*, pages 113–120, Berkeley, CA, 1999.

15. William B. Frakes and Ricardo Baeza-Yates, editors. *Information Retrieval. Data Structures and Algorithms*. Prentice Hall, Upper Saddle River NJ, 1992.

16. Susan Gauch and Guijun Wang. Information fusion with ProFusion. In *Proceedings of WebNet '96: The First World Conference of the Web Society*, pages 174–179, October 1996. Also at www.designlab.ukans.edu/ProFusion.html.

17. Arthur Gill. *Introduction to the theory of finite-state machines*. McGraw-Hill, New York, 1962.

18. Michael Gordon and Praveen Pathak. Finding information on the World Wide Web: The retrieval effectiveness of search engines. *Information Processing and Management*, 35(2):141–180, March 1999.

19. Luis Gravano, Kevin Chang, Hector Garcia-Molina, Carl Lagoze, and Andreas Paepcke. STARTS - Stanford protocol proposal for internet retrieval and search. www-db.stanford.edu/ gravano/starts.html, January 1997.

20. Luis Gravano and Hector Garcia-Molina. Generalising GlOSS to vector-space databases and broker hierarchies. In *Proceedings of the 21st VLDB Conference*, Zurich, Switzerland, 1996. Morgan Kaufmann, San Francisco CA. Also Stanford technical report CS-TN-95-21.

21. D. K. Harman, editor. *Proceedings of TREC-1*, November 1992. NIST special publication 500-207.

22. David Hawking. Scalable text retrieval for large digital libraries. In Carol Peters and Costatino Thanos, editors, *Proceedings of the First European Conference on Digital Libraries*, volume 1324 of *Lecture Notes in Computer Science*, pages 127–146, Pisa, Italy, September 1997. Springer, Berlin.

23. David Hawking, Nick Craswell, Peter Bailey, and Kathleen Griffiths. Measuring the quality of public search engines, 2000. pastimeânuêduàu/TAR/Search_Engines_Conf/.

24. David Hawking, Nick Craswell, and Kathleen Griffiths. Which search engine is best at finding online services? In *WWW10 Poster Proceedings*, May 2001. www.ted.cmis.csiro.au/ dave/www10poster.pdf.

25. David Hawking, Nick Craswell, and Paul Thistlewaite. Overview of TREC-7 Very Large Collection Track. In *Proceedings of TREC-7*, pages 91–104, November 1998. NIST special publication 500-242, trec.nist.gov/pubs/trec7/t7_proceedings.html.

26. David Hawking and Paul Thistlewaite. Relevance weighting using distance between term occurrences. Technical Report TR-CS-96-08, Department of Computer Science, The Australian National University, cs.anu.edu.au/techreports/1996/index.html, 1996.

27. David Hawking and Paul Thistlewaite. Methods for information server selection. *ACM Transactions on Information Systems.*, 17(1):40–76, 1999.

28. David Hawking, Paul Thistlewaite, and Donna Harman. Scaling up the TREC Collection. *Information Retrieval*, 1(1):115–137, 1999.

29. Allan Heydon and Marc Najork. Mercator: A scalable, extensible web crawler. www.research.compaq.com/SRC/mercator/papers/www/paper.html, 1999. Accessed 25 Sep 2001.

30. John E. Hopcroft and Jeffrey D. Ullman. *Formal languages and their relation to automata.* Addison-Wesley, Reading, MA, 1969.

31. Alis Technology Inc. ?'qué? the system for identification of language and character encoding. www.alis.com/castil/silc/. Accessed 25 Sep 2001.

32. H. Garcia-Molina J. Cho and L. Page. Efficient crawling through URL ordering. Efficient crawling through url ordering. In *Proceedings of WWW7*, pages 161–172, Brisbane, Australia, 1998. www7.scu.edu.au/programme/fullpapers/1919/com1919.htm.

33. Fergus Kelledy. *Query Space Reduction in Information Retrieval.* PhD thesis, Dublin City University, Dublin, Eire, 1997. Also available at www.compapp.dcu.ie/asmeaton/FK-thesis/.

34. Steven T. Kirsch. Distributed search patent. U.S. Patent 5,659,732, August 1997. Infoseek Corporation. software.infoseek.com/patents/dist_search/patents.htm.

35. Donald E. Knuth. *The Art of Computer Programming: Sorting and Searching.* Addison-Wesley, Reading MA, 1973.

36. Martijn Koster. The web robots pages. info.webcrawler.com/mak/projects/robots/robots.html.

37. Steve Lawrence and C. Lee Giles. Inquirus, the NECI meta search engine. In *Proceedings of WWW7*, pages 95–105, 1998.

38. Steve Lawrence and C. Lee Giles. Accessibility of information on the web. *Nature*, 400:107–109, 8 July 1999.

39. A. MacFarlane, S.E. Robertson, and J.A. McCann. Parallel computing in information retrieval - an updated review. *Journal of Documentation*, 53(3):274–315, June 1997.

40. Alistair Moffat and Timothy A. H. Bell. *In situ* generation of compressed inverted files. *Journal of the American Society for Information Science*, 46(7):537–550, 1995.

41. National Institute of Standards and Technology. TREC home page. trec.nist.gov/, 1997.

42. Allison L. Powell, James C. French, Jamie Callan, Margaret Connell, and Charles L. Viles. The impact of database selection on distributed searching. In *Proceedings of ACM SIGIR'00*, pages 232–239, Athens, Greece, 2000.

43. S. F. Reddaway. High speed text retrieval from large databases on a massively parallel processor. *Information Processing and Management*, 27(4):311–316, 1991.

44. S. E. Robertson. On term selection for query expansion. *Journal of Documentation*, 46(4):359–364, 1990.

45. S. E. Robertson, S. Walker, M.M. Hancock-Beaulieu, and M. Gatford. Okapi at TREC-3. In *Proceedings of TREC-3*, November 1994. NIST special publication 500-225.

46. J.J. Rocchio, Jr. Relevance feedback in information retrieval. In Gerard Salton, editor, *The SMART Retrieval System – experiments in automatic document processing*, page chapter 14, Englewood Cliffs, NJ, 1971. Prentice-Hall.

47. Gerard Salton. *The SMART Retrieval System – experiments in automatic document processing*. Prentice-Hall, Englewood Cliffs, NJ, 1971.

48. E. Selberg and O. Etzioni. Multi-service search and comparison using the meta-crawler. In *Proceedings of WWW4*, Boston MA, December 1995.

49. Craig Silverstein, Monika Henzinger, Hannes Marais, and Michael Moricz. Analysis of a very large web search engine query log. *SIGIR Forum*, 33(1):6–12, 1999. Previously available as Digital Systems Research Center TR 1998-014 at www.research.digital.com/SRC.

50. Amit Singhal and Marcin Kaszkiel. A case study in web search using TREC algorithms. In *Proceedings of WWW10*, pages 708–716, Hong Kong, 2001. www.www10.org/cdrom/papers/pdf/p317.pdf.

51. Craig Stanfill and Brewster Kahle. Parallel free text search on the Connection Machine system. *Communications of the ACM*, 29(12):1229–1239, December 1986.

52. John A. Swets. Information retrieval systems. *Science*, 141(3577):245–250, July 1963.

53. Anastasios Tombros and Mark Sanderson. Advantages of query biased summaries in information retrieval. In *Proceedings of SIGIR'98*, pages 2–10, Melbourne, Australia, August 1998.

54. Unicode home page. www.unicode.org. accessed 25 Sep 2001.

55. RFC1738: Uniform resource locators (URL). www.w3.org/Addressing/rfc1738.txt. Accessed 25 Sep 2001.

56. Ellen Voorhees. Overview of the TREC-9 question answering track. In *Proceedings of TREC-9*, November 2000. trec.nist.gov/pubs/trec9/papers/qa_overview.pdf.

57. Ellen M. Voorhees. Variations in relevance judgments and the measurement of retrieval effectiveness. In *Proceedings of SIGIR'98*, pages 315–323, Melbourne, Australia, August 1998.

58. Ellen M. Voorhees, Narendra K. Gupta, and Ben Johnson-Laird. Learning collection fusion strategies. In *Proceedings of ACM SIGIR'95*, pages 172–179, 1995.

59. Hugh E. Williams, Justin Zobel, and Phil Anderson. What's next? efficient structures for phrase querying. In John Roddick, editor, *Proceedings of the Tenth Australasian Database Conference, Auckland, NZ*, pages 141–152, Singapore, 1999. Springer Verlag.

60. Ian H. Witten, Alistair Moffat, and Timothy C. Bell. *Managing Gigabytes*. Morgan Kaufmann, San Francisco, 2nd ed. edition, 1999.

61. Justin Zobel. How reliable are the results of large-scale information retrieval experiments? In *Proceedings of ACM SIGIR'98*, Melbourne, Australia, August 1998.

Reducing Information Variation in Text

Agata Savary[1] and Christian Jacquemin[2]

[1] LADL, IGM, Université Marne-la-Vallée,
5, bd Descartes, Champs-sur-Marne 77454 Marne-la-Vallée, France
xsavary@free.fr
[2] LIMSI-CNRS, BP 133, 91403 Orsay, France
jacquemin@limsi.fr,
http://www.limsi.fr/Individu/jacquemi/

Abstract. We discuss the nature and the scope of linguistic (morphological, syntactic and semantic) variation of terms and its impact on two information retrieval tasks: term acquisition and automatic indexing. A review of natural language processing techniques existing in these two areas is done, along with an in-depth presentation of FASTR, a corpus processor for the recognition, normalization, and acquisition of multi-word terms.

1 Introduction

Because of the recent dramatic increase in the number of electronic documents, efficient retrieval of information from texts is a crucial issue. Terminological variation is one of the major obstacles for this task. Consider for example an automatic searching for documents that are relevant to a given subject. One may indicate keywords to be searched for, but the relevant documents may not match them precisely. For instance, while looking for texts concerning the *genetic disease* it is necessary to consider that all of the following variants are valid instances of the query: *genetic diseases* (inflectional variant), *disease is genetic* (syntactic variant), *hereditary disease* (semantic variant), *genetically determined forms of disease* (morphological variant), etc. Conversely, not every co-occurrence of the constituent words of a given term is relevant to this term, e.g. *genetic risk factors for coronary artery disease* is not a correct variant of *genetic disease*. Therefore, a straightforward matching of documents against keywords will result either in misses of relevant responses, if the matching is performed in a rigid way (i.e. by fixed phrases), or in an excess of irrelevant responses, if it is performed loosely (i.e. by a bag of words).

We will show how a compromise may be reached between rigid and loose keyword matching through natural language processing (NLP). We present a survey of existing term extraction tools, with a particular concern for their ability to handle term variation. One of them, FASTR[1] (Fast Term Recognizer), is a shallow parser dedicated to the recognition, normalization and acquisition of compound terms. For a given set of documents and an initial set of controlled terms FASTR produces a set of linguistic

---

[1] FASTR can be downloaded from *http://www.limsi.fr/Individu/jacquemi/FASTR/* and freely used for research projects by noncommercial and academic institutions.

S. Renals, G. Grefenstette (Eds.): Text- and Speech-Triggered Info. Access, LNAI 2705, pp. 145-181, 2003.
© Springer-Verlag Berlin Heidelberg 2003

links between text sequences and initial terms. The exceptional accuracy of the resulting term spotting supports the argument that access to full text documents does not require a complete understanding of their content.

FASTR is a unique combination of several NLP techniques: lexical analysis through large terminological and lexical resources; shallow parsing; novel transformational unification-based techniques, and optimization techniques for fast processing of large corpora. The design of FASTR was based on detailed observation of numerous types of term variations in French and English documents from various specialized domains. The in-depth description of most aspects of the present study is described in [68].

2   Term Variation

Contrary to the traditional view of terms as being fixed labels for well-defined concepts of a given technical sublanguage [99], terms are linguistic objects prone to orthographic, syntactic and denotational fluidity, from both diachronic [55] and synchronic [45] point of view. Therefore ignoring term variability in an automatic information-processing system may result in inability to relate conceptually close but linguistically different occurrences.

For the aim of *term normalization*, i.e. grouping together occurrences of the same multi-word term, we admit the following definition of term variation:

Definition 1. *A morphological, syntactic, or semantic variation is a transformation of a controlled multi-word term that satisfies the following three conditions:*

1. *All "content" words (i.e. words other than prepositions, determiners, etc.)[2] of the controlled term are preserved by the transformation or transformed into any of the 3 types of variants listed in point 2. For instance in French,* moniteur temps réel *(real time monitor) is a variant of* Moniteur en temps réel *(lit. monitor (Noun) in real time), which we will mark* moniteur temps réel → Moniteur en temps réel[3], *but* cell recognition *is not a variant of* Neural cell recognition.
2. *Content words of the variant may be graphically modified, and morphologically or semantically related to those of the controlled term:*
   - *Variations that involve graphic variants of content words or omissions and insertions of word delimiters are called* graphic *variations (e.g.* behavioural model → Behavioral model, lookup → Look-up)[4].
   - *Variations that involve a morphological relationship of inflectional or derivational morphology are called* morphological *variations (e.g.* students union → Student union, image converter → Image conversion).
   - *Variations that involve a semantic relationship are called* semantic *variations (e.g.* speech development → Language development).

---

[2] Sometimes, prepositional or adverbial particles may belong to a term's content words, as in on-line process, parliamentary by-election, etc. If these words are omitted we cannot consider that a variant is valid, (e.g. elections to the parliament is not a variant of parliamentary by-election,) but cases of this kind are difficult to detect in our model.

[3] By convention, the first word of controlled terms is written with a capitalized letter.

[4] Graphic variations are not accounted for in FASTR.

3. *Words may be inserted or deleted and the order of words (or of their graphic, morphological or semantic variants) may be modified but the dependency relations existing between content words of the original term must be preserved in the variant (e.g.* genetic risk factors for coronary artery disease *is not a variant of* Genetic disease *because the syntactic dependency between* genetic *and* disease *is lost). Variations that involve such word insertions/deletions or word order modifications are called* syntactic variations *(e.g.* processing of cardiac image → Image processing*).*

Condition 3 doesn't exclude variants obtained through left or right extensions of a controlled term, e.g. *arterial blood pressure fluctuations, pressure fluctuation diagram,* and *abnormal fluctuations in blood pressure* may all be considered correct variants of *Pressure fluctuation.* In the case of FASTR system, however, only the variants which satisfy the following additional condition are taken into consideration:

4. *The leftmost and the rightmost constituents of a variant must be content words of the original term (thus, the 3 above variants of* Pressure fluctuation *are not dealt with). In particular, the variant should not contain the original term.*

Two reasons account for the extra limitation given in condition 4. On the one hand, the identification of the correct frontiers of variants obtained through left or right extensions of a term cannot be performed reliably in our model. On the other hand, the identification of such frontiers is not our main goal since we essentially wish to be able to point at all text sequences relevant to a given controlled term[5]. Thus, in the example above all text sequences containing e.g. *abnormal fluctuations in blood pressure* will necessarily be identified if only we manage to recognize *fluctuations in blood pressure* as a variant of *Pressure fluctuation.*

Different types of variations may occur together in a variant, for example *disease is familial* and *transmissible neurogenerative diseases* are both syntactic and semantic variants of *Genetic disease.* They are called syntactico-semantic variants.

Variation, as defined above by points 1-3, is a crucial characteristic of terms in corpora. Variants represent approximately one third of the term occurrences in an English scientific corpus [67]. This high percentage is due to the fact that terms in corpora are supposed to satisfy the communication criterion of *appropriateness* ([99], p. 106), i.e. the compromise between two concurrent needs: *precision* (fulfilled by adding modifiers to a term if it is ambiguous in a given context) and *economy* (fulfilled by reusing exiting terms in new combinations to name new concepts, and by using short variants of terms if their full forms can be deduced from the context). For that reason terms in corpora often deviate from their canonical forms found in term banks. Exhaustive listing and in-depth analysis of term variants being often unrealistic, an economical computational treatment of term variation is necessary to help overcome the gap between terms in corpora and in thesauri.

---

[5] The recognition of left and right frontiers of extended terms may though be one of the aims of some term acquisition tools presented in Section 4.

148   Agata Savary and Christian Jacquemin

3 Term Extraction

Identification of terms in textual corpora, called term extraction[6], has several applications: automatic indexing, corpus-based terminology, computer assisted translation, machine translation, etc. Especially the two first of them are concerned in this study. Both are closely related and sometimes tools developed for automatic indexing are used for corpus-based terminology or vice versa, but the essential difference is in the fact that in the former application terms are the means of investigation while in the latter they are its purpose.

Both applications divide into two distinct subfields depending on whether initial terminological knowledge is available or not. The purpose of automatic indexing is to assign to documents terms capable of representing the content of these documents [103]. If this task is performed with reference to a controlled vocabulary it is called *controlled indexing*, in the opposite case it is called *free indexing*. Likewise, the corpus-based terminology, whose purpose is to create terminological thesauri on the basis of term occurrences in corpora, can be either *thesaurus enrichment* if prior terminological knowledge is used, or *term acquisition* otherwise.

Table 1. Subdomains of term extraction

	Indexing	Corpus-based terminology
With initial data	Controlled indexing	Thesaurus enrichment
Without initial data	Free indexing	Term acquisition

Depending on whether we work with single-word terms or multi-word terms, the central issues in the design of a term extraction system are very different:

- Single-word terms are generally polysemous and call for word-sense disambiguation and context analysis.
- Multi-word terms are far less polysemous than single-word terms, but since they have a phrase structure, they are prone to variations. Their identification calls for morpho-syntactic analysers or statistical measures.

In this study we concentrate on multi-word terms. The next section contains a survey of existing concepts and techniques for multi-word term acquisition and for automatic multi-word indexing, called *phrase indexing*. In the following sections we describe FASTR, a term processor whose scope falls into the first line of Table 1.

4 State of the Art in Automatic Term Extraction

Different terminological, morphological and semantic resources, linguistic methods and computational tools contribute to the automatic extraction of terminology nowadays.

---

[6] The notion of "term extraction" is sometimes confused with "term acquisition", which we define below.

Controlled terms are contained in thesauri in which they are often organized in a hierarchical structure and accompanied by various kinds of information. For instance, AGROVOC, a multilingual thesaurus for agronomy [4], has a hierarchical structure. An entry, as the French one in Table 2, consists of a term, its linguistic variants and synonyms (marked *ep*), its generic terms (TG1, TG2,...), its specific terms (TS1), its associated terms (ta), and its equivalents in other languages.

Table 2. A French entry from AGROVOC

Code	Text	Gloss
	IMMUNISATION	[descriptor]
	(immunisation spécifique	
	d'antigène)	[note of usage]
ep	*immunisation active*	[nondescriptor (synonym)]
ep	*immunisation croisée*	—
ep	*sensibilisation immune*	—
TG1	*immunostimulation*	[generic term (level +1)]
TG2	*immunothérapie*	[— (level +2)]
TG3	*thérapeutique*	[— (level +3)]
TG4	*contrôle de la maladie*	[— (level +4)]
TS1	*vaccination*	[specific term (level -1)]
ta	*antigène*	[associated term]
ta	*réponse immunitaire*	—
ta	*résistance aux maladies*	—
ta	*résistance induite*	—
En	*immunization*	[English equivalent]
Es	*immunización*	[Spanish equivalent]

The UMLS (Unified Medical Language System) is a hierarchical meta-thesaurus aimed at unifying medical terminological data from different sources [127]. It allows to assign several kinds of information to terms: lexical variants (e.g. *Atrial fibrillation* and *Atrial fibrillations*), synonyms (e.g. *Atrial fibrillation* and *Auricular fibrillation*), generic/specific relations (e.g. *Atrial fibrillation* **is_a** *Arrhythmia*), concept attributes (e.g. the semantic type *pathologic function* is an attribute of the concept *Atrial fibrillation*), etc. In addition, UMLS contains a semantic network (see Figure 1 for an extract), a map of information sources, and a lexicon which serves the attached NLP module for generating graphical and morphological variants of terms.

4.1   Linguistic Levels of Term Analysis

According to the nature of variation (see definition in Section 2), the normalization of terms is to be done at various linguistic levels: orthographic, morphological, syntactic and semantic.

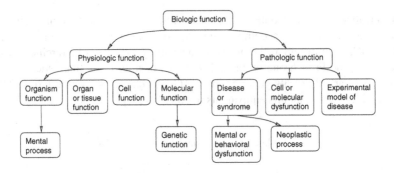

Fig. 1. Hierarchy of *biological functions* in the UMLS.

At the orthographic level, variations may occur either within single words (*flavor - flavour*, *boolean - Boolean*), or at boundaries between adjacent words (*bolthole - bolt-hole*). In both cases, formal methods dealing with string similarities [58] may be useful [39], p. 29, [105], p. 153-156, but they may give many spurious conflations (e.g. *flavor - favor*). Systematic description of orthographic variants [86], [93] is more reliable but labor intensive. Some word separators, such as blanks and hyphens, may be arbitrarily interchanged (e.g. *air(-)conditioning*) but conflating them is not a good strategy in every case, as they may sometimes be disambiguating features. For example, in nominal terms containing an adverbial particle, like *a by-product* or *a take-in*, the hyphen is obligatory and allows to distinguish them from prepositional or verbal phrases. The recognition of orthographic variants of terms is closely connected to the problem of their orthographic correction. In some applications, an error tolerant morphological analysis (as in [94]) may be crucial for the quality of term extraction.

At the morphological—inflectional and derivational—level a word[7] is analysed as a root (a word that cannot be morphologically decomposed), as an inflectional form of a root, or as a word constructed from a root (through suffixing, prefixing, or compounding). Reducing morphological variation means attaching each word to its root (e.g. *beautification* → *beauty*), or to its stem, i.e. a string that is common to morphologically related words (e.g. *denied→deni-*). To this purpose, one of three approaches may be adopted: rule-based, dictionary-based, or hybrid.

In the rule-based approach the inflectional and derivational morphology of words is described with respect to their endings and/or to their prefixes. Rules are conceived through observation of a sufficiently big number of words with common characteristics, and then they are generalized to all words that share these characteristics. The main advantage is robustness and size: each word that belongs to a described paradigm can be analysed, and the size of the set of rules may be kept relatively small. The disadvan-

---

[7] Identification of word and sentence boundaries, called tokenizing, is a preliminary task to higher levels of treatment. It must deal with non trivial problems such as variable status of punctuation marks (spaces, hyphens, apostrophes, dots, etc.) that may either belong to items (as the dots in *a.m.*) or be separators between items (as a full stop at the end of a sentence).

tage is the risk of an erroneous analysis if an exception to a rule has been overseen. The main rule-based approach is stemming. Two significant stemming algorithms for English are the Lovins stemmer [85] and the Porter stemmer [96]. Both are based on rules for suffix stripping (e.g. *absorption* → *absorpt-*) and stem normalization (e.g. *absorpt-* → *absorb-*) that may be applied to words under specified conditions. Stemming of morphologically richer languages like French raises particular issues such as the combination of rules with exception lists [32].

Alternatively, the inflectional and morphological analysis can be based on a dictionary, in which the construction of inflectional and/or derivational forms is explicitly described for each root, like in the word-based approach [20], in the concatenative approach [126], or in the DELAS system [27]. An important dictionary-based approach to computational morphology is the two-level approach [81], which has been applied to numerous languages and stands out as particularly well adapted to morphologically complex, e.g. agglutinative, languages. The advantage of dictionary-based systems is their reliability and extension facility (new words can be added easily). The disadvantages are the high cost and the lack of robustness (unknown words cannot be analysed otherwise than by an additional rule-based guesser). To solve this last problem, dictionary-based and rule-based approaches may be combined into hybrid systems [26].

The inflectional and morphological analyses of compounds raise particular problems discussed in the following section.

After inflectional and morphological analyses words may remain ambiguous with respect to their part-of-speech and inflectional features. This ambiguity may be dealt with in corpus through increasingly available grammatical taggers, such as [18] and [98] for English, or [22] and [83] for French.

At the syntactic level the analysis of multi-word terms aims at determining different syntactic structures of a given term that preserve its conceptual content. A number of linguistic studies have been carried out in areas closely related to this problem. Their main idea is that some groups of words, called idioms or compounds, have limited syntactic flexibility with comparison to free constructions. For example, in French, *une chambre est froide* (a room is cold) is not an acceptable variant of the complex word *Chambre froide* (a refrigerated place used for cold storage), while *une chambre est aérée* (a room is ventilated) is a variant of the free noun compound *chambre aérée* (ventilated room).

This phenomenon has been analysed in an introspective approach [53] inspired by the notion of lexicon-grammar [54]. In this approach, a set of generic transformations is first established for each syntactic structure. Then, for each compound of the given structure, and for each transformation, a linguist gives her/his judgement of acceptability which is reported in a boolean table, such as Table 3. This method has been applied to a relatively high coverage of standard French compounds, but it is less appropriate for large-scale terminology description for two reasons: it is very labor-intensive due to the high number of terms and corresponding variants, and it requires not only a linguistic competence but also a deep technical knowledge in the particular domain of description.

An alternative approach by Barkema is based on a large-scale corpus investigation [10]. It consists in building a *flexibility profile* of idioms by determining the list and the

Table 3. Examples of acceptabilities for Noun-Adjective compounds: predicativity (e.g. *la nuit est blanche* → *Nuit blanche*), nominalization (e.g. *l'historicité de ce fait* → *Fait historique*), selective restriction (e.g. *accent aigu* → *Accent grave*).

Compound	Predicativity	Nominalization	Selection restriction on adjective
Accent grave (grave accent)	−	−	+
Cinéma muet (silent films)	+	−	−
Fait historique (historic event)	+	+	−
Nuit blanche (a sleepless night)	+	−	+

number of forms (including external or internal modifiers, and coordinations) that each idiom takes in a reference corpus.

At the semantic level variations of terms can be detected through identifying semantically related words. This can be based on terminological resources like thesauri which contain semantic classes or semantic relations, as those described above. A method of conceptual indexing is proposed in [5] and [134]. It relies on the *kind-of* relationship described in a knowledge representation system. A controlled term, such as *automobile steam cleaning*, is extended to a set of conceptually related terms containing *automobile cleaning*, *automobile upholstery cleaning*, *automobile washing*, and *car washing*. In [59] non-transitive synonymy relations between single words are used in order to recognize semantic variants among candidate terms produced by an automatic term extractor.

4.2 Morphological Analysis of Compounds

The conflation of inflectional variants of compounds is often handled by stemming or lemmatizing of their component words, as in WordNet[8] thesaurus: *morphy* module) or in automatic term acquisition systems, e.g. in ACABIT. This method may give erroneous results in some cases.

First, a compound's base form may be in plural. For instance, *bits and pieces* doesn't have the singular form, while its lemmatizing performed on a single word basis yields the incorrect form **bit and piece*[9]. One may agree that such a form be an "abstract" reference form, as it is the case in stemming of single words (e.g. *deni* for *denied*). However, this is inconvenient for two reasons: it makes any human postfiltering tedious, and it may result in spurious conflations with free forms, as in *think a bit and piece the jigsaw together*.

Second, some compounds, such as *cross-roads*, have their singular and plural form identical. Here again a simplistic lemmatizing produces an incorrect form **cross-road*.

---

[8] WordNet is available from *http://www.cogsci.princeton.edu*.

[9] The * symbol preceding a text sequence indicates that it is an invalid occurrence of a term in this context.

In the general case, the lemma of a compound may contain words that are not lemmas themselves. For instance, the singular of *customs duties* is *customs duty* instead of **custom duty*.

Third, a single word may carry an inflection or derivation mark (or both) of a compound although this word has no inflection/derivation as an individual lexical item. For instance, in *court martials, good-for-nothings, stand-bys, take-aways, cure-alls, forget-me-nots, has-beens, johny-come-latelies*, etc. the underlined words cannot be lemmatized by a standard dictionary-based morphological analyser. Similarly, in *up-to-dateness, captain-generalcy,* and *ivory-towerist,* the underlined words are no valid derivations of the corresponding single words *date, general,* and *tower.* Such cases may be handled by a stemmer though.

The lemmatizing of compounds in French is even more complex due to the gender inflection of nouns and adjectives, as well as to the important number of compounds with a non-standard nominal construction, e.g. *un porte-avions* (aircraft carrier), *une deux-chevaux* (a car with a two horsepower engine).

Such non-standard cases of compounds' inflected forms may be lemmatized in a reliable way only if they have been explicitly described. This can be done either in a static approach, in which all inflected forms of controlled compounds are generated beforehand, or in a dynamic approach, in which the relevant inflected form of a controlled compound is calculated on demand during the runtime of the morphological analyser. In ([114], pp. 98-100) it is argued that the static approach is preferable for the morphological analysis of compounds. In ([105], pp. 48-101) a detailed analysis of inflection irregularities of compounds in English, French and Polish is shown, together with a formalism and an algorithm for automatic generation of their inflected forms.

4.3   Computational Techniques

Computational techniques most frequently used in NLP tools for information extraction are: finite-state machines, context-free and unification-based grammars, and statistical measures [23].

Many aspects of a natural language can be seen as formal languages described by regular expressions. For instance, in [73] the following part-of-speech pattern is used to extract well formed noun phrases in English: $((A \mid N)^+ \mid (A \mid N)^* (N P) (A \mid N)^*) N$. The symbols A, N and P stand for adjective, noun and preposition respectively, alignment of symbols stands for concatenation, "|" stands for union, "+" for one or more occurrences of a symbol, and "*" for zero or more occurrences. Thus, the possible patterns matching this regular expression include AN, NN, AAN, ANN, NAN, NNN, NPN, ... Regular expressions are equivalent to finite-state automata, i.e. for every regular expression there is a unique minimum deterministic finite-state automaton defining the same language, and vice versa. Finite-state transducers are more complex tools than automata because of their two-way functioning based on an input alphabet and an output alphabet. They are applied to many areas of natural language processing: phonology [74], [82]], morphology [81], part-of-speech tagging [98], and parsing [97]. In the field of information extraction, a transducer cascade is an efficient technique. A cascade is a set of transducers that are applied to a text one after another. Each transducer parses the text and performs some transformations on it. The resulting transformed text becomes the input for the following transducer. Three of the systems using this technique are Cass [3], FASTUS [62] and INTEX [46].

One of the reasons why finite-state automata and transducers are widely used in NLP in their classical and extended [80] versions is their time and space efficiency obtained by determinization (sequentialization) and minimisation [133], [28], [92], [48]. These two properties can be characterized as follows. For each non-deterministic finite-state automaton there exists a minimal deterministic finite-state automaton recognizing the same language [63], [64]. In the general case, due to the determinization process, the number of states of the resulting automaton may theoretically increase exponentially, but for some subclasses of finite-state automata the worst-case space complexity of determinization is far lower [87]. The problem of minimisation and determinization of finite-state transducers is more complex than that of finite-state automata. A transducer may be interpreted as a simple automaton whose alphabet contains couples of input and output symbols. Then, the minimisation algorithms designed for automata may also be applied to transducers. However, a word lookup in such a transducer may not be deterministic. A transducer which is deterministic with respect to its input alphabet is called a sequential transducer. Not all transducers can be sequentialized, but their sequentiability is decidable [48].

Unification-based grammars, that stem from context-free grammars, represent languages that are more complex than the regular expressions, in particular they may describe arbitrarily distant dependencies and deep recursive structures. Context-free grammars are composed of rewriting rules with a unique nonterminal as the left component, and with concatenation of nonterminals and terminals as the right-hand component. For example, the following context-free grammar describes some well-formed English noun phrases, like *bone marrow, normal bone marrow, blood and bone marrow, blood and bone marrow cell*, etc.

$$\langle \text{NP} \rangle \rightarrow \langle \text{PreMod} \rangle \langle \text{Noun} \rangle \tag{1}$$

$$\langle \text{PreMod} \rangle \rightarrow \langle \text{PreMod} \rangle \ and \ \langle \text{PreMod} \rangle \tag{2}$$

$$\langle \text{PreMod} \rangle \rightarrow \langle \text{PreMod} \rangle \langle \text{PreMod} \rangle \tag{3}$$

$$\langle \text{PreMod} \rangle \rightarrow \langle \text{Adj} \rangle \mid \langle \text{Noun} \rangle \tag{4}$$

$$\langle \text{Adj} \rangle \rightarrow normal \tag{5}$$

$$\langle \text{Noun} \rangle \rightarrow blood \mid bone \mid cell \mid marrow \tag{6}$$

The language generated by such a grammar is the set of all sequences of terminal symbols (words) obtained by derivations starting from a particular nonterminal called the start symbol (here $\langle \text{NP} \rangle$). A derivation can be displayed either as a bracketing of the resulting sequence, or as a derivation tree in which leaves are terminals, interior symbols are non-terminals, and each interior node with its daughters corresponds to a rewriting rule. A sequence is ambiguous if it has more than one parse tree (bracketing) in the same grammar. For example, *blood and bone marrow cell* is ambiguous in the above grammar as its two possible bracketings (in simplified notation) are: ((*blood and (bone marrow)) cell*) and (((*blood and bone) marrow) cell*).

The classical context-free grammars have been extended to more complex models in which the mechanism of *unification* [1] allows for an efficient description of some dependencies between words, e.g. agreement rules. Such extended models contain the Lexical Functional Grammar (LFG, [17]), the Generalized Phrase Structure Grammar (GPSG, [50]), the Tree Adjoining Grammar (TAG, [72]), and the Head-Driven Phrase Structure Grammar (HPSG, [95]). As far as the computational complexity is concerned, these models are equivalent to various classes of formal grammars: HPSG has the complexity of a Turing machine, LFG of a context-sensitive grammar, GPSG of a context-free grammar, and TAG of a "slightly context-sensible" grammar.

Two classical approaches to parsing standard and extended context-free languages are the top-down and the bottom-up approach, in which the derivation is done by applying the rewriting rules, respectively, from left to right or from right to left. Both approaches may encounter serious efficiency problems [2] due to non-determinism in the derivation process. Various optimisation techniques [76], e.g. the left-corner parsing, may speed-up the parsing, but the gain seems not to be satisfactory enough for large-corpus applications such as information retrieval. Therefore, most of the term extraction systems presented below rely on less precise but faster NLP techniques, like tagging or shallow parsing or a combination of both.

Statistical techniques are very frequently used for term extraction. They rely on the hypothesis that words building a multi-word term tend to co-occur more frequently than if they were independent. The simplest statistical observations about two words w_1 and w_2 are: the frequency of their co-occurrence within a window of a given size, and the frequencies of their isolated occurrences, which form the following contingency table ([30], chap 4.3.2):

	w_2	$w' \neq w_2$
w_1	$a = f(w_1, w_2)$	$b = \sum_{w' \neq w_2} f(w_1, w')$
$w \neq w_1$	$c = \sum_{w \neq w_1} f(w, w_2)$	$d = \sum_{w \neq w_1, w' \neq w_2} f(w, w')$

An information-theoretic measure called *Mutual Information* ([43], ch.2), based on the above table, is widely used in computational linguistics (e.g. [116], [25], and [19]):

$$MI(X,Y) = \log_2 \frac{P(w_1, w_2)}{P(w_1)\, P(w_2)} = \log_2 \frac{a}{(a+b)(a+c)} \ . \tag{7}$$

Other statistical measures used to compute word associations or document similarities in information retrieval are: Dice coefficient [36], Jaccard coefficient [125], Cosine coefficient [102], log-likelihood ratio [38], etc. The statistical methods of term extraction have two important drawbacks. The first one is the risk of conflating co-occurrences of words which represent different concepts, like *horse race* et *race horse* ([30], p.113). The second drawback is the difficulty of dealing with terms that occur rarely in corpora. Such terms are very numerous and in some applications must not be ignored. With [106], in a 280,000 word corpus from the domain of computer science submitted to a pattern matching term extractor, the term hapax legomena (i.e. terms occurring only once in a given corpus) are twice as many as other terms. To remedy such and other problems statistical measures may be accompanied by linguistic methods to build hybrid systems [79].

4.4   Evaluation of Term Extraction

Whatever technique is used to extract terms from corpora it is necessary to evaluate the outcome of term extractors. The goal of automatic term extraction, being to retrieve all occurrences of terms and their variants and only them, is never fully attained in practice. This results in a certain level of *noise* (wrongly retrieved occurrences), and a certain level of *silence* (correct but unretrieved occurrences). The two main measures of quality of term extraction systems, the *precision* and the *recall*, are taken from the evaluation in information retrieval [101]. Precision P is the proportion of relevant occurrences within all retrieved occurrences, and recall R is the proportion of retrieved occurrences within all relevant occurrences. A complementary measure is *fallout* (F), the proportion of retrieved occurrences within all irrelevant occurrences. In the following formulas I stands for the set of all occurrences, I_E for the set of retrieved occurrences, and I_R for the set of relevant occurrences.

$$P = \frac{|I_E \cap I_R|}{|I_E|} . \tag{8}$$

$$R = \frac{|I_E \cap I_R|}{|I_R|} . \tag{9}$$

$$F = \frac{|I_E \setminus I_R|}{|I \setminus I_R \cdot|} \tag{10}$$

All three measures have values within 0 and 1. The bigger are precision and recall, and the smaller is fallout, the higher the quality of term extraction. However, precision is a decreasing function of recall, in the sense that tuning a system toward a higher precision results in lower recall and vice versa. Hence, a trade-off is necessary between these two factors, according to the needs of the particular application.

The actual difficulty of the evaluation of term extraction lies in the determination of the set of relevant occurrences (I_R) of terms in a given corpus. In the classical approach, this set is supposed to be a correct and exhaustive reference list, elaborated a priori by an expert after a manual or semi-manual analysis of the corpus. Unfortunately, the definition of a relevant term occurrence is far from being clear because it depends on the particular application of term extraction. For instance, a term like *disease is genetic* may be relevant in the context of automatic indexing because it may be a good descriptor of a document's content, but it may not be relevant in the same document for thesaurus enrichment because of its non-compound structure. In other applications, like computer aided translation, term relevance may have as complex conditions as: text origin (due to a company's internal terminology), date (some old terms may be out-of-date), translation contract (a reference list of terms and their translations may be an integral part of this contact), etc. [52].

As [12] put it, the terminology of a given technical domain is not a set of predefined labels attributed to rigid concepts, that need only be discovered. The terminology should be *textual* rather than metalinguistic, in the sense that it should be constructed individually for each new application by a terminologist accompanied by a technical expert of the given domain. In conclusion, an objective evaluation of a term extraction system is only possible with respect to a particular application.

The evaluation of FASTR system presented below is less complex than in the general case (at least as far as the variant recognition is concerned) because a list of valid terms is an input provided by the user. Thus, an extracted occurrence is considered as relevant if and only if it is one of the formally defined variants of a controlled, i.e. a proiri relevant, term.

In the following two sections we present a survey of existing tools for term acquisition and automatic phrase indexing (see also [57] and [21]).

4.5 Term Acquisition

All automatic term acquisition tools presented below take a raw or a tagged corpus as input, and provide, as output, a list of candidate terms, possibly enhanced with conceptual links. We deliberately exclude tools for term management from our consideration, since the term extraction is only a small subcomponent of such tools.

ACABIT ([30] and [31]) is a term acquisition tool based on a hybrid - linguistic and statistical - approach. The corpus is first tagged with part-of-speech categories and morphological features, and analysed by a finite-state shallow parser which extracts various noun phrase patterns, lemmatizes them and normalizes them by attaching variants to canonical binary forms such as NN, AN or NPN. For example, the following sequences: *permanent failure, permanent failures, permanent physical failure*, and *failure is permanent*, are all recognized as variants of the canonical binary term candidate *permanent failure*. Such conflated binary term occurrences are then submitted to different statistical filters (frequency, log-likelihood, mutual information, etc.) which are evaluated with respect to their ability to separate valid term candidates from non-terminological candidates. The recognition of variants is based on syntactic transformations:

- coordination of binary terms: *assemblage de paquets* (packet assembly) + *désassemblage de paquets* (packet disassembly) → *assemblage/désassemblage de paquets* (packet assembly/disassembly),
- overcomposition of binary terms: *réseau à satellites* (satellite network) + *réseau de transit* (transit network) → *réseau de transit à satellites* (satellite transit network),
- insertion of a modifier in a binary term: *liaison par satellites* (satellite link) → *liaisons multiples par satellites* (multiple satellite links),
- shifting of a modifier from epithet to attribute position: *permanent failure* → *failure is permanent*.

ANA [39] is a fully statistical termer which uses a raw untagged corpus with no linguistic analysis (therefore it is language independent). Its input is a bootstrap containing some controlled terms that are used to discover new terms. A new term candidate may be either a frequent co-occurrence of bootstrap terms, or a frequent co-occurrence of a bootstrap term and of any other word (not belonging to a stop-list), possibly combined by a function word (preposition or determiner). Term discovery is incremental: newly discovered terms are included in the bootstrap, and the process is repeated until no new terms can be found. Different morphological forms of single words are conflated through approximate string matching based on string edit distance [132].

LEXTER [13], [14], and [15]) performs term acquisition in French through shallow parsing, without any statistical measure, which allows for a high recall of extraction of both frequent terms and single-occurrence terms (hapax legomena). The corpus is tagged, lemmatized and bracketed through noun phrase frontier detection (e.g. a past participle followed by any preposition except *de* builds a right frontier). The resulting chunks—called maximal noun phrases—are then decomposed into binary term candidates (e.g. *rejet d'air froid* [cool air exhaust] → *rejet d'air* [air exhaust] + *air froid* [cool air]). Then an endogenous disambiguation process retains only those ambiguous candidates which are encountered anywhere else in the corpus in a nonambiguous situation. Finally, a terminological network is created by grouping candidate terms sharing the same head (*vanne motorisée* [powered valve], *vanne d'isolement d'enceinte* [zone insulation valve],...) or the same extension (*vanne manuelle* [manual valve], *commande manuelle* [manual control], *lignage manuel* [manual lining],...).

TERMINO ([33] and [34]) is another linguistic approach based on a partial parser. Rule-based morphological analysis and lemmatizing are performed on the corpus. A partial parser allows for word disambiguation and extraction of noun phrase nuclei (e.g. in the sequence *un traitement de texte très performant* [a very efficient word processor] only *traitement de texte* [word processor] is extracted). A term recognizer filters the output of the parser in order to discover nested structures (e.g. *système de gestion de bases de données* [database management system] → *gestion de bases de données* [database management], *base de données* [database]), and ambiguous or nonambiguous expansions (e.g. the participle *intégré* [integrated] in *logiciel intégré* [integrated software] may either be attached to the head noun *logiciel* [software] or not). Obtained term candidates are filtered and ordered according to some heuristics like stop-lists and endogenous disambiguating process similar to the one in LEXTER. Finally, a term base management module allows for visualization and classification of term candidates.

TERMS ([73]) is based on matching the following regular expression pattern in an untagged corpus: $((A \mid N)^{+} \mid (A \mid N)^{*} (N P) (A \mid N)^{*}) N$. Part-of-speech ambiguities are handled by a simple noncontextual preference selection and a stop-list. All extracted sequences appearing only once are rejected, all others are retained. TERMS was the inspiration for a term extractor for Japanese, JBrat ([47], sec. 3.2).

Xtract ([115]) is intended for extraction of collocations (e.g. *heavy smoker*, *agree to*, *to hit a record*) which are a wider class of word co-occurrences than terms. Xtract is a hybrid system which, contrary to ACABIT, applies statistical filters before linguistic ones. It is presumed that components of a collocation appear together more often than expected by chance, therefore term discovery starts with statistical observation of word couples. For each couple, the co-occurrences within a 5-word window are summarized by a histogram that describes the possible relative positions of the two words. Then the first statistical filter retains only frequent pairs of words, and the second retains only those that co-occur most often in the same relative position. The whole procedure is reiterated to expand binary collocation candidates into *n*-ary ones. The resulting sequences are analysed by a parser and only syntactically correct expressions are retained. The

Chinese version of Xtract ([47], sec. 3.1) must deal, additionally, with the lack of word delimiters which calls for a sophisticated preliminary tokenizing task.

Table 4 presents a comparative summary of all mentioned term extraction systems.

Table 4. Comparative features of term acquisition tools

		ACABIT	ANA	LEXTER	TERMINO	TERMS	XTract
1	Tagging	×		×			×
2	Morphological analysis				×	×	
3	Stemming		×				
4	Syntactic patterns	×		×		×	×
5	Grammar				×		
6	Statistical filtering	×	×			×	×
7	Text simplification		×				
8	Incrementality		×				
9	Language	Fr/En/Mal[10]	∀	Fr	Fr	En	En

The term acquisition tools presented above are concerned with term variation to a variable extent.

ACABIT's approach allows for conflating inflected forms by lemmatizing, and provides a good coverage of syntactic variants (coordinations, overcompositions, modifier insertions, attributive structures).

ANA attaches some inflected or derived forms to their roots through approximate string matching, which may conflate some orthographic or morphological term variants (e.g. *behavioral model - behavioural model, compiler option - compile options*), but approximate string matching is usually not enough to detect syntactic or semantic variants (except some "accidentally" morphologically close synonyms like *multiple output - multiple outlet*, etc.).

LEXTER includes lemmatizing, and treats some term overcompositions by decomposition rules, but no morphological or semantic variants are taken into account.

The lack of consideration of term variants, such as coordinations (*programmation locale ou subrégionale*) or acronyms (*émetteur AM*), is one of the main reasons of the limited precision of TERMINO, according to [84].

---

[9] Malagasy.

In TERMS, the matching pattern based on observation of terms in specialized dictionaries does not take into account that dictionaries contain only normalized forms of terms, while term occurrences in a corpus are prone to variation.

In Xtract, variation is only partially dealt with. On the one hand, collocation variants rarely exceed the 5-word window, therefore they contribute to the collocation's frequency examined by the first, statistical, filter. On the other hand, the collocations whose structure is not fixed are most prone to be rejected by the second, histogram-based, filter. Moreover, the linguistic analysis doesn't allow to conflate different forms having the same root or the same meaning (*rise - rose, rise - go up*, etc.).

Let's have a closer look to why variant recognition should be useful for term acquisition. The first reason is a statistical one. If any kind of frequency count is used to filter term candidates, as e.g. in ACABIT, ANA or Xtract, the results are always more accurate if term variants are conflated. For instance, if the following sequences: *permanent failure, permanent failures, permanent physical failure*, and *failure is permanent* are seen as different term candidates, their respective frequencies are much lower, and so their chance to be retained is smaller, than if they are conflated into one candidate. Besides, some terms may never appear in the corpus in their base forms, but may nevertheless be acquired from occurrences of their variants, as in the case of e.g. ACABIT. The second reason is ergonomic: if different variants of a term candidate are extracted but not conflated, the resulting list is longer and its validation more tedious. The third reason is the recall and the precision of the acquisition. If a sequence is recognized as a variant of a controlled term, or of a highly ranked term candidate, this sequence (or its subgroup) may itself be a relevant new term candidate. For example, if *permanent failure* is supposed to be a relevant term, then it is probably also the case for *permanent physical failure* and *permanent failure detection*. Speculations of this type prove to be justified in systems like ANA, Xtract and FASTR. They are also with relation to the problems referred to as *nested collocations*, i.e. collocations that are included inside each other [24] and [44], and *interrupted collocations*, i.e. collocations joined together to build lager collocations [65] and [113]. The fruitful association of term acquisition and variant conflation is illustrated through a combination of FASTR and LEXTER in [16]. Candidate terms produced by LEXTER are clustered by FASTR and placed into a relational database with an expert interface for human term validation.

Due to the coming up of new NLP general purpose tools like parallel corpora alignment (cf the evaluation project Arcade, [129]), term acquisition gains a bilingual dimension useful for the construction of translation aid tools. The usual procedure is to perform alignment of sentences in two parallel corpora one of which is the translation of the other. Then a monolingual term acquisition takes place in either corpus, and finally the extracted terms are aligned. In this kind of approach the acquisition phase is usually not the central issue, and is performed either through relatively simple regular expression matching [128], [29] and [49] or statistical measures [116]. The interesting issue concerning the term acquisition for bilingual thesauri, as opposed to monolingual acquisition, is that an equivalent for a term in one language does not necessarily have a terminological status in the other language (that supports also our discussion in Section 4.4 on the status of relevant terms). Therefore, the extraction needs to be performed loosely enough in order to be able to provide such non terminological associations.

4.6 Phrase Indexing

The purpose of automatic indexing is to assign content descriptors to documents in order to fulfil the three following purposes [77] and [103]:

1. Locate items within a document that deal with a given topic.
2. Build hypertext links that connect documents with similar content.
3. Assist information retrieval by predicting the relevance of individual documents with respect to a query.

Automatic indexers are generally parts of larger applications for information access. Extracted content descriptors (called *terms*, even if they are not always genuine terms), may be either single words or multi-word units. In the former case, the basic indexing techniques consist of: text simplification (based on stemming and on a stop-list of high frequency words), selection of best indices (usually based on a frequency criterion), and ranking indices according to their relevance for information retrieval. In our study, we are more interested in *phrase indexing*, i.e. indexing through multi-word units, which consists of two stages ([42], sec. 1.4): *phrase identification* and *phrase normalization*. The latter is used to group phrase indexes with different forms and similar meanings, in the same way that term variants are conflated for term acquisition. At present, we proceed to the presentation of a survey of some existing phrase indexing tools.

CLARIT [40] contains three large-scale NLP modules: a lexicon-based morphological analyser, a disambiguation module based on a probabilistic grammar, and a context-free parser for identifying noun phrases (NPs). The NPs extracted by the last module are submitted to a filtering and matching module which enriches them with statistical scores. The system is able to perform free indexing as well as controlled indexing. In the latter case extracted NP indexes are matched with initial terms in such way that partial overlaps are tolerated. Two further studies, [41] and [136], concentrate on enhancing *CLARIT's* output in that the structure of extracted NPs is submitted to a statistically driven disambiguation.

The *Constituent Object Parser* (COP, [88], [90], and [89]) also relies on large grammatical and lexical data. First, it filters documents through keywords contained in the query, and then parses the query and the sentences in the selected documents to produce binary trees expressing dependency relations. Such trees are simpler and more easily obtained than fine-grained syntactic structures. A tree matching algorithm allows to rank each document according to the number of dependencies it shares with the query. No explicit phrase indexes are produced.

COPSY [109] and [110]) also performs the extraction of dependency relations but, contrary to *COP*, does it for noun phrases rather than for entire sentences. After pre-filtering of documents through query keywords, and a stemming procedure based on a suffix tree and exception lists, noun phrases are isolated through detection of noun phrase delimiters (verbs, punctuations, etc.). Then, the dependency structure of these noun phrases is calculated by applying syntactic rules that make the head/modifier relations explicit. Finally, the dependency trees of the noun phrases in the query and of those in documents are matched (possibly partially).

Fagan's syntactic phrase indexer[11] [42] relies on the output of a general-purpose syntactic parser, PLNLP [61]. The parser produces parse trees, each of which is composed of a head word, premodifiers and/or postmodifiers. Then, the trees are recursively reduced by encoding rules and stop-lists of semantically empty premodifiers and heads (*the, four, also, abundant, ability, procedure*, etc.) to create binary phrase indexes. The categories of phrases treated in this way are:

- general noun phrases: *the efficiency of these four sorting algorithms* → *algorithm efficiency + sorting algorithm,*
- conjoined noun phrases: *the philosophy, design and implementation of an experimental interface* → *interface philosophy + interface design + interface implementation + experimental interface,*
- adjective phrases: *a system for encoding, automatically matching, and automatically drawing chemical structures* → *automatically matching+ automatically drawing + structure encoding + structure matching + structure drawing + chemical structure,*
- verb phrases: *the machine coding these chemical structures* → *machine coding + structure coding + chemical structure,*
- phrases with semantically empty heads (belonging to a stop-list): *an automated document clustering procedure* → *an automated document clustering* → *automated clustering + document clustering.*

The most serious problem caused in this system by the generative phrase parsing is the lack of structural disambiguation which results in incorrect descriptors due to wrongly identified dependency relations (e.g. *they design software for browsing interfaces* → **interface browsing + browsing software*). Nevertheless, Fagan's work paved the way for exploitation of large coverage parsers in information retrieval.

FASIT [37] is based on text simplification techniques. In the process of morphological analysis words are looked up in several small exception dictionaries (i.e. lists of frequent words, of semantically empty words, of domain-dependent words, etc.), and if they are not found, they are submitted to a suffix-based stemming. Then, multiply tagged words are disambiguated through contextual rules (some ambiguities are replaced by single multi-category tags such as *Adjective|Noun*). Finally, a set of 161 syntactic patterns is applied to the tagged document in order to extract single-word or multi-word indexes. Synonymous indexes are conflated into canonical forms through deletion of function words, stemming and word sorting (*library catalogs, library cataloging, catalogs of library* → *catalog librar*).

IRENA [7] and [8] uses NLP techniques for phrase recognition and term normalization. First, a tagger, a shallow parser and a syntactic normalizer allow to extract noun and verb phrases and represent them in a canonical form containing the head and the list of modifiers (*air pollution, pollution of the air* → [*air, pollution*]). Then, each inflected word is reduced to its lemma by the Porter stemmer enhanced with an exception dictionary. Complex phrases are decomposed into binary dependencies. Finally,

---

[11] Fagan also proposes a statistical phrase indexing method which we will not present here as it is a generalization of the approach presented in [104].

the normalization of semantic variants is done through discovery of synonymy and hyperonymy relations between heads or modifiers, based on semantic resources such as WordNet. This pipeline of processing modules is applied both to the query and to documents. Documents are ranked according to which types of query term variants they contain, and how distant the components of each variant are in their text occurrences.

NPtool [131] is a finite-state noun phrase parser not meant for the term extraction as such but adapted for this task by [9]. A raw corpus is first processed by a two-level morphological analyser, followed by a morphological and syntactic disambiguation module, based on the *Constraint Grammar* [75], which may leave some ambiguities unresolved. Then, two parallel noun phrase parsers are run upon the tagged corpus: an NP-friendly parser, and an NP-hostile parser. They retain, respectively, the longest and the shortest possible sequences of tags that may constitute a correct noun phrase. For instance, if the sequence *cylinder head* may be interpreted either as a pair of nouns or as a noun followed by a verb, the NP-friendly parser will favor the first interpretation and extract *cylinder head*, while the NP-hostile parser will only retain *cylinder*. The final NP candidates are obtained by the intersection of the outputs of both parsers.

In the phrase matcher by Sheridan and Smeaton [117] and [111], the query and the corpus are first analyzed by a two-level morphological analyser accompanied by local disambiguation rules. Dependencies between heads and arguments of phrases are marked by syntactic tags. Then, phrases with their morphological and syntactic tags are transformed into partially ambiguous binary trees. No explicit indexes are produced. A tree matching algorithm is used instead for pairing texts and queries.

The variant generator by Sparck Jones and Tait [119] and [118] uses a conventional syntactic analyser [11] in order to transform the query into a parse tree, in which nodes are words accompanied by syntactic and semantic labels (noun, verb, determiner, etc. and man, thing, kind, etc.), and branches are labelled with thematic roles (agent, object, recipient, etc.). Then, candidate terms are extracted from the query's parse tree, and rich sets of their possible syntactic variants are generated. For example, a sub-tree corresponding to the term *circuit detail* yields, in particular, the following variants: *the details about the circuits, detail about the circuits, details about a circuit, the detail of circuits*. The variants are converted into boolean queries which are applied to documents.

SPIRIT system [6] results from a large project for exploitation of NLP tools in information retrieval. Its inputs are both the document and the query. They are first processed by a morphological analyzer, whose two main particularities are: linking of words to their derivational families (e.g. in French, *taxer* [to tax], *taxation* [taxation], *taxable* [taxable]), and recognition of semantically opaque frozen expressions (e.g. *afin de* [in order to]). Then, a contextual disambiguation of syntactic tags takes place. Finally, the compound recognition module, based on Debili's parser [35], splits sentences into maximal-length verbal and nominal chunks, and recognizes, possibly ambiguous, head-modifier dependencies within the chunks. The dependency ambiguities are resolved through a corpus-based learning, similar to the one existing in *LEXTER* and in *CLARIT*. The retained dependencies are directly transformed into binary indexes, enhanced with frequency-based weights. The distance between a query and a document is a function of the number of common indexes, their weights, and the nature of the syntactic dependencies holding between these indexes.

TTP [124], [121], [122], and [123] is a fast and robust parser allowing to recover from ill-formed or too complex inputs, and from structures not covered by the grammar. Its first stage is part-of-speech tagging which associates each word with a unique syntactic category. A dictionary-based morphological analysis conflates inflected words with their lemmas and verb nominalizations with the corresponding verbs (e.g. *implementation* → *implement*). Then, parsing based on wide-coverage *Linguistic String Grammar* [100] produces a normalized representation of each sentence, where both head-modifier and predicate-argument relations are explicitly described. Finally, a termer extracts binary head-modifier terms and organizes them into similarity classes. For example, the sentence:

> *The former Soviet president has been a local hero aver since a Russian tank invaded Wisconsin.*

yields the following set of binary indexes: *president soviet, president former, hero local, tank russian, tank invade, invade wisconsin.*

Table 5 presents a comparative summary of the automatic phrase indexing tools presented here. Their three main differentiating characteristics seem to be: (a) the depth of the morphological analysis, whether restricted to inflectional morphology or extended to derivational morphology, (b) the nature of structural description, whether text fragments (chunks), interword links (dependencies), or traditional phrase structures, (c) the possible concern for term variations.

As far as the third differentiating aspect is concerned, the following remarks can be made with respect to the phrase indexing systems presented above.

In *CLARIT*, different inflectional forms of single words are conflated with their roots, but as far as multi-word units are concerned, variation is not treated deeply. The extracted NP indexes are matched against controlled terms only on the adjacent subsequence basis, i.e. a noun phrase ABCD is decomposed into ten adjacent substrings: A, B, C, D, AB, BC, CD, ABC, BCD, ABCD, that are compared to substrings derived from controlled terms. Thus only few syntactic transformations are accounted for, except (partially) overcompositions.

COP allows to decompose coordination term variants due to a fine-grained grammar for conjunctions. Its first part, the *equal-grammar*, allows to analyse coordinations of syntactically similar constituents (*the robber with the gun and the cop with the dog*). Its second part, the *unequal-grammar*, describes coordinations of constituents that need to be complemented if appearing alone (*he is a cop and good at it*).

In *COPSY* the stemming of single words as well as the conversion of noun phrases into dependency trees allow to normalize some cases of syntactic variation, but its simplistic model of dependencies in noun phrases may produce erroneous conflations, like *transport in containers, transport of containers,* and *transport from containers.*

Fagan's indexer covers a large variety of syntactic transformations that allow to combine binary terms into complex variants, including nominal, adjectival and verbal phrases.

FASIT performs index grouping through nonlinguistic techniques (function word deletion, stemming, word reordering) which allows to account for some syntactic and

Table 5. Comparative features of phrase indexing tools

		CLARIT	COP	COPSY	Fagan	FASIT	IRENA
1	Morphological analysis	×	?			×	
2	Stemming		?	×		×	×
3	P-o-s disambiguation	Probabilities	?			Rules	
4	Chunks	×					
5	Dependency relations		×	×			×
6	Phrase structures	×	×			×	×
7	Structural disambiguation	×					
8	Variant generation						
9	Variant conflation	×		×	×	×	×
10	Language	En	En	En	En	En	En

		NPtool	Sheridan and Smeaton	Sparck Jones and Tait	SPIRIT	TTP
1	Morphological analysis	×	×	?	×	×
2	Stemming			?		
3	P-o-s disambiguation	Rules	Rules	?	Rules	Probabilities
4	Chunks				×	
5	Dependency relations	×	×		×	
6	Phrase structures		×	×		×
7	Structural disambiguation				×	×
8	Variant generation			×		
9	Variant conflation		×		×	
10	Language	En	En	En	Fr	En

morphological variants, but also results in incorrect conflations like of *school library* and *library school*.

IRENA recognizes three families of variations: syntactic, inflectional and lexicosemantic, the first of which is treated most deeply through syntactic normalization and unnesting of complex phrases into binary dependencies.

In *NPtool*, whose prime interest is the noun phrase extraction and not particularly the identification of terms, the issue of terminological variation is not raised. However, the term extractor by [9] based on *NPtool* performs a noun phrase normalization in that the extracted NPs of different syntactic structures are transformed into a canonical "germanic" form in which the head noun is preceded by all its modifiers. The normalization procedure works by placing a postmodifying prepositional phrase between the modified head and its nominal premodifiers except possessive nouns, and the premodifying adjectives and possessive nouns. In NP's with multiple heads, this procedure is performed recursively. For instance the following NP: *exact form of the correct theory of quantum gravity* is transformed into *exact correct quantum gravity theory form*.

In Sheridan and Smeaton phrase matcher the morphosyntactic term variation is accounted for in the tree matching algorithm, even if the description of acceptable variants is not explicit enough. Query phrases and document phrases are matched with respect to nodes and dependencies existing in their binary trees, as well as with respect to textual sequences separating the matched words. For example, the query phrase *classification systems* and the textual phrase *the development of a classification schema using library system theory* don't match because of the verb *using* present in the residual structure.

The approach of Sparck Jones and Tait is opposite to other variant recognition tools. Instead of normalizing extracted phrases into canonical forms, they treat query terms as base forms which they expand into possible syntactic variants resulting from inflection, addition of determiners, and production of syntactic synonyms. The generated variants are searched for in documents on a string matching basis.

Two modules of *SPIRIT* benefit from the conflation of term variants. First, in the process of parsing, the ambiguities of head-modifier dependencies are resolved due to a corpus-based learning module which accounts for syntactic, morphological and semantic variation. For example, if a nonambiguous dependency is discovered in a sequence like *affichage mural* (wall posting), it is extended to the derivational families of the constituent words. Thus, the dependencies present in the sequences like *affichage sur les murs* (posting on the walls) and *afficher sur les murs* (post on the walls) are also considered as nonambiguous. Second, the binary dependecies are represented in an normalized form: they are ordered couples of words abstracted from their textual realization in the corpus. Therefore, the distance measure between queries and documents based on such binary dependencies, allows for syntactic and morphological variant conflation.

TTP system encompasses normalization of inflected forms of terms, as well as of some morphological variants (those involving verb nominalizations). Moreover, the full exploitation of head-modifier and predicate-argument dependencies existing in a whole sentence permits the discovery of a wide range of syntactic variations, although this issue is not explicitly illustrated in the reference papers.

In conclusion, some general remarks that can be made on the tendencies existing in term acquisition and phrase indexing tools:

- The benefit of phrase indexing with respect to single-word indexing is a subject of debate in the information retrieval community. [42] suggests that phrase indexing does not outperform classical single-word indexing. In [51] it is shown that retrieval efficiency decreases when phrases are used as indexing terms unless the query is precise. [91] presents a study of statistical and syntactic phrase indexing based, respectively, on co-occurrences and on tag patterns. Neither approach proved to do significantly better than single-word indexing, except in determining the relative ranks of low-ranked documents.
- Most acquisition and indexing systems concentrate on extracting noun phrases, although verbal and adjectival phrases may be equally informative. The few approaches in which this argument is at least partially taken into account are: Constituent Object Parser, Fagan's indexer, IRENA, Sheridan and Smeaton's matcher, and TTP.
- Many of the presented methods rely on decomposing complex phrases into binary dependencies (ACABIT, LEXTER, IRENA, TTP, etc.), and propose resulting binary phrases as term candidates or document descriptors. On the one hand, this technique must cope with the problem of phrase structure ambiguities that may result in incorrect decompositions (e.g. *dynamic information processing* → **dynamic information + information processing*). On the other hand, sets of binary substructures may be far less informative than the original complex structures. In [106] an evaluation experiment of term acquisition is presented concerning ACABIT in particular. Some binary term candidates extracted by ACABIT as basic terms, such as *history table, significant bit, number generator*, appear only within strongly terminological complex terms, like *absolute address history table* (*AAHT*), *most (least) significant bit,* and *random number generator* (*RNG*). Such binary substructures seem to be far less adequate term candidates than the corresponding complex terms.

In the following sections we present the outline of FASTR, a shallow parser dedicated to the recognition, normalization and acquisition of compound terms.

5   Variant Conflation in FASTR

FASTR is a natural language processor essentially meant for controlled indexing. It is implemented in a unification-based framework, inspired by *PATR-II* [112] and *OLMES* [56]. However, the efficiency problems typical for general unification-based grammars are not encountered in FASTR because it is a *shallow* parser: few or no recursive dependencies between terms need to be described.

The input of FASTR is a corpus and an initial set of controlled complex terms that are analyzed morphologically and transformed into syntactic rules. The output is a set of linguistic links between text sequences and initial terms. In order to attain this goal, FASTR relies on three levels of description:

1. A word level in which single words are accompanied by morphological and semantic features and links.
2. A terminological level in which terms are represented by syntactic structures.

3. A metaterminological level in which variations are implemented by local rules that transform term structures into variant structures.

For example, the following rule indicates that *compensation* is a noun derived from the canonical verb root *compens* through appending of the suffix *-ation*. Its inflectional number is 1, which means that the two suffixes corresponding to the singular and the plural form are the empty string and *-s*, respectively.

Word '*compensation*' :
$\langle cat \rangle \doteq 'N'$; $\langle inflection \rangle \doteq 1$; $\langle root\ cat \rangle \doteq 'V'$;
$\langle root\ lemma \rangle \doteq 'compens$; $\langle history \rangle \doteq 'ation'$.

Another rule states that *genetic* is and adjective with inflection number 1 and 6 synonyms.

Word '*genetic*' :
$\langle cat \rangle \doteq 'A'$; $\langle inflection \rangle \doteq 1$;
$\langle syn \rangle \doteq ('familial',A) \mid ('genetical',A) \mid ('genic',A) \mid ('hereditary',A) \mid$
$('inherited',A) \mid ('transmitted',A)$.

The data for the inflectional and derivational morphology of English words come, respectively, from the Tree-Tagger (http://www.ims.uni-stuttgart.de), and the CELEX base (over 52,000 English lemmas corresponding to more than 160,000 word forms, http://www.kun.nl). The semantic data for English is obtained from WordNet. Synonym sets (*synsets*) of *WordNet* thesaurus (95,000 simple words and compounds, http://www.cogsci.princeton.edu) are compiled in such a way that each word is mapped to the union of all synsets containing this word.

Controlled complex terms which are given as input to the system are first automatically recycled into syntactic rules by a morphological analyser and a generic noun phrase grammar. For instance, the rule below results from the input term *Umbilical artery* which contains an adjective with lemma *umbilical* and inflectional number *1* (no gradation), as well as a noun with canonical lemma *arter* and inflectional number *2* (suffix *-y* for singular and suffix *-ies* for plural). The rule is linked to the lexical item *arter*, called the *lexical anchor* (notion adopted from the LTAG formalism, [107]).

Rule $N_1 \rightarrow A_2\ N_3$:
$\langle N_1\ lexicalization \rangle \doteq N_3$; $\langle A_3\ lemma \rangle \doteq 'umbilical'$; $\langle A_3\ inflection \rangle \doteq 1$;
$\langle N_3\ lemma \rangle \doteq 'arter'$; $\langle N_2\ inflection \rangle \doteq 2$;
$\langle N_1\ agreement \rangle \doteq \langle N_3\ agreement \rangle$.

In such a rule it is possible to express dependencies between lexical items which are either at the same level of analysis (here: A_2 and N_3) or at two neighbouring levels (here: N_1 and A_2, or N_1 and N_3). For example, the last constraint indicates that agreement features (here: the number of nouns) are propagated from the head noun to the whole complex term. However, in FASTR's formalism the syntactic term rules may also be embedded one within another when nested term structures are to be described. For instance, the following rule describes the complex term *Measure of [arterial pressure]*:

Rule $N_1 \rightarrow N_2\ P_3\ (N_4 \rightarrow A_5\ N_6)$:
$\langle N_1$ lexicalization$\rangle \doteq N_2$; $\langle N_2$ lemma$\rangle \doteq$'*measure*'; $\langle N_3$ inflection$\rangle \doteq 1$;
$\langle P_3$ lemma$\rangle \doteq$'*of*'; $\langle A_5$ lemma$\rangle \doteq$'*arterial*'; $\langle A_5$ inflection$\rangle \doteq 1$;
$\langle N_6$ lemma$\rangle \doteq$'*pressure*'; $\langle N_6$ inflection$\rangle \doteq 1$;
$\langle N_1$ agreement$\rangle \doteq \langle N_2$ agreement$\rangle$;
$\langle N_4$ agreement$\rangle \doteq \langle N_6$ agreement$\rangle$.

This mechanism gives the formalism the descriptive power similar to the one in LT-AGs: the dependencies between distant nodes of a lexical entry may be expressed. This property is called *extended domain of locality*. In the rule above, the feature agreement is described between adjacent nodes only: N_1 and N_2, as well as N_4 and N_6, but other dependencies could also be expressed between non neighbouring nodes, like N_6 and N_2, or N_6 and N_1, etc.

The description of terminological variation in FASTR stems from the Harissian notion of *transformation* [60]: term variants result from base terms through application of relevant linguistic transformations. The transformations are represented by metarules (concept introduced into a number of formalisms, such as GPSG [50] and FB-LTAG [120], in order to reduce the size of the grammar). For instance, the following metarule:

$$\text{Metarule Coor}(N_1 \rightarrow A_2\ N_3) \equiv N_1 \rightarrow A_2\ C_4\ A_5\ N_3:\ .$$

when unified with the rule for *Umbilical artery* introduced previously, produces the following new rule which matches coordination variants such as *umbilical or carotoid artery*:

Rule $N_1 \rightarrow A_2\ C_4\ A_5\ N_3$:
$\langle N_1$ lexicalization$\rangle \doteq N_3$; $\langle A_2$ lemma$\rangle \doteq$'*umbilical*'; $\langle A_2$ inflection$\rangle \doteq 1$;
$\langle N_3$ lemma$\rangle \doteq$'*arter*'; $\langle N_3$ inflection$\rangle \doteq 2$;
$\langle N_1$ agreement$\rangle \doteq \langle N_3$ agreement$\rangle$

The descriptive power of metarules is enhanced by regular expressions and constraints. For example, the following metarule covers any variants of Noun-Noun terms, e.g. of *Tumor cell*, in which the noun modifier N_2 can be coordinated with another modifier containing up to 3 words, as in *tumor or nontumorous hepatic cells*. The constraint on the number of N_2 allows to filter out incorrect variants such as ...(*but failed to lyse*) *tumors or K562 cells*, which result most often from the fact that frontiers between syntagms cannot be detected reliably without a full syntactic analysis of a sentence.

$$\text{Metarule Coor}(N_1 \rightarrow N_2\ N_3) \equiv N_1 \rightarrow N_2\ \langle C\ \langle A \mid N \mid A_{pp} \rangle^{1-3}\rangle\ N_3:$$
$\langle N_2$ agreement number$\rangle \neq$'*plural*'.

Another role of metarules' constraints is to describe morphological and semantic term variants[12]. The rule below states that an Adjective-Noun ($A_4\ N_3$) sequence is a valid variant of a Noun-Noun term if the head nouns (N_3) are equal and if the adjective (A_4) belongs to the same morphological family (i.e. has the same root) as the modifier noun (N_2). For instance, *enzymatic activity* is a valid variant of *Enzyme activity* extracted by using the following metarule:

---

[12] By the same means, the description of some graphic variations could be obtained if FASTR were coupled with an adequate database of single words' graphic variants.

Metarule NountoAdj($N_1 \rightarrow N_2\ N_3$) $\equiv N_1 \rightarrow A_4\ N_3$:
$\langle N_2\ \text{root} \rangle \doteq \langle A_4\ \text{root} \rangle$.

Similarly, the following metarule allows for the replacement of the modifier adjective (A_2) by another adjective (A_4) which has the same semantic value (e.g. which belongs to the same set of synonyms [*synset*] in *WordNet*), as in *hard lens* → *Rigid lens*.

Metarule SemArg($N_1 \rightarrow A_2\ N_3$) $\equiv N_1 \rightarrow A_4\ N_3$:
$\langle A_2\ \text{syn} \rangle \doteq \langle A_4\ \text{syn} \rangle$.

During the construction of FASTR's metagrammar, various types of variants have been deeply studied for both binary and *n*-ary terms. For each suggested metarule its context-free skeleton was first applied to a training corpus. Then, the extracted sequences were analyzed manually and constraints were added gradually to the metarule in order to filter out as many spurious occurrences as possible, without eliminating correct variants.

As a result, the following syntactic variations can be extracted by FASTR's 113 metarules[13]:

- Permutation of a nominal modifier: *effect of light* → *Light effect*.
- Modification (or a substitution) by an additional modifier: *blood mononuclear cell* → *Blood cell*, (*red blood cell* is obtained by an insertion out of the controlled terms range and is not considered as a valid variant, according to condition 4 of the definition of variation in Section 2).
- Coordination of heads or arguments: *axillary artery and vein* → *Axillary vein*, *intercostal and bronchial arteries* → *Intercostal arteries*, *central venous or oesophageal pressure* → *Central venous pressure*.

Some of the 113 syntactic metarules describe compositions of these elementary variations[14]. For instance, *expression of lymphokine gene* may be recognized as a variant of *Gene expression* through a permutation (*expression of gene*), followed by a modification (*expression of lymphokine gene*). Such sequence of transformations is implemented by the following metarule:

Metarule Perm($X_1 \rightarrow X_2\ X_3$) = $X_3\ P_4\ X_5\ X_2$

As far as morphological transformations of words are concerned, inflections and derivations are treated differently by FASTR. Inflections are not really considered as variants since both the rules' constituents and the corpus words are lemmatized by the part-of-speech tagger so the conflation of inflected forms is instantaneous. Conversely, affixing is seen as a genuine variation and needs to be described by metarules. Variations

---

[13] In particular, elision variants, such as *Kerr effect* → *Kerr magnetooptical effect*, have been studied but not retained for the design of FASTR due to their poor extraction results (precision value as low as 34%).

[14] Alternatively, compositions of variations could be implemented through successive application of metarules corresponding to simple variations. This solution has been discarded due to its higher computational cost.

that involve morphological transformations of words are most often morphosyntactic variations, and only rarely pure morphological variations. The reason is that morphologically transformed words usually change their category which deeply modifies the syntactic structure of the whole term. This fact makes it necessary for FASTR to cover non-nominal phrase structures: verbal, adjectival, and adverbial phrases. Since these structures are of a great syntactic diversity, their description calls for an extensive use of regular expressions. The types of morphosyntactic variants retained in FASTR are:

- Noun to adjective variants: *disease of the abdomen → Abdominal disease, sparse data → Data sparseness, error tolerant → Error tolerance.*
- Noun to verb variants: *consolidate those loans → Loan consolidation, estimating gestational age → Age estimation.*
- Adjective to adverb variants: *observed simultaneously → Simultaneous observation, simultaneously obtained measurements → Simultaneous measurement.*
- Noun to noun and adjective to adjective variants: *air ventilation filter → Air filtration, analytic methods → Analytical method.*

As soon as the input terms have been recycled into a grammar of syntactic rules, and the metarules describing adequate syntactic, morphological and semantic variations have been experimentally tuned, such lexicalized grammar can be applied to a tagged corpus. For each sentence in the corpus the set of active grammar rules (term rules) is determined by verifying if the sentence contains all of a rule's lexical items or their morphologically or semantically related words (method inspired by LTAGs [108]). The parsing of the sentence takes place in two steps. In the first step, the input string is matched on the bottom-up basis against the context-free skeleton of each active grammar rule and its *lemma* features, while all other feature equations are ignored. Only if this first matching step succeeds the remaining features are unified. If the unification succeeds the parsed sequence is reported as a valid term occurrence together with a link to the corresponding term. If the unification fails all metarules relevant to the given rule are activated to generate new rules which in turn are applied to the sentence.

This two-step parsing mechanism—context-free parsing and unification—allows to speed-up the parsing considerably because the unification rarely fails when the context-free parsing step succeeds. The parsing efficiency grows even more due to the *lexicalization of the grammar* [66], i.e. the distribution of rules' lexical anchors in such a way that each single word is the anchor of possibly smallest number of rules. The parsing speed is a function of the size of the terminological and transformational data. When indexing a medical corpus with a list of about 72,000 terms and a set of 115 metarules, on a Pentium (300 Mhz), 32 Mbytes main memory running Linux, the average speed is 25,000 words/min. With a 10 times smaller list of terms, the parsing speed is 6 times higher.

6   Term Enrichment in FASTR

Apart from FASTR's primary goal, i.e. controlled indexing, its variant recognition results may also have a secondary utility: term enrichment. Most variants involve more than one term in their construction. At least one of these terms must appear in the controlled vocabulary so that the variant can be recognized by FASTR. Other terms that contribute to the variant may be absent from the controlled vocabulary but they may be spotted relatively easily due to the fact that they are associated with a controlled term. For example, having recognized *uterine and carotid artery* as a variant of *Uterine artery* we may suppose that *carotid artery* is itself a correct although unlisted term.

The case of coordinated binary terms is simple to decompose: given a binary term and its coordinated variant, there is only one possible binary candidate, such as *carotid artery* in the above example. Where ternary terms are coordinated there are two possible candidates, only one of which must be selected. For instance, *inflammatory and erosive joint disease* which is a variant of *Inflammatory joint disease* may yield either a binary candidate *erosive joint* or a ternary one, *erosive joint disease*. An experimental study ([68], pp. 244-246]) shows that the latter choice, i.e. the choice of the longest candidate, is most often the correct one. If the two candidates are of equal length the one which is a continuous substring of the variation is preferable.

The case of a substitution variation is similar to the one of coordination. For instance, *regional cerebral blood flow* which is the variant of *Regional blood flow* yields three candidates: *cerebral blood*, *cerebral flow*, and *cerebral blood flow*. Here again the latter, i.e. the longest, candidate is expected to be the best one.

The analysis of the more complex cases: compositions of substitutions, compositions of coordinations, and compositions of permutations and substitutions is presented in ([68], pp. 246-248).

Once the term candidates have been obtained from the extracted variants, a postprocessing is necessary to produce terminologically valid candidates. For instance, the variant *performance of an expert system* → *System performance* yields the candidate *an expert system* in which the leading determiner needs to be cut off in order to obtain the standard nominal compound structure *expert system*. In addition, candidate terms which already belong to the controlled vocabulary need to be discarded. The retained candidates are ranked according to an association ratio, as well as to a symbolic criterion which advantages the candidates obtained from several variants of different types. For instance, the candidate *bile duct* is produced both from a coordination variant (*pancreatic and bile duct* → *Pancreatic duct*), and from a modification variant (*hepatic bile duct* → *Hepatic duct*), which suggests that it is probably a secure candidate term.

The term enrichment is implemented in FASTR as an incremental process. Acquired candidates may be considered as controlled terms, and given as input to a new step of variant recognition and term enrichment. This processing chain may be reiterated until no new terms are found. This allows to increase the number of acquired terms, as well as to build a conceptual network of terms and candidates. The latter task is realised due to the supposition that terms acquired from coordination variants share a common hypernym with the original term, while those acquired from substitution variants are more specific than the original term.

The term enrichment by FASTR is an original and, relatively to other term acquisition methods, a very reliable way of discovering new terms but has a limited scope because only terms involved in terminological variants can be acquired. The number of such terms is not very high. In the evaluation experiment described in the following section a corpus of 120,000 words and the initial vocabulary of 6,621 terms yielded only 165 new correct term candidates.

Another method of term enrichment using FASTR's output is described in ([68], pp. 228-240). Due to a statistical calculus the extracted substitution variants are filtered in order to retain only those that have the biggest chance to be correct new terms, while the use of statistical measures allows to disambiguate their structure.

7 Results

The quality of term extraction by FASTR has been evaluated in terms of precision (P), recall (R), and precision of fallout (P_F), which is a complementary measure to fallout ($P_F = 1 - F$) and has the advantage that the better are the results the higher is its value, while it is the opposite for fallout. Two different evaluation experiments have been performed for different types of variations. Table 6 presents their summary results.

Table 6. Precision, recall and fallout of the term extraction by FASTR

	Precision P	Recall R	Prec. Fallout P_F
Syntactic variants	94.5%	71%	96.5%
Morphosyntactic variants	46% 74% 80%	58% 70% 58%	73% 76.5% 91%
Semantic variants	91% 78% 55% 29%	not evaluated	not evaluated
Term acquisition	79%		

The evaluation of syntactic and morphosyntactic metarules has been done with a 120.000 word corpus from the metallurgy domain, a list of 6,621 terms in the same domain, and the morphological data from CELEX database containing 160,000 word forms.

While tuning the syntactic metarules, the precision of extraction has been preferred to recall, which is reflected by the experimental results: 94.5% vs. 71%. The syntactic variants proved to be pervasive: they constitute as much as 28% of all term occurrences. The most frequent type of syntactic variation is modification of a binary term.

The qualitative evaluation of the morphosyntactic metarules depends on two factors: whether prefixed words are included in the morphological families (since they most often result in incorrect variants, e.g. *surface interaction* is not a variant of *Surface reaction*), and whether prefixed hyper/hyponyms and antonyms are considered as valid variants (e.g. *magnetic/electromagnetic, dioxide/monoxide*). Each cell of the second line of Table 6 is divided into three parts: the first two parts contain the results in the case when both nonprefixed and prefixed variants are taken into account. In the first part antonyms/hypernyms/hyponyms are considered as incorrect, and in the second part as correct. The third part describes only nonprefixed cases.

The precision of the semantic term extraction has been evaluated for French [67] with a 1.2 million word corpus from the agricultural domain, and two types of semantic data: links from the AGROVOC thesaurus [4] and links from Microsoft Word97 the-saurus. The results for both thesauri are given, respectively, in the first and in the second part of the third line in Table 6. The precision is calculated separately for pure semantic variants (91% and 78%) and for hybrid, i.e. morphosyntactico-semantic variants (55% and 29%).

The evaluation of term enrichment by FASTR was done with the same data as for syntactic variant recognition. The total precision obtained is of 79%. The recall and the fallout were not calculated because the set of all correct terms in a corpus is very difficult to determine.

8   Conclusion

This chapter has presented several tools for term extraction: term acquisition for corpus-based thesaurus construction and term recognition for machine-aided indexing. Most of these studies show a concern for term variant conflation. The weakest approaches correspond to "bags of stems", the most elaborated ones correspond to conceptual analysis and paraphrase detection. FASTR lies somewhere in the middle by combining large scale shallow parsing and systematic variant generation. It offers a reasonable and how-ever efficient means for recognizing and grouping term variants. The kind of conflation performed by FASTR is positively evaluated in a framework of machine-aided indexing [69].

The application has been designed to support extensions to other languages. Cur-rently, French [70], [78], and [71], Spanish and Catalan [130], German, and Japanese [135] have been considered in addition to the English language. But the scope of variant recognition is wider than core automatic indexing. In Section 6 variant deconstruction and variant ranking both serve the purpose of term enrichment. In ([68], chap. 8) it is suggested how variant recognition can also be useful in cross-lingual information re-trieval, document filtering in Web search, or corpus-based morphological acquisition. More elaborated approaches to linguistic normalization such as paraphrase detection can have applications in document summarization, information extraction, and open domain question answering. Since these fields tend to be very active at present, other developments in variation reduction should be expected in the near future.

References

1. A. Abeillé. *Les nouvelles syntaxes. Grammaires d'unification et analyse du franais.* Ar-mand Colin, Paris, 1993.
2. A. Abeillé. Grammaires et analyseurs syntaxiques. In J.-M. Pierrel, editor, *Ingénierie des langues.* Hermes Sciences, Paris, 2000.
3. S. Abney. Partial parsing via finite-state cascade. In *Proceedings, Workshop on Robust Parsing, 8th European Summer Schol in Logic, Language and Information*, pages 8–15, Prague, Czech Republic, 1996.
4. AGROVOC. *AGROVOC - Multilingual Agricultural Thesaurus.* Food and Agricultural Or-ganization of the United Nations, 1995. http://www.fao.org/catalog/Book/products/v9669-e.htm.

5. Jacek Ambroziak and William A. Woods. Natural language technology in precision content retrieval. In *Proceedings, Natural Language Processing and Industrial Applications (NLP+IA'98)*, Moncton, New Brunswick, 1998. University of Moncton.

6. A. Andreewsky, Fathi Debili, and Christian Fluhr. Computational learning of semantic lexical relations for the generation and automatic analysis of content. In *Proceedings, IFIP Congress*, pages 667–73, Toronto, 1977. IFIP.

7. A. T. Arampatzis, C. H. A. Koster, and T. Tsoris. IRENA: Information retrieval engine based on natural language analysis. In *Proceedings, Intelligent Multimedia Information Retrieval Systems and Management (RIAO'97)*, pages 159–75, Montreal, 1997. CID, Paris.

8. A. T. Arampatzis, T. Tsoris, C. H. A. Koster, and Th. P. van der Weide. Phrase-based information retrieval. *Information Processing and Management*, 34(6):693–707, 1998.

9. A. Arppe. Term extraction from unrestricted text. ¡*http://www.lingsoft.fi/doc/nptool/term-extraction.html*¿, 1995.

10. Henk Barkema. Determining the syntactic flexibility of idioms. In Udo Fries, Gunnel Tottie, and Peter Schneider, editors, *Creating and using English language corpora*, pages 39–52. Rodopi, Amsterdam, 1994.

11. Bran K. Boguraev and Karen Sparck Jones. A natural language front end to databases with evaluative feedback. In Bran K. Boguraev and Karen Sparck Jones, editors, *New Applications of Databases*. Academic Press, London, 1984.

12. D. Bourigault and M. Slodzian. Pour une terminologie textuelle. *Terminologies Nouvelles*, 19, 1999.

13. Didier Bourigault. An endogeneous corpus-based method for structural noun phrase disambiguation. In *Proceedings, Sixth Conference of the European Chapter of the Association for Computational Linguistics (EACL'93)*, pages 81–86, Utrecht, 1993. ACL.

14. Didier Bourigault. *LEXTER un Logiciel d'EXtraction de TERminologie. Application à l'extraction des connaissances à partir de textes*. Thèse en mathématiques, informatique appliquée aux sciences de l'homme, École des Hautes Études en Sciences Sociales, Paris, 1994.

15. Didier Bourigault. LEXTER, a Natural Language tool for terminology extraction. In *Proceedings, Seventh EURALEX International Congress*, pages 771–79, Göteborg, 1996. EURALEX.

16. Didier Bourigault and Christian Jacquemin. Term extraction + term clustering: An integrated platform for computer-aided terminology. In *Proceedings, Ninth Conference of the European Chapter of the Association for Computational Linguistics (EACL'99)*, pages 15–22, Bergen, 1999. ACL.

17. J. Bresnan, editor. *The Mental Representation of Grammatical Relations*. MIT Press, Cambridge, MA, 1992.

18. Eric Brill. A simple rule-based part of speech tagger. In *Proceedings, Third Conference on Applied Natural Language Processing (ANLP'92)*, pages 152–55, Trento, 1992. ACL.

19. Peter L. Brown, Vincent J. Della Pietra, Peter V. deSouza, Jennifer C. Lai, and Robert L. Mercer. Class-based *n*-gram models of natural language. *Computational Linguistics*, 18(4):467–79, 1992.

20. Roy J. Byrd, Judith L. Klavans, Mark Aronoff, and Frank Anshen. Computer methods for morphological analysis. In *Proceedings, 24th Annual Meeting of the Association for Computational Linguistics (ACL'86)*, pages 120–27, New York, 1986. ACL.

21. Maria Teresa Cabré Castellví, Rosa Estopà Bagot, and Jordi Vivaldi Palatresi. Automatic term detection: A review of current systems. In Didier Bourigault, Christian Jacquemin, and Marie-Claude L'Homme, editors, *Recent Advances in Computational Terminology*. John Benjamins, Amsterdam, 2001.

22. J.-P. Chanod and P. Tapanainen. Statistical and constraint-based taggers for french. Technical report, Xerox Research Centre Europe, Grenoble, France, 1994.

23. Eugene Charniak. *Statistical Language Learning*. A Bradford Book. MIT Press, Cambridge, 1993.

24. Kuang-Hua Chen and Hsin-Hsi Chen. Extracting noun phrases from large-scale texts: A hybrid approach and its automatic evaluation. In *Proceedings, 32nd Annual Meeting of the Association for Computational Linguistics (ACL'94)*, pages 234–41, Las Cruces, NM, 1994. ACL.

25. Kenneth W. Church and Patrick Hanks. Word association norms, Mutual Information and lexicography. *Computational Linguistics*, 16(1):22–29, 1990.

26. D. Clemenceau. Finite-state morphology: Inflections and derivations in a single framework using dictionaries and rules. In Emmanuel Roche and Yves Schabes, editors, *Finite-State Language Processing*, pages 383–406. MIT Press, Cambridge, MA, 1997.

27. B. Courtois. Un système de dictionnaires électroniques pour les mots simples du franais. *Langue Française*, 87, 1990.

28. J. Daciuk, S. Mihov, B. Watson, and R. Watson. Incremental construction of minimal acyclic finite state automata. *Computational Linguistics*, 26(1):3–16, 2000.

29. Ido Dagan and Kenneth W. Church. *Termight*: Identifying and translating technical terminology. In *Proceedings, Fourth Conference on Applied Natural Language Processing (ANLP'94)*, pages 34–40, Stuttgart, 1994. ACL.

30. Béatrice Daille. *Approche mixte pour l'extraction de terminologie : Statistique lexicale et filtres linguistiques*. Thèse en informatique fondamentale, Université de Paris 7, Paris, 1994.

31. Béatrice Daille. Study and implementation of combined techniques for automatic extraction of terminology. In Judith L. Klavans and Philip Resnik, editors, *The Balancing Act: Combining Symbolic and Statistical Approaches to Language*, pages 49–66. MIT Press, Cambridge, 1996.

32. Georgette Dal, Nabil Hathout, and Fiammetta Namer. Construire un lexique dérivationnel: Théorie et réalisations. In *Proceedings, Conférence de Traitement Automatique du Langage Naturel (TALN'99)*, pages 115–24, Cargèse, 1999. ATALA, Paris.

33. Sophie David and Pierre Plante. De la nécessité d'une approche morpho-syntaxique dans l'analyse de textes. *Intelligence Artificielle et Sciences Cognitives au Québec*, 3(3):140–54, 1990.

34. Sophie David and Pierre Plante. Le progiciel TERMINO : de la nécessité d'une analyse morphosyntaxique pour le dépouillement terminologique des textes. In *Colloque International sur les Industries de la Langue: Perspectives des Années 1990*, pages 71–88, Montréal, 1990. Office de la Langue Fran caise et Société des Traducteurs du Quebec.

35. Fathi Debili. *Analyse syntaxico-sémantique fondée sur une acquisition automatique de relations lexicales-sémantiques*. Thèse de doctorat d'état en sciences informatiques, University of Paris 11, Orsay, 1982.

36. Lee R. Dice. Measures of the amount of ecologic association between species. *Journal of Ecology*, 26:297–302, 1945.

37. Martin Dillon and Ann S. Gray. FASIT: A fully automatic syntactically based indexing system. *Journal of the American Society for Information Science*, 34(2):99–108, 1983.

38. Ted Dunning. Accurate methods for the statistics of surprise and coincidence. *Computational Linguistics*, 19(1):61–74, 1993.

39. Chantal Enguehard and Laurent Pantera. Automatic natural acquisition of a terminology. *Journal of Quantitative Linguistics*, 2(1):27–32, 1995.

40. David A. Evans, Kimberly Ginther-Webster, Mary Hart, Robert G. Lefferts, and Ira A. Monarch. Automatic indexing using selective NLP and first-order thesauri. In *Proceedings, Intelligent Multimedia Information Retrieval Systems and Management (RIAO'91)*, pages 624–43, Barcelona, 1991. CID, Paris.

41. David A. Evans and Chengxiang Zhai. Noun-phrase analysis in unrestricted text for information retrieval. In *Proceedings, 34th Annual Meeting of the Association for Computational Linguistics (ACL'96)*, pages 17–24, Santa Cruz, 1996. ACL.

42. Joel L. Fagan. Automatic phrase indexing for document retrieval: An examination of syntactic and non-syntactic methods. In *Proceedings, Tenth Annual International ACM SIGIR Conference on Research and Development in Information Retrieval (SIGIR'87)*, pages 91–101. ACM, 1987.

43. Robert M. Fano. *Transmission of Information: A Statistical Theory of Communications.* MIT Press, Cambridge, 1961.

44. Katerina T. Frantzi and Sophia Ananiadou. Retrieving collocations by co-occurrences and word order constraints. In *Proceedings, 16th International Conference on Computational Linguistics (COLING'96)*, pages 41–46, Copenhagen, 1996. ACL.

45. Karen A. Frenkel. The human genome project and informatics. *Communications of the ACM*, 34(11):41–51, 1991.

46. N. Friburger and D. Maurel. Finite-state transducer cascade to extract proper nouns in texts. In *Proceedings, 6th Conference on Implementations and Applications of Automata*, pages 97–106, Pretoria, South Africa, 2001.

47. Pascale Fung. *Using Word Signature Features for Terminology Translation from Large Corpora.* PhD dissertation, Graduate School of Arts and Science, Columbia University, New York, 1997.

48. T. Gaál. Is this finite-state transducer sequentiable? In *Proceedings, 6th Conference on Implementations and Applications of Automata*, pages 107–115, Pretoria, South Africa, 2001.

49. Éric Gaussier. Flow network models for word alignment and terminology extraction from bilingual corpora. In *Proceedings, 36th Annual Meeting of the Association for Computational Linguistics and 17th International Conference on Computational Linguistics (COLING-ACL'98)*, pages 444–50, Montreal, 1998. ACL.

50. Gerald Gazdar, Ewan Klein, Geoffrey K. Pullum, and Ivan A. Sag. *Generalized Phrase Structure Grammar.* Harvard University Press, Cambridge, 1985.

51. Julio Gonzalo, Anselmo Peñas, and Felisa Verdejo. Lexical ambiguity and information retrieval revisited. In *Proceedings, Joint SIGDAT Conference on Empirical Methods in Natural Language Processing and Very Large Corpora (EMNLP/VLC'99)*, pages 195–203, University of Maryland, CollegePark, 1999. ACL.

52. D. Gouadec, editor. *Terminologie et Phraséologie pour Traduire - Le concordancier du Traducteur.* La Maison du Dictionnaire, Paris, 1997.

53. Gaston Gross. Degré de figement des noms composés. *Langages*, 90:57–72, 1988.

54. Maurice Gross. *Grammaire transformationnelle du français, 2: Syntaxe du nom.* Systématique de la langue française. Cantilène, Paris, 1986.

55. Louis Guilbert. *La formation du vocabulaire de l'aviation.* Larousse, Paris, 1965.

56. Benoît Habert. *OLMES*: a versatile and extensible parser in CLOS. In *Proceedings, Fourth International Conference on Technology of Object-Oriented Languages and Systems (TOOLS'91)*, pages 149–60, Paris, 1991. Prentice-Hall, Englewood Cliffs, NJ.

57. Benoît Habert and Christian Jacquemin. Noms composés, termes, dénominations complexes : Problématiques linguistiques et traitements automatiques. *Traitement automatique des langues*, 34(2):5–42, 1993.

58. Patrick A. Hall and Geoff R. Dowling. Approximate string matching. *Computing Surveys*, 12(4):381–402, 1980.

59. Thierry Hamon, Adeline Nazarenko, and Cécile Gros. A step towards the detection of semantic variants of terms in technical documents. In *Proceedings, 36th Annual Meeting of the Association for Computational Linguistics and 17th International Conference on Computational Linguistics (COLING-ACL'98)*, pages 498–504, Montreal, 1998. ACL.

60. Zellig S. Harris. *Mathematical Structure of Language*. John Wiley, New York, 1968.
61. G. E. Heidorn. Augmented phrase structure grammars. In R. Schank and B. L. Nash-Webber, editors, *Theoretical Issues in Natural Language Processing: An Interdisciplinary Workshop in Computational Linguistics, Psychology, Linguistics, and Artificial Intelligence.*, pages 10–13. Lawrence Erlbaum Associates, Hillsdale, NJ, 1975.
62. Jerry R. Hobbs, Douglas Appelt, John Bear, David Israel, Megumi Kameyama, Mark Stickel, and Mabry Tyson. FASTUS: A cascaded finite-state transducer for extracting information from natural-language text. In Emmanuel Roche and Yves Schabes, editors, *Finite-State Language Processing*, pages 383–406. MIT Press, Cambridge, 1997.
63. John E. Hopcroft. An $nlogn$ algorithm for minimizing the states of in a finite automaton. In Z. Kohavi and A. Paz, editors, *The Theory of Machines and Computations*, pages 189–96. Academic Press, New York, 1971.
64. John E. Hopcroft and Jeffrey D. Ullman. *Introduction to Automata Theory, Languages, and Computation*. Addison-Wesley, Reading, 1979.
65. Satoru Ikehara, Satoshi Shirai, and Hajime Uchino. A statistical method for extracting uninterrupted and interrupted collocations from very large corpora. In *Proceedings, 16th International Conference on Computational Linguistics (COLING'96)*, pages 574–79, Copenhagen, 1996. ACL.
66. Christian Jacquemin. Optimizing the computational lexicalization of large grammars. In *Proceedings, 32nd Annual Meeting of the Association for Computational Linguistics (ACL'94)*, pages 196–203, Las Cruces, NM, 1994. ACL.
67. Christian Jacquemin. Syntagmatic and paradigmatic representations of term variation. In *Proceedings, 37th Annual Meeting of the Association for Computational Linguistics (ACL'99)*, pages 341–48, University of Maryland, CollegePark, 1999. ACL.
68. Christian Jacquemin. *Spotting and Discovering Terms through NLP*. MIT Press, Cambridge, MA, 2001.
69. Christian Jacquemin, Béatrice Daille, Jean Royauté, and Xavier Polanco. In vitro evaluation of a program for machine-aided indexing. *Information Processing and Management*, 2001. forthcoming.
70. Christian Jacquemin, Judith L. Klavans, and Evelyne Tzoukermann. Expansion of multi-word terms for indexing and retrieval using morphology and syntax. In *Proceedings, 35th Annual Meeting of the Association for Computational Linguistics and Eighth Conference of the European Chapter of the Association for Computational Linguistics (ACL-EACL'97)*, pages 24–31, Madrid., 1997. ACL.
71. Christian Jacquemin and Evelyne Tzoukermann. NLP for term variant extraction: A synergy of morphology, lexicon, and syntax. In Tomek Strzalkowski, editor, *Natural Language Information Retrieval*, pages 25–74. Kluwer Academic Publisher, Boston, 1999.
72. Aravind K. Joshi. An introduction to Tree Adjoining Grammars. In Alexis Manaster-Ramer, editor, *Mathematics of Language*, pages 87–115. John Benjamins, Amsterdam, 1987.
73. John S. Justeson and Slava M. Katz. Technical terminology: some linguistic properties and an algorithm for identification in text. *Natural Language Engineering*, 1(1):9–27, 1995.
74. R. Kaplan and M. Kay. Regular models of phonological rule systems. *Computational Linguistics*, 20(3), 1994.
75. Fred Karlsson, Atro Voutilainen, Juha Heikkilä, and Arto Anttila, editors. *Constraint Grammar A Language-Independent System for Parsing Unrestricted Text*. Mouton de Gruyter, Berlin, 1995.
76. M. Kay. Algorithm schemata and data structures in syntactic processing. In *Proceedings, Nobel Symposium on Text Processing*, pages 35–70, Gotheborg, Danemark, 1980. reprint in Grosz, B., Sparck Jones, K., Webber, B. (eds.) *Readings in Natural Language Processing*, Morgan Kaufman.

77. E. M. Keen. On the generation and searching of entries is printed subject indexes. *Journal of Documentation*, 33(1):15–45, 1977.

78. Judith L. Klavans, Christian Jacquemin, and Evelyne Tzoukermann. A natural language approach to multi-word term conflation. In *DELOS Workshop on Cross-Language Information retireval*, ETHZ, Zurich, Switzerland, 1997. ERCIM: European Consortium for Informatics and Mathematics.

79. Judith L. Klavans and Philip Resnik, editors. *The Balancing Act: Combining Symbolic and Statistical Approaches to Language*. MIT Press, Cambridge, 1996.

80. A. Kornai. *Extended Finite State Models of Language*. Cambridge University Press, Cambridge, UK, 1999.

81. Kimmo Koskenniemi. *Two-Level Morphology: A General Computational Model for Word-Form Recognition and Production*. PhD dissertation, University of Helsinki, Helsinki, 1983.

82. E Laporte. Rational transductions for phonetic conversion and phonology. In Emmanuel Roche and Yves Schabes, editors, *Finite-State Language Processing*. MIT Press, Cambridge, 1997.

83. E. Laporte and A. Monceaux. Elimination of lexical ambiguities by grammars: the *ELAG* system. *Linguisticae Investigationes*, 22, 1998. John Benjamins Publishing Company.

84. Andy Lauriston. Automatic recognition of complex terms: Problems and the TERMINO solution. *Terminology*, 1(1):147–70, 1994.

85. Judith Beth Lovins. Development of a stemming algorithm. *Translation and Computational Linguistics*, 11(1):22–31, 1968.

86. Michel Mathieu-Colas. Orthographe et informatique: Établissement d'un dictionnaire électronique des variantes graphiques. *Langue Française*, 87:104–11, 1990.

87. B. Melishar and J. Skryja. On the size of deterministic finite automata. In *Proceedings, 6th Conference on Implementations and Applications of Automata*, pages 203–216, Pretoria, South Africa, 2001.

88. Douglas P. Metzler and Stephanie W. Haas. The Constituent Object Parser: Syntactic structure matching for Information Retrieval. *ACM Transactions on Information Systems*, 7(3):292–316, 1989.

89. Douglas P. Metzler, Stephanie W. Haas, Cynthia L. Cosic, and Charlotte A. Weise. Conjunction ellipsis, and other discontinuous constituents in the Constituent Object Parser. *Information Processing and Management*, 26(1):53–71, 1990.

90. Douglas P. Metzler, Stephanie W. Haas, Cynthia L. Cosic, and Leslie H. Wheeler. Constituent Object Parsing for Information Retrieval and similar text processing problems. *Journal of the American Society for Information Science*, 40(6):398–423, 1989.

91. Mandar Mitra, Chris Buckley, Amit Singhal, and Claire Cardie. An analysis of statistical and syntactic phrases. In *Proceedings, Intelligent Multimedia Information Retrieval Systems and Management (RIAO'97)*, pages 200–14, Montreal, 1997. CID, Paris.

92. Mehryar Mohri. Compact representations by finite-state transducers. In *Proceedings, 32nd Annual Meeting of the Association for Computational Linguistics (ACL'94)*, pages 204–08, Las Cruces, NM, 1994. ACL.

93. A. Monceaux. Le dictionnaire des mots simples anglais: mots nouveaux et variantes orthographiques. Sèrie Informes IGM 95-15, Institut Gaspard Monge, Université de Marne-la-Vallée, Noisy-le-Grand, France, 1995.

94. K. Oflazer. Error-tolerant finite-state recognition with applications to morphological analysis and spelling correction. *Computational Linguistics*, 22(1):73–89, 1996.

95. Carl Pollard and Ivan A. Sag. *Information-Based Syntax and Semantics. Volume 1: Fundamentals*. CSLI Lecture Notes vol. 13. Chicago University Press, Chicago, 1987.

96. M. F. Porter. An algorithm for suffix stripping. *Program*, 14:130–37, 1980.

97. E. Roche. Parsing with finite state transducers. In Emmanuel Roche and Yves Schabes, editors, *Finite-State Language Processing*. MIT Press, Cambridge, MA, 1997.

98. Emmanuel Roche and Yves Schabes. Deterministic part-of-speech tagging with finite-state transducers. In Emmanuel Roche and Yves Schabes, editors, *Finite-State Language Processing*, pages 205–40. MIT Press, Cambridge, 1997.

99. Juan C. Sager. *A Practical Course in Terminology Processing*. John Benjamins, Amsterdam, 1990.

100. Naomi Sager. *Natural Language Information Processing : A Computer Grammar of English and Its Applications*. Addison-Wesley, Reading, 1981.

101. Gerard Salton. *Automatic Text Processing : The Transformation, Analysis and Retrieval of Information by Computer*. Addison-Wesley, Reading, 1989.

102. Gerard Salton and Michael E. Lesk. Computer evaluation og indexing and text processing. *Journal of the Association for Computational Machinery*, 15(1):8–36, 1968.

103. Gerard Salton and Michael J. McGill. *Introduction to Modern Information Retrieval*. McGraw-Hill, New York, 1983.

104. Gerard Salton, C. S. Yang, and C. T. Yu. A theory of term importance in automatic text analysis. *Journal of the American Society for Information Science*, 26(1):33–44, 1975.

105. A Savary. *Recensement et description des mots composés — méthodes et applications*. Thèse de doctorat, Université de Marne-la-Vallée, Noisy-le-Grand, France, 2000.

106. A. Savary. Etude comparativee de deux outils d'acquisition de termes complexes. In *Proceedings, Conference Terminologie et Intelligence Artificielle (TIA-2001)*, INIST-CNRS, Nancy, 2001.

107. Yves Schabes, Anne Abeillé, and Aravind Joshi. Parsing strategies with 'lexicalized' grammars. In *Proceedings, 12th International Conference on Computational Linguistics (COLING'88)*, pages 578–83, Budapest, 1988. ACL.

108. Yves Schabes and Aravind K. Joshi. Parsing with Lexicalized Tree Adjoining Grammar. In Masaru Tomita, editor, *Current Issues in Parsing Technologies*. Kluwer Academic Publisher, Boston, 1990.

109. Christoph Schwarz. Content-based text handling. *Information Processing and Management*, 26(2):219–26, 1989.

110. Christoph Schwarz. Automatic syntactic analysis of free text. *Journal of the American Society for Information Science*, 41(6):408–17, 1990.

111. Paraic Sheridan and Alan F Smeaton. The application of morpho-syntactic language processing to effective phrase matching. *Information Processing and Management*, 28(3):349–69, 1992.

112. Stuart M. Shieber. *An Introduction to Unification-Based Approaches to Grammar*. CSLI Lecture Notes vol. 4. Chicago University Press, Chicago, 1986.

113. Sayori Shimohata, Toshiyuki Sugio, and Junji Nagata. Retrieving collocations by co-occurrences and word order constraints. In *Proceedings, 35th Annual Meeting of the Association for Computational Linguistics and Eighth Conference of the European Chapter of the Association for Computational Linguistics (ACL-EACL'97)*, pages 476–81, Madrid, 1997. ACL.

114. Max Silberztein. *Dictionnaires électroniques et analyse automatique de textes : Le système INTEX*. Masson, Paris, 1993.

115. Frank Smadja. Xtract : An overview. *Computer and the Humanities*, 26:399–413, 1993.

116. Frank Smadja, Kathy R. McKeown, and Vasileios Hatzivassiloglou. Translating collocations for bilingual lexicons: A statistical approach. *Computational Linguistics*, 22(1):1–38, 1996.

117. Alan F. Smeaton and Paraic Sheridan. Using morpho-syntactic language analysis in phrase matching. In *Proceedings, Intelligent Multimedia Information Retrieval Systems and Management (RIAO'91)*, pages 415–29, Barcelona, 1991. CID, Paris.

118. Karen Sparck Jones and John I. Tait. Automatic search term variant generation. *Journal of Documentation*, 40(1):50–66, 1984.
119. Karen Sparck Jones and John I. Tait. Linguistically motivated descriptive term selection. In *Proceedings, Tenth International Conference on Computational Linguistics (COLING'84)*, pages 287–90, Stanford, 1984. ACL.
120. B. Srinivas, D. Egedi, C. Doran, and Tilman Becker. Lexicalization and grammar development. In *Proceedings, KONVENS'94*, pages 310–19, Vienna, 1994. ÖGAI.
121. Tomek Strzalkowski. Robust text processing in automatic information retrieval. In *Proceedings, Fourth Conference on Applied Natural Language Processing (ANLP'94)*, pages 168–73, Stuttgart, 1994. ACL.
122. Tomek Strzalkowski. Natural language information retrieval. *Information Processing and Management*, 31(3):397–417, 1995.
123. Tomek Strzalkowski and Peter G. N. Scheyen. Evaluation of the Tagged Text Parser. In Harald Bunt and Masaru Tomita, editors, *Recent Advances in Parsing Technology*, pages 201–20. Kluwer Academic Publisher, Boston, 1996.
124. Tomek Strzalkowski and Barbara Vauthey. Information retrieval using robust natural language processing. In *Proceedings, 20th Annual Meeting of the Association for Computational Linguistics (ACL'92)*, pages 104–11, Newark, DE, 1992. ACL.
125. T. T. Tanimoto. An elementary mathematical theory of classification. Technical report, IBM, 1958.
126. Évelyne Tzoukermann and Mark Liberman. A finite-state processor for Spanish. In *Proceedings, 13th International Conference on Computational Linguistics (COLING'90)*, Helsinki, 1990. ACL.
127. UMLS. *Unified Medical Language System, UMLS Knowledge Source*. National Library of Medicine, sixth experimental edition, 1995. http://www.nlm.nih.gov/research/umls-/UMLSDOC.HTML.
128. Pim Van der Eijk. Automating the acquisition of bilingual terminology. In *Proceedings, Sixth Conference of the European Chapter of the Association for Computational Linguistics (EACL'93)*, pages 113–19, Utrecht, 1993. ACL.
129. J. Véronis and Ph. Langlais. Evaluation of parallel text alignement systems: Arcade. In J. Véronis, editor, *Parallel Text Processing*. Kluwer Academic Publisher, Dordrecht, 2000.
130. Jorge Vivaldi Palatresi. *Extracción de candidatos a término mediante combinación de estrategias heterogéneas*. Tesi doctoral, Universitat Politécnica de Catalunya, Barcelona, Spain, 2001.
131. Atro Voutilainen. *NPtool*, A detector of English noun phrases. In *Proceedings, Workshop on Very Large Corpora : Academic and Industrial Perspectives*, pages 48–57, Columbus, Ohio, 1993. ACL.
132. Robert A. Wagner and Michael J. Fisher. The string-to-string correction problem. *Journal of the Association for Computational Machinery*, 21(1):168–73, 1974.
133. B. Watson. *Taxonomies and Toolkits of Regular Language Algorithms*. PhD. Thesis, University of Technology, Eindhoven, the Netherlands, 1995.
134. William A. Woods. Conceptual indexing : A better way to organize knowledge. Technical Report SMLI TR-97-61, Sun Microsystems Laboratories, Mountain View, 1997.
135. Fuyuki Yoshikane, Keita Tsuji, Kyo Kageura, and Christian Jacquemin. Detecting japanese term variation in textual corpus. In *Proceedings, Fourth International Workshop on Information Retrieval with Asian Languages (IRAL'99)*, pages 97–108, Academia Sinica, Taipei, Taiwan, 1998.
136. Chengxiang Zhai. Fast statistical parsing of noun phrases for document indexing. In *Proceedings, Fifth Conference on Applied Natural Language Processing (ANLP'97)*, pages 312–19, Washington, DC, 1997. ACL.

Open Research Questions for Linguistics in Information Access

Jussi Karlgren

Swedish Institute of Computer Science
Box 1263, SE 164 29 Kista
Sweden
jussi@sics.se

Abstract. Information access systems based on standard mechanisms can be improved. Not because of any obvious drawbacks in the mechanisms themselves: they provide consistent and stable results, with variation from system to system surprisingly small; the reason to continue work is that the stable results are not only consistent but consistently mediocre. This paper claims linguistic research has a important role to play in the future of information access.

1 A Role for Linguistics

Why would linguists be interested in information access as an application area and an inspiration for research? And why would information access system developers need linguistics to improve their systems?

Accessing information is a primarily linguistic activity, and the documents available for retrieval in information access systems of today are for the most part texts. Linguists know about texts, and should know about discourse and dialog. It should not be difficult to figure out how information access research should need linguists.

On the other hand, linguists and linguistics should be able to make good use of the experience of designing and deploying information access systems. Furthermore, the application of statistics on large bodies of language data itself is a form of study of language. The information found is not in an explicit form, but if a result from practical systems is that two content words within a four word span from each other tend to form content-bearing associations where longer spans do not, this in itself ought to be interesting for the study of language. Finding generalizable topical clusters of documents irrespective of the language they are written in ought to be interesting for the study of language in itself. If retrieval of admittedly shoddy output from speech recognition systems works on average as well as retrieval of carefully proof-read texts this ought to be interesting in itself for the study of language. But results such as these are not appreciated by linguists or information scientists, for other than motivation for engineering efforts.

1.1 The Standard Model for Information Retrieval

The standard model for information retrieval is roughly as shown in figure 1. There is a body of texts; information requests are put to a system which handles this body

S. Renals, G. Grefenstette (Eds.): Text- and Speech-Triggered Info. Access, LNAI 2705, pp. 182-191, 2003.

of texts; the texts are analysed by some form of analysis procedure to yield a non-textual representation of the same; the information requests are likewise analysed by an identical or similar procedure to yield a query. The two representations are then matched. The texts with the best matches are presented as potential information sources to fulfil the request.

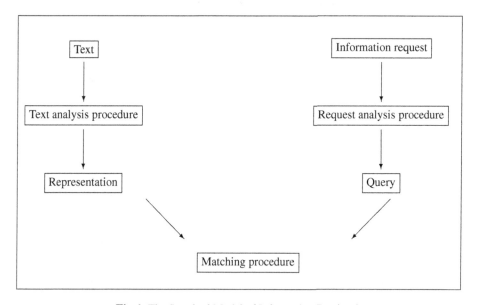

Fig. 1. The Standard Model of Information Retrieval.

The point of the analysis operations is typically taken to be (a) to reduce the amount of information in order to make the representations manageable—and the noise caused by language and the freedom human languages afford their users are crucially important to reduce to that end—and (b) straighten out the vagueness and indeterminacy inherent in natural language in order to facilitate matching. The representations are in some way assumed to be a-linguistic and amenable to pure formal manipulation.

This quite intuitive and in many ways appealing model hides the complexity of human language use from the matching procedure, which can then be addressed using formal methods. This is not entirely to the benefit of the enterprise. The very same mechanisms which make the matching complicated—the vagueness and indeterminacy of human language—are what makes human language work well as a communicative tool; awareness of this is typically abstracted out of the search process. The major difference between using an automated information-retrieval system and consulting with a human information analyst is that the latter normally does not require the request to be transformed to some invariant and unambiguous representation; neither does the human analyst require the documents to be analyzed into such an representation. A human analyst not only copes with but utilizes the flexibility of information in human language:

it is not an obstacle but a feature. For non-trivial retrieval as performed by humans, concepts glide into each other painlessly and with no damage done to the knowledge representation they utilize, and documents that have previously been thought to be of some specific type or topic can be retrieved for perfectly unexpected and new purposes.

2   What Is a Document? — Two Views

Information retrieval systems view documents as carriers of topical information, and hold words and terms as reasonable indicators of topic. The techniques used for analysis and and organization of document collections are primarily focused on word and term occurrence statistics. Non-textual documents must be addressed in a different but analogous way.

Linguists believe linguistic expressions are composed of words which form clauses which in turn form text or discourse. Words have predictable, situation-, speaker- and topic-independent form and structure which can be described formally. Clauses have largely predictable, situation-, speaker- and topic-independent structure which can be described formally. Texts have largely unpredictable situation-, speaker-, and topic-*dependent* structure, which cannot be described formally. Not with the same type of formalisms. Non-textual documents are typically not interesting.

Given that linguistics focuses on the theory of clause structure, and information retrieval on appearance of words and texts, the lack of contact between the fields may not be entirely surprising.

> "What is needed is a theory of language which makes it possible to make fairly gross statements about large units of text, and this is a matter on which linguistics has had very little to say." [3],

But an optimistic later quote by Karen Sparck Jones och Martin Kay seems to indicate that some progress is being made to broach the divide:

> "We take heart particularly from two facts: first, linguists are turning their attention more and more to larger units of discourse than the sentence, and second, on-line retrieval systems are likely to involve retrievable units smaller than traditional documents. We believe that the relevance of these fields to one another will become more apparent as the size of the text units they deal with becomes more commensurable." [4].

Research on larger units of language use such as texts, dialogs or discourse in general has not succeeded in providing generalizable results. The goal is less concrete: texts are not regular in the sense sentences are, and when formalization is attempted, it only succeeds in prototypical cases. Still, there is reason for optimism. With large amounts of texts available for automatic analysis of texts, linguists can test, discard, verify, and refine methods for large-scale analysis with the same efficiency clause-level analysis was performed earlier.

3 Linguistic Methods in Information Retrieval

But so far, relatively few results have been evident. Morphological analysis is used both for variant conflation and compound term analysis. Syntactic analysis of entire sentences for the purpose of matching analyses to analyses of information requests have been experimented with for a long time [15, e.g.], [16], and syntactic analysis is used to generalize over relations between entities in the text, to cluster term variants (cf. Figure 2) — but this latter sort of relation can, at least for English, be captured almost as well by extracting content terms within some short distance from each other.

Content analysis Analysis of content Systems that analyze content ... When content is being analyzed ...	analysis+content

Fig. 2. Example of normalization of syntactic variants of multi-word terms.

So what is wrong with syntactic analysis? Why does it not help? Apparently structure on a clausal level is insufficient to clearly improve word based indexing schemes, and to back this up, there is some psycholinguistic evidence that the surface appearance of clauses is promptly forgotten after the clause has been analyzed and internalized.

The implicit semantic models in today's systems are based on single word occurrence and, occasionally, cooccurrence between words. This takes us a bit of the way, but not far enough for us to claim we have text understanding within reach. Words are besides vague both polysemous and incomplete: every word means several things and every thing can be expressed with any one of several words.

Semantic models for information access work either with lexical resources or knowledge bases or ontological networks of some sort; some schemes such as Latent Semantic Analysis [12], [1], Hyperspace Analogue of Language, and Random Indexing [7], work with clustering words based on occurrence patterns, and thus have a semantic model based on term occurrence, but on a higher level of abstraction. The lexically based models are brittle and do not age well, and share with the statistically based models the limitation that they model relatively atomic units of meaning, or senses — not relations, dependencies, actions or events: the stuff whereof discourse is made.

We need far better semantic models: better in the sense that they model language *use* rather than Language in the abstract. We need a better understanding of how meaning is negotiated in human language usage: fixed representations do not seem practical, and do not reflect observed human language usage. We need more exact study of inexact expression, of the *homeosemy*, (homeo- from Greek *homoios* similar) or near and close synonymy of expressions of human language [8]. This means we need to understand the temporality, saliency, and topicality of terms, relations, and grammatical elements — it means modeling the life cycle of terms in language, the life cycle of referents in discourse, and the connection between the two.

4   Multilinguality

Multi-lingual retrieval needs to be explored, for the obvious reason that interesting material may be available in the wrong language. Equally crucially, multi-lingual retrieval may improve retrieval in general by clearing the decks from the linguistic bias of results so far.

A strong case for continuing experiments on indexing schemes even in the face of the reasonably stable results obtained to date, is the fact that no substantive research has been performed on other than English text. English is a typologically special language in that it relies more on word order than on inflection than most other languages; this can be expected both to decrease the value of normalization through morphological analysis and the utility of linear precedence based statistical metrics. If we can expect words to appear adjacently in a predictable order with minimal variation from occurrence to occurrence, the systems we build will be very different than if we assume there are long range dependencies between haphazardly appearing words marked with agreement features.

5   How Textuality Could Be Utilized Better

Texts do have structure — that much is evident. So far, little of this structure has been used explicitly for information retrieval. There are numbers of experiments that wait to be performed: if a text can be structured by some means, and its components indexed separately, such a composite index might well provide a richer picture of text topic than a simple list. Clause weighting approaches, topic-focus detection, foreground-background clause identification, summarization, and subtopic segmentation are all techniques available for experimentation: these show promise to perform differently from the single word and multi-word term frequency based indexing schemes detailed in the previous section.

Understanding more of why texts are texts rather than word containers, and why texts in important ways are more like pictures than dictionaries will give more depth to text analysis. The objective is some level of topical or semantic analysis, and from the discussion above and in the introduction, it seems abundantly clear this should be performed in interaction with the intended reader of the text. The reader or user is not a single one-shot question submission module — the user is accessing text for some reason, and this reason is not irrelevant for information retrieval purposes.

However, studying topical progression in a text is complex. Local effects — the distinction between given and new information in a clause, say — have been studied and partially formally described, but not robustly enough to be useful for predictive work, which is what information retrieval requires. "It is not easy to identify the topic and focus of a printed sentence, especially in such a language as English, where the surface word order is grammatically bound to a great extent." [14] And later experiments cover — by author admission — prototypical cases only. [2] There is a systematic problem in automatic text analysis in that text in itself is an entire semantic object, and has transcended much of the syntactically governed constraints that clause structure adheres to: surface cues give us only incidental traces of semantic linking of text. [5, e.g.], [6]

But it is clear that human understanding of text hinges crucially on *expectations* and *hypotheses* on the part of the reader as well as the data itself as encoded in the text. It is not the structure of the text alone but of the *story* that leads readers right. And we need to ask readers about it to learn more.

Beyond finding texts, information may need to be composed from events and facts from databases, unorganized data or as produced by text analysis tools of various kinds. Building a legible, understandable, and hopefully enjoyable text from unorganized data is not only impossible for computers today but difficult for people. The conventions we use to organize an incoherent whole into an enjoyable story are difficult to master (and people who do so are deservedly held in high esteem) but do have a clear reality for readers. The narrative form of discourse is fundamental to human cognition and communication and can be found in all aspects of life from learned factual reporting to folklore. Language itself is organized as tool for narration in linear sequence. Stories arrange information in a way that arguably is most easily accessible to humans, with a beginning, a resolution and steps in between comprised of informational as well as emotional progression communicated through focus, emphasis, linear structure, non-linear references, and often mediated through emotionally charged characters. This structure is non-trivial and possibly impossible to describe generally and difficult at best to select, identify, and use specifically. But we should try. And we as linguists do not — who will?

6   Other Properties of Texts

Further, texts have many kinds of properties besides being topical. Texts can be characterized, described and categorized in numerous ways. None of the criteria are independent of each other; some of them are weak and unreliable; all are not applicable to all items. Texts can be vague, abstract, legal, discussions, monologues, illustrated, difficult, short, repetitive, lucid, persuasive, focused, ungrammatical, schizophrenic, annoying, newsprint, offensive, obsolete, trendy — and so forth. Many of these types of stylistic or genre characteristics are salient for readers, and *could* be used in retrieval contexts.[10, e.g.], [9]

And when further modalities come into play, a more general view must be taken. For instance, experiments with audio database indexing involve not only a textual representation of the spoken data, but type of speech: dialog, monolog, etc. [11], [13] Whatever dimensions of variation can be accepted as valid for an area or a set of texts, it is clear that a mono-modal text representation — whatever it is, and however well it is designed — simply will not be able to capture more than very simple characteristics of a text, and thus will ultimately constrain the utility of the matching functionality.

7   Reading — and Who Is the Reader?

Given the variation in different types of knowledge about text, we understand that texts give many each in themselves weak signals to the reader. Still the reader judges texts quickly and efficiently. What is the connection between text and reading experience?

What clues can we as system designers find and utilize? How can we merge several weak knowledge sources to make simple polar or near-polar judgments?

But the decisions made by users — even if they boil down to a polar "will read" or "won't read" are made by way of judgments on a relatively high level of abstraction. A reader will judge a text according to its authenticity, its suitability, its quality, as perceived.

We must formalize the subjective aspects of text categorization. And in practice, for system design, we need to investigate how to create and make use of several different indexing methods simultaneously.

And to understand reading better, we must have a way of understanding readers and users better. We cannot discuss reading in the abstract. In fact, general designs are likely not to be useful in building usable systems: tailoring systems to a specific set of goals will probably be better. But to get here we need to systematize the acquisition of knowledge about users, tasks, and goals. Readers come in many shapes, but they are not likely to be haphazard or disorganized. We will be able to understand trends and typical cases if we try.

8   Interaction Between Human and System

With the recent introduction of new types of computing and new categories of user population it is time to reexamine some of the basic assumptions of interactive information access system design. Most systems so far have been built for goal-oriented computational tasks in a workplace setting. The result of the interaction has been delivered in as timely a manner as the system is able to. The evaluation of the system has been made by efficiency in terms of time and system capacity. Typically the user is made to work with single users. The interaction models have been assumed to be general and useful in any of several envisioned situations and user populations. The introduction of the information access system in whatever task environment it has been envisioned for (if any) has been viewed as a productivity or quality raising measure with no further ramifications for the task and user.

8.1   New Types of Interaction

Many of these assumptions bread down when we deal with mobile interaction, with ubiquitous computing systems, with systems built to be sensitive to social context, situation, physical location, and emotional and affective factors in interaction.

Computers have originally been built to sit in office environments, with text entry and review of tabular data as main interactive activities. Systems have fixed screens, fixed key keyboards and pointer devices, and invest most of user focus on the visual channel. These limitations are neither necessary nor desirable as the computer as a system moves from the desktop to the ... wherever. We are ready to make real use of other modalities of interaction and other physical manifestations of interaction points with information processing.

We want to be able to allow readers access to the information services and sources they are prone to use independently of physical location but sensitive to situation. We want to allow readers to create, access, maintain, and share information services with other readers in the digital world much as they would in the physical. This will change many of the basic tenets today's systems are designed for.

Without an office environment with files, folders, shelves, and paper clips our understanding has changed of what it means to organize, store, and retrieve useful information in a timely manner. The concept of relevance cannot be divorced from the situation the information will be used in: building information access devices to deliver information correctly and tailoring information sources to provide the conversationally correct type and amount of relevant information must be well founded in the where and why.

8.2 Relevance Is a Function of Situation

Stepping away from the task-oriented design for computer systems, we find that computer systems are not solely used for atomic one-shot computational problems. Computers are used in situations that extend over time and across the entire spectrum of what it means to be human. Systems are being used for purposes that are hard to describe in terms of quantifiable performance metrics; as machinery in situations less vectored towards efficiency and more towards emotional fulfilment of the user. Building systems for fun, for expressivity and for protracted interaction will require new design principles and a new understanding of how interaction can be evaluated.

Whatever the application, the situation, the user population, or the intended use - it is becoming clear that there is no general case. There is no single best solution for interaction with computer systems. To provide relevant information, to entertain appropriately, to connect someone to the pertinent group of peers at the right time we need an understanding of situation, context, individual background and, most crucially of *perspective*: where readers are, why they are there, and why they believe they are where they believe they are.

This means that the concept of relevance as we now know it must be modified. There is no given model to follow in the information sciences — but understanding how readers read text in various situations and what in a text is most pertinent given an information need is a task for linguists. Or should be.

9   Beyond ASCII

A picture says more than a thousand words. Building a system for accessing non-linguistic data will focus on several problems that must be addressed for textual and other linguistic systems as well. We do not have recourse to the short-cut words afford us. And this, in fact, may be to our benefit: the fact that text consists of readily identifiable words with obviously regular local dependencies to each other could be said to have lead language engineering up the impractical path of compositional semantics. Most likely, text retrieval and text access cannot be understood in any real way until more general questions, e.g. image access, have been understood well enough to have been posed.

The utility of the notion of homeosemy, introduced above, becomes all the more clearer if we raise our perspective beyond that of text retrieval to attempting retrieval of non-textual documents. It is the task of linguists to make obvious the connection between picture and text. No-one else will.

10   System Evaluation

The standard evaluation metric — the combination of *precision* and *recall* — which is in current and widespread use has its drawbacks: it suffers from a disregard for user and usage aspects. In general, evaluating interactive systems formally is difficult: incidental factors such as screen contrast, network induced time lags, background noise, task formulation, and subject briefing make experimental testing prohibitively expensive to perform reliably. Most importantly, motivation to perform the given task, or pursuit of the given goal, vary from user to user and context to context — which make real life evaluations difficult to replicate across conditions.

11   What Do We Need?

We need to study texts, systems, and users reading. The first and the last of those three study objects are arguably linguistic questions. The second may be.

We need to understand texts better. We obviously need *more* than the syntactic and semantic models of today can offer us. We need a *better* semantic theory than word occurrences. We also need to study more *global* textual phenomena rather than the local information organization and argument structure. To this end we need good and reliable syntactic analysis — the sort of tools that are being made available today. While the immediate utility of these tools for information retrieval purposes is unclear, they are absolutely necessary for any further steps.

We need to understand aspects of language use through studies of the practice of human question answering outside laboratories rather than study of models of question answering in model worlds. We need to understand how users combine large amounts of data into a simple judgment of relevance. We need to understand the concept of relevance better.

And after providing various ways of enriching the representation of texts, and enriching our understanding of users and their needs, tasks, and goals, we must improve human-machine dialog, by building search systems that cope with such enriched representations.

References

1. Sue Dumais, George Furnas, Tom Landauer, and Scott Deerwester. Using latent semantic analysis to improve information retrieval. In *Human Factors in Computing Systems, CHI '88*, pages 281–285. ACM, 1988.
2. Eva Hajičová, Hana Skoumalová, and Petr Sgall. The organization and use of information: An automatic procedure for topic-focus identification. *Computational Linguistics*, 21:81–95, 1995.
3. Karen Sparck Jones and Martin Kay. *Linguistics and Information Science*. Academic Press, New York, 1973.

4. Karen Sparck Jones and Martin Kay. Linguistics and information science: A postscript. In Walker et al. [17].

5. Gunnel Källgren. Deep case, text surface, and information structure. *Nordic Journal of Linguistics*, 1:149–167, 1978.

6. Gunnel Källgren. *InnehRall i text, Ord och Stil 11*. Studentlitteratur, Lund, 1979.

7. Pentti Kanerva, Jan Kristofferson, and Anders Holst. Random indexing of text samples for latent semantic analysis. In LR Gleitman and AK Josh, editors, *Proceedings of the 22nd Annual Conference of the Cognitive Science Society*, page 1036, Mahwah, New Jersey, 2000. Erlbaum.

8. Hans Karlgren. Homeosemy – on the linguistics of information retrieval. In Walker et al. [17].

9. Jussi Karlgren. Stylistic experiments in information retrieval. In Tomek Strzalkowski, editor, *Natural Language Information Retrieval*. Kluwer, Boston, 1999.

10. Jussi Karlgren and Douglass Cutting. Recognizing text genres with simple metrics using discriminant analysis. In *Proceedings of the 15th International Conference on Computational Linguistics*, volume 2, pages 1071–1075, Kyoto, Japan, August 1994. ICCL.

11. Donald Kimber, Lynn Wilcox, Francine Chen, and Thomas Moran. Speaker segmentation for browsing recorded audio. In *Human Factors in Computing Systems, CHI '95, Conference Companion*, pages 212–213, Denver, Colorado, April 1995. ACM.

12. Tom Landauer and Sue Dumais. A solution to Plato's problem: The latent semantic analysis theory of acquisition, induction and representation of knowledge. *Psychological Review*, 104:211–240, 1997.

13. Douglas W. Oard. Speech-based information retrieval for digital libraries. In *Notes from AAAI Spring Symposium on Cross-Language Text and Speech Retrieval*, Stanford University, California, 1997. AAAI.

14. Petr Sgall. Relevance of topic and focus for automatic question answering. In Ferenc Kiefer, editor, *Questions and Answers*. Reidel, Dordrecht, Holland, 1980.

15. Edward H. Sussenguth, Jr. The sentence matching program - graph. In Gerard Salton, editor, *Information Storage and Retrieval, Scientific report No. ISR-7 to the National Science Foundation*. The Computation Laboratory of Harvard University, Cambridge, Massachusetts, 1964.

16. Donald E. Walker. Computational linguistic techniques in an on-line system for textual analysis. In *Proceedings of the 3d International Conference on Computational Linguistics*, SRanga-Säby, Sweden, September 1969. ICCL.

17. Donald E. Walker, Hans Karlgren, and Martin Kay, editors. *Natural Language in Information Retrieval - Perspectives and Directions for Research*. Skriptor, Stockholm, 1976.

Index